More Acclaim for *Over the Moat*

"James Sullivan is the best kind of guide—adventurous, intelligent, and desperately interested. *Over the Moat* takes the reader on a whirlwind tour of the country and the culture, never letting us forget that, as Americans, we're just visitors."

—Stewart O'Nan,
author of *The Names of the Dead*
and editor of *The Vietnam Reader*

OVER the MOAT

OVER
the
MOAT

LOVE AMONG THE RUINS OF
IMPERIAL VIETNAM

James Sullivan

PICADOR

NEW YORK

Picador® is a U.S. registered trademark and is used by St. Martin's Press under license from Pan Books Limited.

www.picadorusa.com

Library of Congress Cataloging-in-Publication Data

Sullivan, James.
    Over the moat : love among the ruins of imperial Vietnam / James Sullivan.
    p. cm.
    ISBN 0-312-42237-7
    1. Vietnam—Social life and customs.   2. Courtship—Vietnam.   3. Hue (Vietnam)—Description and travel.   4. Sullivan, James, 1965—Travel—Vietnam. I. Title.

DS556.42.S96   2004
959.704'4'092—dc22
[B]

                                                                2003062335

First Edition: January 2004

10 9 8 7 6 5 4 3 2 1

For Xuân Thùy

ACKNOWLEDGMENTS

The author would like to thank Tom Barbash, Jack Beaudoin, David Oliver Relin, and Don Snyder for their friendship, vision, and counsel and Josh Kendall, Ellen Levine, and Louise Quayle for their finesse.

The author would also like to thank the James Michener and Copernicus Society of America for its support.

OVER the MOAT

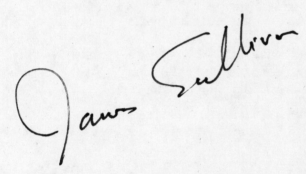

CHAPTER ONE

Even in broad daylight, the cyclo drivers were trying to line up clients. "You go boom-boom?" a driver asked, coasting to a stop beside me.

"No boom-boom," I said.

"I know good place you go boom-boom."

"No."

"Ma-sah?" he asked. "Very good ma-sah near here."

Massage was the euphemism for *boom-boom*. I looked back at the door to the Hotel Trang An. I was sure, when I left our room, that Relin was almost ready to go. But in the last couple of days, I'd been realizing that I couldn't be sure about anything anymore.

The cyclo driver asked several more questions, which I ignored, then came down off the high saddle of his rickshaw pedicab, pulled up the brake, and circled my mountain bike, appraising the technology as a fellow cyclist.

"Not Russian," he said, confirming it.

"Khong lien xo," I said, repeating his words in Vietnamese.

He caught his breath, astonished. It didn't take much.

From across the street, a savvy young student in a red kerchief, the vanguard of a whole bunch of kids trudging home from school, hailed me with a sharp salute. "Hello *do-la,*" he called out.

Soon I was surrounded by earnest young students, chirruping questions: What your name? Where are you from? How old are you? What the time? What your job? I humored them with fibs about Fred from Alaska. They didn't care about my responses, only that they could elicit one. An older student then embarked upon an advanced set of getting-to-know-you questions, common all over the country: How much you earn for one month? Do you have a lover?

"It's like a greatest-hits package," Relin called down from our Trang An window. "The whole trip all over again. The kids, the cyclo driver. And look, here comes the banana saleswoman."

I looked at a wristwatch I wasn't wearing. "Isn't there a train to catch?"

"I was just letting you have this moment," Relin said, ducking back inside. "The trip's a rap, Fred," I could hear him saying out of sight. "We pulled it off."

"Not French," the cyclo driver said, confirming that.

I shook my head.

"Australian?"

He was circling around, I could tell. "American."

"Ohhhhh," he stepped back, as if floored, but rebounded with a grin. "First time you come back my country?"

I looked at him. He was older than me by a generation, and his shirt front was a pastiche of nonsensical English phrases: Delightful Mind. Enjoyed the Members. Three Dear Boys Have a Top Sense Feeling. I tried to remember if I'd run across him during my previous five days in Hanoi or anywhere else in the two months I'd been bicycling up from Saigon. I didn't think so.

"Come back? Come back since when?" I asked.

My question seemed to make him shy, as if I'd asked for the revelation of an embarrassment. He flicked his fingers beside either ear, puffed his cheeks, and imitated the sounds of bombs exploding. Since the war? Was this my first time back since the war?

This was January 1993. In the States, they were still asking for my I.D. But this was Vietnam, where much had petrified since 1975, including the cyclo driver's perception of what an American looked like. To him, perhaps, we would always be young and earnest and up to something.

"My first time in Vietnam. I'm twenty-seven," I said.

"When you come back America?"

"Go back" was what he meant. "Two days."

Across the street, two boys lit firecrackers from a burning stick of joss and flipped them shamelessly into the wheels of passing traffic, fast, one after another, like addicts. The driver frowned with exaggerated disgust. He counted the digits of one hand with the thumb of his other. "In four days, the Tet New Year."

I followed Relin through dense downtown traffic, most of it two-wheeled and some of it four-legged. Though midday, it looked as if many people were returning home for the holiday already, carrying boughs of vibrant pink peach blossoms like torches; strapped to the backs of many bicycles were tiny potted orange trees called kumquats. I kept losing sight of Relin as he weaved through the traffic, and every time I caught sight of his Day-Glo yellow Gore-Tex he was a little further ahead. Beside a lime-juice vendor, he stopped and waited.

"Fancy me waiting for you," he said.

"My chain needs oil."

"No it doesn't. You got a grand total of one, maybe two more kilometers to go before we box these boys."

He refolded his map of Hanoi, squaring off a grid that would take us to the station. I ordered a lime juice from the old woman and oiled my chain just in case.

"We don't have time," he said, glancing at a watch that bulged off his wrist.

He'd shaved the goatee he'd grown over the previous two months. In one of the mesh side pockets of his panniers, there was a Thailand guidebook he'd bought used at a travelers' café. We'd made reservations on a Thai Air flight out of Saigon. One week to recoup on an island in the Andamann Sea, where we would also write a magazine article about our trip, then back to the States.

"Do they celebrate Tet in Thailand?" I asked.

"No, just lethargy, and on Koh Pi Pi, the sunset."

Relin rarely got ahead of himself this way. He was the most unhurried person I'd ever met. But it had been raining since we'd ridden in to Hanoi, the ceiling of clouds lower every day, the faint, gray drizzle casting a spell over everything. It would be sunny on that island.

In the maze of streets that lay between us and the train station, I lost him. As trailer, it was my responsibility to keep my eye on Relin; we'd decided this on the bike trip. But I'd lost him somehow and now found myself following four high school girls, pedaling side by side in formation. They sat perfectly erect on their bike seats, their long black hair fanned out beneath their sun hats, immaculate in their white *ao dai* dresses, like a mobile tableau en route to another exhibit.

I made several uninformed turns, operating on hunches, before I stopped, really lost now, and looked down at the transparent map case on my handlebar pannier. I hadn't changed the map since Hue. It was drawn in blue pen on a four-by-six-inch spiral notebook page. Thuy could have pointed out her address on a city map, but

I'd asked her to draw one and then watched her, the peculiar decisions she made for iconography: parallel lines for the roads we'd take, crescents for gates and bridges, a square box for the landmark bazaar near her house, all rendered in a hand so light and so steady, she could have been at homework.

We were to visit for tea. That was all, tea and light conversation as we'd been having all the way up Highway 1. That afternoon before tea, Relin and I had worked on our language skills, reading from disintegrating phrase books we'd picked up in Saigon. I memorized new questions and worked on pronunciation with a hotel concierge who bolstered my confidence, telling me I spoke "Vietnamee very goose."

I also figured on a number of ways to work Relin's girlfriend into the conversation. Something about the years they had been together. How he valued the gymnastics of witty banter in a relationship. How compatible they were. I knew otherwise. I'd paid attention to a recent phone call and heard lots of disgruntled sighs and expensive gaps of silence. But I needed her now. That evening, as we'd pedaled over Hue's Perfume River, I asked about Deborah.

"Why are we talking about her now?" Relin asked.

"I'm sure we'll be talking about her later," I said.

"No lover," Relin said, braking to make his point. "If they ask the question about the lover tonight, I don't have one."

"Judas."

"Don't flatter me."

I looked upriver as passengers on a sampan leaned over the gunwales and let loose a flotilla of colorful paper lanterns, each guttering votive light symbolic of a wish released. "No promises," I said.

"Okay, then what was the name of that girl who lived in the guest house next to ours on Bui Vien in Saigon?"

"The girl I bought bananas from?"

"Bananas? It looked like more than bananas to me."

"Baloney."

"Right, but I'm the only one who'll know it. Tonight, no Deborah."

At the flag-tower bastion, a giant billboard rendition of Ho Chi Minh, illuminated by klieg lights, smiled down on us. We turned right off Le Duan Street and tunneled fifty feet through one of the Citadel's arched gates, per the salesclerk's directions.

Inside, the neighborhood was blacked out, and the clouds were spitting rain. At roadside, vendors sold liter bottles of amber-colored petrol, made luminescent by an oil lamp set among them. We spanned another body of water, a canal perhaps, and I checked my bearings against the map. My cheap Chinese flashlight lit a gatepost numbered in the thirties. The numbers dropped at the next gatepost, then rose again.

We doubled back to the Citadel gate and made a fresh start. The house numbers rose sequentially, then plummeted suddenly, then began to seesaw randomly. Sometimes there were two numbers, separated by a slash mark; other times, a letter was affixed to the numeral; other times there was a tiny *bis* superscript.

After twenty minutes up and down, I steered into the small front yard of a home that didn't have a numeric designation but looked to be the right place. Motorcycle frames littered the front yard, and tarpaulin rice bags covered the windows. A bare-chested man came to the door, smoking a cigarette.

"Day la nha gia dinh Nguyen?" I asked. Is this the Nguyen home?

"Vang," he said. Yes.

Three more men filled the doorway behind him, one carrying an oil lamp, another with a clear jug of rice wine in which I could see the coil of a large drowned snake. "Where you from?" one of the drunks blurted.

"*Nha gia dinh Nguyen?*" I repeated my question.

"*Vang,*" the first man said again. He didn't move. He tossed his cigarette into a puddle, and I listened to the fizzle.

I kicked down the stand of my bike. The house was tiny, a single room, and I could see the legs of someone jutting into the light of the doorway.

"I've read about those snakes in rice wine," Relin said, setting his kickstand. "They only drown the poisonous ones, often for medicinal purposes, as a cure for night blindness, but as an aphrodisiac too."

"*Thuy o' day?*" I asked.

"*Khong,*" the bare-chested man said. No.

"*Day la nha so muoi sau?*" Relin asked. Is this house number sixteen?

"*Khong,*" he said.

We wheeled out quickly but drew no closer to number sixteen. In other peoples' courtyards, they'd give my map a cursory glance, turn it over, find nothing interesting, and invite us in for tea.

In the midst of our search, the power flickered on. A satisfied groan of half-surprise went up in the neighborhood, like people responding to marginally impressive fireworks. But finding the right number sixteen proved no more promising in the light. More than forty minutes late now, I remembered the time a girl had given me her phone number, and it turned out to be a joke shop. When I saw her again, I told her she had given me the wrong number, and she told me she had not.

"Want to call it a night?" Relin asked.

"One more house."

I went on to another house, and another, and another. I shined my flashlight in the faces of other people, most of whom actually answered to the name Nguyen. A maze of Nguyens. A house of mirrors, I thought, pulling out of one courtyard a second time. Relin stopped following me. He parked beneath a streetlight, and I passed him, going one way and volleying back the other.

I went over a bridge and coasted down, straining to listen more carefully now, as if that's what I hadn't been doing. Beyond the motorbikes and the erratic buzz of a broken fluorescent light tube, I could hear the plaintive call of a small girl's voice, *"My . . . my . . . my."* She was standing in her pajamas between two gate pillars, disconcertingly short in the darkness, piping the one word at regular intervals. The word meant "American," and for one seized moment as the girl fastened her eyes on me, I had this feeling that I'd been found out here in this less traveled part of the city. But the word, inflected another way, the way she was sounding it, was the word for "bread." She was simply calling for one of the bread peddlers who were out on their nightly rounds.

Relin joined me, and we started back in silence. I was trying to persuade myself that this map did not lead to a joke shop and at the same time trying to figure out why the hell that mattered if it did. I was on a bike trip. In Vietnam. In a small city I could not have placed on a map six months earlier. All of that was supposed to preclude the disappointment that now had a grip on me. It was ridiculous, and the light laughter we heard from the bicyclists trailing us seemed to confirm that.

When those cyclists flanked us, I glanced at two women, cloaked in hooded ponchos and rigidly attentive of the road ahead. They kept to our pace in silence as we passed into a brightly lit stretch outside the local market, and when I glanced over again, I found

Thuy, her profile glistening with beads of rain that had begun falling again.

"You're very late," she said without looking over.

"We had trouble."

"I know. Do you know, when you didn't come my house, my
young sister and I, we came to look for you?"

I craned my head to the side and nodded at her sister, then
looked back at Thuy. The drawstring of her hood was tightened
so that only her face showed, small and pear-shaped like a silent
film actress. Her lips were shining with gloss and moisture, and for
a desperate moment I wished for something to go wrong here, for
the revelation of a broken tooth or a cloud in her eye not seen
before, something to let me off the hook, to let me turn away and
remember that she was beautiful except for that. Instead, she
swerved her eyes to glance at Relin, who was moving in off the
road, then swerved them back, a gorgeous little gesture that floored
me: She looked like this and did things like that.

"Why so much trouble?" she asked.

I didn't want to blame her map or my inability to count house
numbers. I told her it was tricky, and left it at that, but she knew
I'd had trouble with her map, and maybe she had guessed that I
had second-guessed her ability to provide directions. She produced
a small flashlight from beneath her poncho and shined it on my
map cover. "Do you see, here is the market?" She snapped off her
light, case closed.

A nervous silence possessed me, and I shuddered with it, wondering what I might say to her and why I should be feeling this
way. I was here on a bike trip. Hers was a face I was supposed to
photograph, and keep that way, no other. That was all.

"I . . . we were trying to follow the house numbers," I said finally.
"To number sixteen."

"Yes, I see," she said. "I'm sorry. But my mother, she doesn't like."

"What doesn't she like?"

"Number 116. In fact, we live at 116. But my mother, she doesn't like such the number. The fortune-teller advised against it. She likes better the number, for example, 16."

"So she just took 100 numbers away from your house?" I wondered. "Doesn't that make problems?"

"No." She laughed. "Do you know, my city is very small and many people know my family."

Until the previous spring, Vietnam had meant little to me. I knew where Asia was and knew some people who'd traveled there, but that was it. I didn't have a history of fascination with the Far East, like Relin, or with the Vietnam War, like guys in my generation who could quote from *Apocalypse Now*, chapter and verse. I'd never taken a class in East Asian studies. When I thought of Buddhism, I thought of Jack Kerouac.

When I graduated from school that year, I planned to go home to Boston with my master's degree. I looked forward to it. I'd lived away since college, in Maine and California and Iowa, and for a while I had thought I would never go back home. But after two years in the Midwest, I'd begun to believe that my previous distaste for the city and the culture I had grown up in was a phase that was over now. And then one day after class, David Relin mentioned plans to spend the following year in Bangkok.

"What's in Bangkok?"

"A staging area," he said. "A hub, right in the middle of it all. Angkor Wat. Plain of Jars. Vietnam. Vietnam's opening up. They're letting travelers in now, and I've been looking at some maps, at a highway built by the colonial French. It runs up the coast from Saigon to Hanoi, and it looks perfect for motorbike or mountain bike."

Relin had this slow, methodical way of speaking. His words seemed to come up out of a deep well and only after a few more beats of deliberation than you expected, as if he were distilling them or writing them to ensure they had adequate potency. He drove a BMW motorcycle and wore a Swedish policeman's leather jacket that had an elementary school pin on the lapel that read FOR PROGRESS IN WRITING. The leather was horsehide, which held up better than "cow," Relin said, if you spilled. He was twenty-nine, and though he was not from Brooklyn, I had only just learned that.

I mentioned a long-distance bike trip I'd started in 1987, after graduating from college. A friend and I had dipped our rear wheels in the Atlantic at a rocky little beach where I'd worked as a clam digger summers during college. A photographer from the local paper snapped our picture. Five hundred miles later, the trip petered out in a small Pennsylvania town when an old soccer injury flared, and my classmate had to quit.

"So you interested?" Relin asked.

"In what?"

"Going over."

"Where you're going?

"Yeah."

"No. I'm moving back home."

"Move back home. We take off in the fall, at the tail end of the monsoon season. Three months, you're in, you're out, and you got a few more stories to tell when you're an old man and all those Sullivan grandkids start asking what the world was like in the twentieth century."

A week later, driving up to the bar we regrouped in after class, Relin showed me a collection of bike company catalogues from Trek, Specialized, and Cannondale. He was certain he could persuade one of their flaks to donate a couple of high-end models to a couple of guys who'd ride up Highway 1 in Vietnam and write a magazine article about it.

"You're kidding," I said.

"No joke."

The glossy pictures of the bikes dazzled me, the components made of space-age composites I'd never heard of, the brilliant enamel paint. I was sure he couldn't reel them in, and then, unbelievably, he did, and I made a capitulation, this time in the form of a letter, a query to *Bicycling* magazine. A few days after I mailed the letter, my phone rang and an editor at *Bicycling* told me he was mailing a contract.

I signed the contract, but going to Vietnam was still an unreal proposition. I wasn't a traveler. Yes, California, but I'd lived with an uncle. Yes, Iowa, but I had school to structure my agenda. I'd spent my junior year abroad, and when people asked where, I sometimes tried to get away with saying Europe. But that was a ruse. I'd spent that year in Ireland, in Cork, not more than fifty miles from a town where most people seemed to carry Sullivan as their surname. One of my father's brothers had spent a couple of years in Vietnam during the war, but otherwise the country was off all of my maps.

Then Northwest Airlines agreed to fly us round-trip to Bangkok, gratis, business class. It was more than I could resist. "Three months," I said to Relin.

"In and out," he said.

That summer, I tended bar on Martha's Vineyard, and Relin moved in with his girlfriend in Charlottesville, though he never seemed to be in Charlottesville that summer. As we coordinated plans for the trip, my calls to Virginia invariably wound up on a machine while Relin and Deborah were in San Francisco, or Seattle, or several islands in the Caribbean for a little "decompression time." Decompression from what, I'd wondered.

He went to Paris, and Moscow, where he purchased an infrared night-vision mask at an underground army surplus warehouse near the Kremlin.

"There probably won't be streetlights in Vietnam," he told me after Moscow. "If we get stuck out pedaling after dark, it might come in handy."

In response, I mentioned my new flashlight and all my extra Eveready batteries, and he didn't say anything.

I began to dread his phone calls for what they did to my very fragile trip budget. He'd suggested I get not one but two spare tires; self-repairing tire tubes; a self-inflating mattress pad; Mr. Tuffy tire liners; a spare, titanium Hyper-glide chain; a saddle lock; Gore-Tex socks; Gore-Tex boots; and a water-bottle fanny pack to supplement the two cages on the bike frame and the four pouches on the panniers. He talked about asthma inhalers though neither of us had asthma, about prescriptions for Flagyl, Lomotil, and a myriad of antibiotics I'd never heard of. He spoke with the authority of someone who'd traveled widely, to the remotest islets of obscure Indonesian archipelagos, to India, and, as of this summer, behind the Iron Curtain.

He didn't need half of what he brought, and he'd had to make a series of jettisonings, at a college friend's flat in Bangkok, at our Saigon guest house, and after the first day on the road in Xuan Loc. But still, he managed to hold on to some of his gadgets: a Casio electronic encyclopedia, two camera bodies, and all his Gore-Tex. I put my clothes in plastic bags. He put his in Gore-Tex stuff sacks. Mornings packing, he took great care to make sure his clothes and gear were neatly folded and stowed in his panniers, as if at any moment some outdoors-catalogue photographer might want a cross-section shot of the contents.

I'd come to believe he was overly circumspect, and I knew he thought I was recklessly optimistic. In the searing afternoon heat of a day on the road, as we gauged the distance to our next destination, he tended to think we had twice as far to go as we actually did, and I always reckoned we were half as far. Since we were each willing to compromise and accede, things worked out.

It had been Relin's idea that we retereat to Thailand after the bike trip. Though I'd agreed, now that we were actually on our way to Thailand, I was having trouble picturing my departure from Vietnam.

After losing Relin that morning in Hanoi, I asked several vendors for the way to the train. They prompted me with outstretched arms and anxious looks, as if they knew I was running late. When I finally arrived at the station, Relin was waiting out front if only to glance knowingly at his watch and enjoy the small bit of vindication that comes from being right. He'd suggested we leave very early for the train.

"I thought you might have said the hell with it and started back down," he said now.

"I don't mind putting the bikes up."

"You hate putting the bikes up. But wait till you see Pi Pi. The world doesn't get any better."

Outside the city, the low gray cloud ceiling lifted and lightened, and further south, broke into a field of rubble with blue sky beyond. Boys led water buffalo along the paddy dikes of bright green rice fields, a vignette that was as prevalent in real life as it was on the lacquered mother-of-pearl art for sale in the towns. There was the

Vietnam you imagined and the Vietnam that was, and sometimes they were the same thing.

"If the train's on time, we'll make that flight out tomorrow," Relin said, looking up from a Thai Air timetable, "unless there's any reason to hang around Saigon another day."

"No, there's nothing in Saigon."

At dusk, the sun dropped behind the western mountains, pulling the roseate sky light down after it through a cleft between two peaks, as magically fast as a genie into its lamp. I believed I could almost hear its departure, the light being sucked toward another day, in another place, illuminating chance and possibility elsewhere.

The train rolled south through the night, clacking time over inexpertly welded rail joints with metronomic regularity, halting at Thanh Hoa, Ninh Binh, and Vinh. As the train stopped, I listened for the footsteps of the conductor and the intonation of another place-name, the towns of our trip north scrolling by in reverse, all of it being undone.

Shortly before dawn, we stopped again. I waited for the conductor's footsteps, but none came. I listened for the night vendors who tapped at the windows to ply us with fruit and bottled water, but there were no murmurs outside the window, only the distant, disconnected idle of the engine further downtrack.

I looked at Relin in the upper berth across from me, his head cocked back on the small plaid pillow he traveled with, the mouth slightly ajar, his unencumbered sleep. In Iowa City he had confessed to a "thing" for Asian women, a low-grade gravitational pull from West to East, and yet, here, he had managed to resist the lure. He'd initiated contact with Thuy. And his interest in her through that first tea encounter and evening at her house had been as obvious as mine. But after that, he ceded the initiative.

I knew part of the reason. At the end of that first evening, Thuy's younger sister was flipping through his phrase book when she encountered a series of phrases, written in Vietnamese, that he'd asked a waiter in Nha Trang to jot down for him: *I like you too much. / I am single. / Let me hold you. / I want to kiss you.* When Thuy seized my phrase book, indicting me with a smirk as she hurried into my end pages, the absence of any "Don Juan poems," as she put it, conferred upon me a nobility of intention that Relin had lost.

Still, I was persuaded that Relin's reluctance to engage her, or any of the Asian women he had a thing for, was rooted elsewhere, in a sophistication, perhaps, that I lacked. He might indulge whims or infatuations, but he wouldn't let them reorient his life. It wasn't what you let happen with chance encounters in Southeast Asia.

The night after our first tea, I'd returned to Thuy's house again alone, carrying a package of coconut biscuits imported from China and a sorry excuse about having come empty-handed the previous evening and feeling bad about it. Our talk roamed erratically, from the inconsistency of Hue's power supply, to the floodlines on the interior walls of her living room, to the painted portrait of a woman I suspected was Thuy. It wasn't; it was an older sister, Vui, who Thuy said was very beautiful at that time, when she was young. "And how old is she now?" I asked.

"Twenty-six."

Her English, even as she bungled grammar and pronunciation, never wrenched her face into contortions. It traipsed along at the same pace and volume as her Vietnamese. We spoke English mostly, but regularly she shunted the talk back into Vietnamese, forcing me to fumble gracelessly for understanding and to wrack my head for decipherable sentences. She didn't ask any questions

about me, or America. Toward the end of that second evening, I'd
proposed that we meet again at a café.

"When?" she asked.

"Tomorrow? After work?"

"I'm busy." She said it so flatly I thought of a high school girl
painting her nails at the other end of the phone line while I trembled through my bid for a date. I suggested then that we go out
some other time.

"When?" she asked. Her tone was urgent, as if I'd backed her
into a corner.

"When's good for you?"

"When I have some free time."

When I stopped by her shop the following day and asked if she
had some free time tomorrow, again she told me she was busy. I
closed my eyes, nodding, letting her know I got the message. As I
straddled the top tube of my bicycle, she called me back. "Jim," she
said, using my name for the first time, "when you have some free
time, you may come to my house to play."

I'd been playing her words over in my head ever since I'd pedaled
out of Hue and especially again this evening, rolling south, rolling
home. As the train's engine continued to idle, I climbed out of my
berth and went to the space between the cars. I leaned out to see
if we'd arrived at some unaccountable station, but there was nothing, just the long green arc of cars and morning moonlight spread
over the rice paddies. Raised paddy dikes wandered randomly away
from the track's berm, partitioning my view into puzzle pieces. In
the near distance, an oil lamp burned in the window of a small
thatched home.

I climbed onto the sill of the window and sat there as something
gave in my stomach. I rocked back and forth, the way I had as a

boy, standing on successively higher ledges of granite swimming quarries in Quincy, wondering whether this leap was beyond my courage. I looked at the house again as something momentarily shielded the light of the lamp.

From the States, Relin and I had thought such homes would provide our lodging at the end of day. They never did. We played it safe, every night, cycling on to the next town. We stayed in guest houses, never chancing the serendipity of invitations to bunk down in a private home. This was partly my doing. I'd insisted we stay on schedule. I'd made sure we met self-imposed deadlines, that we stuck to the itinerary, that we pedaled ten, twenty, or thirty more kilometers to that day's goal, no matter how tired, no matter the weather. We'd budgeted four days for Nha Trang; we stayed four days in Nha Trang. At the end of the day, I wanted a win, an uninterrupted bicycle ride of more than two thousand kilometers from Saigon to Hanoi. No support vehicles. No trains. No buses. No unredeemed portages. Laying our own tread all the way to Hanoi had been important to me from the start. It's why I'd come: to accomplish that. That had been less important to Relin. Getting to Hanoi "by a combination of means if necessary," as he'd once said, was not anathema. Detours and indulgences, an extra day or week here, wouldn't have bothered him. That was the essence of travel and might have been the essence of the difference between us. He'd been traveling through Vietnam, and I just thought I'd come here on a bike trip.

I straightened my arms, lifting my seat off the sill, and dropped silently onto the gravelly slope below. In the wake of my noise, I hushed, listening. Something moved in the tall grass bordering the railway. Another light illuminated a nearby home, and it occurred to me that I had a choice.

I took a step forward, away from the train, and felt my old fear

of heights siphoning strength from my arms and legs. I took another step, hauling my lungs full of the night air, the fumes of
diesel fuel, creosote, and some other fragrance carried in the breeze.
One more step, and the train jerked. The muscles in my groin went
numb as they do when a plunge takes you into the coldest depths.

I hadn't felt fear on this trip, not once since we'd arrived, not in
Chu Lai when a sentry outside an army base marched us at the
point of an AK-47 down a deserted stretch of road (to his barracks
and commander, who reprimanded us for snapping photos), not
pedaling after dark in the central coast when three men on motorbikes tailed us on a lonely road for several kilometers. I'd hoped to
be afraid. I'd wanted this trip as a bike ride but as an adventure
too. Instead, I felt detached, as if none of it were really happening
to me. I wasn't really here; my life wasn't. I had armor on, a suit
I wouldn't take off until later, back in the States.

Two more steps, and I was holding on to a long blade of grass,
hearing the echo of Thuy's voice and seeing her face, an image I
had been telling myself should stay within the white-bordered
frame of a journalist's photograph. That, I'd been saying over and
over again, was where she belonged, there with all the other Vietnamese we'd met. I had come here on a bike trip, and that was
over now, but as one of the lights went out in the house nearby
and the train bucked again, I had a feeling that my journey had
only just begun.

Wait a minute, wait a minute," Relin said, following me down the
corridor. He laughed, a giddy uncharacteristic laugh. "You know
what you're doing?"

"No."

My duffel bag kept wedging in the corridor, and several times I
had to yank it free. At the exit, I embraced the duffel vertically and

stepped onto the platform. I hailed a uniformed porter and showed him my baggage claim. *"Xe dap,"* I said, gesturing at the freight car.

He looked at my ticket. *"Di Saigon."*

"Toi doi thanh pho," I said.

"Changing cities?" Relin said. "I don't believe this. It's too rash."

He picked the right word. I knew I had tendencies in rash, overly optimistic directions. My governor was susceptible to intermittent failure, and Relin knew I worried about this.

"You spent one evening with her," Relin said. "Two." He was standing beside me while the porter unlodged my bicycle from the freight that had banked against it. Relin had laid an even keel in his voice, and it was sailing right into the storm of wavering indecision that had gripped me since we'd left Hanoi the day before.

The porter passed my bicycle down.

"Is that enough to . . . I don't know, is that enough to jump ship?"

"No."

The train lurched, and Relin hopped onto the metal steps. "This is ridiculous."

The train lurched again and stayed moving, slowly. "You're serious," he said.

"If I don't catch up with you in Saigon, I'll . . ."

But I didn't know what I'd do, and by then the train had pulled far enough away that he couldn't hear me anyway.

At the Hue railway station, I hitched my panniers and merged into a thick stream of midday traffic on Le Loi Street. The students were out at lunch, and several shadowed me but only so far. This close to Tet, the esplanade along the Perfume River was a whirl of kiddie rides and carnivalesque attractions. Photographers had propped out kitschy replicas of the Eiffel Tower and two-dimensional cartoon characters like Doremon, the Japanese cat: You provide the face. Anticipation was as palpable as the wind.

If my reception at the boutique went one way, to spare further humiliation, I was prepared to lie. I would mention my departure the following morning. I would lead her to believe I was bicycling back to Saigon. Despite the resolve that propelled me from the train, a small piece of me yearned for this in the same way I sometimes hoped to be disappointed by a closer look at a woman first glimpsed from a distance. I could go home then, without guilt, knowing I'd not backed down.

On Tran Phu Street, traffic filled the road, gutter to gutter: bicycles, motorbikes, carts drawn by oxen, a Lambro ferrying old women to the riverside bazaar, one cyclo so laden with torpedo-shaped baskets it was difficult to see the cyclo. Holiday shoppers streamed thickly along the sidewalks, the way people shopped Main Street in the '40s and '50s. I was grateful for the cover. With all my gear rigged to the bike, I couldn't risk parking in a corral. I had to go directly to the shop. I had to barge my way through the pedestrian traffic, excusing myself in my pitifully pronounced Vietnamese.

She probably heard me before she saw me, for the only way to keep the nervousness from my voice was by raising it: *"Xin loi, xin loi."* Embarrassed, I reverted to English. "Sorry, sorry."

They opened a path for me with alacrity. Thuy stood behind the glass counter. Her hair was pinned back on one side, and her mouth, as she glimpsed me, opened slightly. I couldn't read anything in her face, and I wasn't yet close enough to say anything. She glanced once at her sister, and then back to me quickly, without changing her expression.

She had chenille sweaters draped over her forearm: maroon,

cream-colored, and olive. Her lips were moist. She looked more gorgeous than I'd remembered, no matter what hyperbole did to memory.

"I came back—" I said, halting momentarily, "to write my magazine article. And to see if you had any free time."

Her eyes opened wider. "I have free time now." She turned and walked past her sister, through the holiday shoppers to my side. "Let's go."

"Thuy oi Thuy!" Oanh called.

Thuy turned, but Oanh couldn't say anything, she was laughing too hard. Finally, she raised her forearm, in hysterics now, before collapsing in laughter behind the counter.

Thuy looked at her arms, still draped with sweaters, then looked up at me. "I'll need these?" she asked, narrowing her eyes hard against her thoughtlessness and what that revealed.

I hope so, I thought, getting way ahead of myself.

CHAPTER TWO

THE FIRST TIME I'D EVER heard of Hue as a real place in a real country, and not in reference to a battle the U.S. Marines fought in 1968, was in the bank I'd gone to for traveler's checks before leaving home. I'd purposely queued in the line of a Vietnamese teller, curious about the reaction she'd make to what tellers inevitably ask of people getting traveler's checks. After I sprang my answer on her, I ticked off the place-names on my itinerary. "It's not *Hugh*," she'd said when I got to Hue. "It's *Hway*." She was from Saigon herself, "boat people," and though she'd never visited the imperial capital of Vietnam, she cast the city for me in one neat gesture. Stepping back from her window, she made a half-pirouette and placed her hand at a right angle to the small of her back, which was how long, she said, the girls in Hue grew their hair.

Hue inspired that kind of poetry in people. Pedaling north on Highway 1, I'd found that the Vietnamese loved Hue unconditionally. It didn't matter whether you were from the north or the south, a truck driver told me outside Saigon. "Everybody agree about Hue." It wasn't the guidebook stuff he was talking about, not the

Imperial Citadel or the Forbidden Purple City or the pagodas so much as it was something else, less easily defined, qualities better communicated by gesture, by the aroma swirling off a bowl of *bun bo Hue* soup and a limning of moonlight over the Perfume River, by whispers and by secret. An old woman in Danang had told me that on quiet nights gold seeped out of the ground in Hue: Believe it. Back in Hue now, I was prepared to believe that anything was possible.

The day before Tet, Thuy's father, Mr. Bang, was sitting with friends on his porch when I showed up. Bamboo fishing poles leaned against the wall beside them and the day's catch was subdued in a bucket at their feet. Thuy had told me her family hated when her father fished the rice paddies. They figured all that time in the sun was sapping his health. They might have been right. His face looked drained of fat, his cheeks caved in and whiskered. His eyes were sunk deep in their sockets and capped with eyebrows that arched severely in the middle. He'd soldiered with the Americans during the war, but he was "retired" now, although *retirement* was more like a euphemism for the dire straits of his employment opportunities since 1975.

His given name, Bang, meant "blackboard." He was Mr. Blackboard, but if I thought that was funny, the way he pronounced my name, *Ca Rem*, among his grandchildren, was even funnier. To him, and to them, I was Mr. Popsicle.

When I entered the courtyard, Mr. Bang shocked his friends with the revelation of my bike's price tag—$1,500. One man repeated the price, looking to me for confirmation, then added the kind of cluck that passed for a stateside whistle. Incredulous, he came down for a better look. He lifted the bike, communicated its weight to the others, and then through his own analysis of cost, weight, and worth, determined, I think, that I'd been had. He patted me on the shoulder and resumed his place on the porch.

Another man returned from behind the house, zipping his trousers. *"Troi oil!"* he said, taking in me and the bike at a glance. An American with a space bike might have been the last thing he expected to see after a trip to the john. Mr. Bang hurriedly explained who I was and how much the bike cost.

The old man shook my hand and took it for granted that I understood French. *"Since 1975,"* he said. *"I'm working on bikes."*

Abruptly, he squatted beside the rear derailleur. While I steadied the handlebars, he lifted the back wheel, spun it, and flicked his fingers for me to work the levers. The chain links were beveled for easier slips from sprocket to sprocket, and the derailleur was renowned for its hypersmooth action. With every effortless gear change, he made the characteristic Vietnamese tsking sound, admiring technology that had evolved fifty years beyond the simple one-speeds he worked on. While I played the chain up and down the freewheel, he counted the seven sprockets on the freewheel, the three chain rings up front, multiplied, and came up with *vingt et un!* combinations. Delighted, he stood up and shook my hand, as if I were not only the proud owner but the draftsman as well.

"Number one," he assured me in English. He ushered me to the platform where the men were sharing a drink from a clear jug that had a brown patty on the bottom.

Mr. Bang revealed what he'd learned of my bike trip from his daughter. He mentioned the terminal cities, the total distance in kilometers, and the time frame. Astonishment gave way to guffaw and scrutiny of my size and shape as if therein lay the evidence they'd need for credence.

"Difficile," the bike mechanic said, frowning bitterly.

I shot back the rice-wine shooter and sprung my Vietnamese on them. *"You were soldiers?"* I asked.

"Vous parlez Vietnamee tres bien?" the mechanic told me.

"He does not," Thuy called out from inside the house.

I asked Thuy's father when he joined the army, and the bike mechanic translated his response. From the village of his birth, just outside Hue, he had followed his oldest brother into the Viet Minh's war against the French in 1951. When he contracted malaria, he was sent back to his village. During his recuperation, Vietnamese forces allied with the French coerced him to fight on their side.

"La Jaunissement," the mechanic said. "The Yellowing," as the French had termed their efforts to put a Vietnamese face on their efforts to retain control. When the Americans took control of the government of South Vietnam and its army in the 1950s, Mr. Bang drifted into an Army of the Republic of Vietnam (ARVN) unit. At the same time, his brother fought for the Viet Minh and its descendent resistance cadre, the Viet Cong.

Trying Vietnamese again, I asked Mr. Bang what his job had been during the war. I thought he hadn't understood me, then he cocked his ear and I asked again.

"Howitzer 1-0-5," he said, giving me the number in English.

I told him he had spoken English very well, but I wasn't loud enough. He unbuttoned his shirt and pulled it down off his left shoulder. There was a four-inch scar on his upper arm. "Quang Tri," he said, naming the city where he'd been wounded.

They didn't seem to want to talk about the war anymore, so I turned my attention to the glass jug. What, I wanted to know as Thuy stepped onto the porch, arms akimbo, was the brown patty?

They grinned, every one of them. The mechanic tried to remember the word in French, but failed. Finally, they offered me

the Vietnamese word, *con khi*. I still didn't know. When I turned
to Thuy, she gestured a translation, quickly scratching fingers above
the hips. Monkey. The patty was residue of a monkey, dropped
alive, wriggling and howling, in a vat of boiling water and cooked
until all of him, or her, settled to the bottom of the pot.

For New Year's Eve, Thuy was dressed in a white silk *ao dai*, a
long, form-fitting dress with a tunic collar and side seams split from
ankle to hip. The material was fine and shimmered in the fluorescent light shed by a tube buzzing over the doorway inside. From
beneath the hem of her flared slacks, I could see the toes of low-
heeled pumps spangled with tiny stars and crescents. Her hair fell
indulgently long and in tresses to the center of her back, hair not
unlike the Breck girls I'd dreamed about as a boy, with heft and
swing, and that was not straight as rain like most Asian women's.
She'd referred to her hair as curly.

"Curly?" I laughed. "Your hair's not curly."

"No?" She plucked a single strand and brought the light down
on it. The strand was wavy, surprisingly so. "It curls this way," she
said, tracing her forefinger over it, "then it curls this way. So what
is the adjective for that action?"

Inside, the home had been made over for the New Year. On a
table set before the ancestor altar was a gangly bough of yellow
apricot blossoms vased in a brass shell casing with a jagged lip. A
pencil sketch of Zefferelli's Romeo and Juliet hung from walls
freshly painted in aquamarine green. By the door was an old portrait of a military man, of evident rank and stature, decked in dress
whites; a saber in a scabbard hung at his side, and his chest was
cluttered with medals.

"Your father?" I asked.

"My grandfather."

"He looks famous."

"Maybe."

While I waited for elaboration, my head was busy with calculations, dating her father and then her father's father to find that this man's heyday had to have been during the 1930s and 1940s, while the emperor still reigned.

"Did he know the emperor?"

"Bao Dai King?"

"Yes."

"Maybe. But I'm not sure."

She stared into the photo with me, placing a forefinger on a lower eyetooth, as if viewing it for the first time. As I leaned forward under the pretext of a closer look, my arm brushed her shoulder, and then as if by accident stuck there, maintaining the pressure. That otherwise indifferent swatch of arm suddenly turned on, sensate, in a way I'd never known possible, dispatching bolts of sheer feeling.

In the time we'd known each other, I had yet to touch her. She declined to shake hands, even in parting. After my first night at her house, when I put out my hand to say good-bye, she'd crossed her arms and smiled. "We don't do that in Vietnam," she said. But in that brief moment, before she moved beyond me, I confirmed what I suspected, that her skin had a tacky, adhesive quality to it, a consequence of climate and luck. At her sister's shop, when customers asked which brand of cold cream she used—as they often did—she pulled the expensive tubs of Noxema out from the glass display case. The truth was she didn't use cold cream.

"Do you need to know?" she asked.

I opened my palms, feigning little regard for the follow-up I was suddenly desperate to know: Was she descended from one of those fallen families?

"Because it's better we don't talk about my family before 1975. For example, your magazine."

"No, no. Not for the magazine."

"A-ko."

Her mother stepped through a side door, carrying a translucent pink carousel dish. A small buck-toothed granddaughter followed with a tea service. Mrs. Bang was buttoned up in a long heavy coat, and her still-long hair was pinned in a bun at the back of her head. Though nearly sixty, the skin around her eyes was taut, shaded through the worst sunlight for years by a conical hat. I nodded at her, bowing slightly, solicitously, and kept from looking too closely at her mouth, certain that any glance at her face would rivet my gaze on her mouth, and she would know, the way young women with dyed mustache hairs know, that my assiduous avoidance of looking *there* was evidence of my captivation.

Thuy's mother's teeth were jet black, not from corrosion and not stained like women in the market who chew betel nuts for the caffeinated high, but from deliberate lacquering. Catching the fluorescent doorway light, they were lustrous, and daunting.

"Please wait for me some minutes," Thuy said, sweeping her arm toward the tea table. "Some tea and snakes."

Brown monkey patty and now snakes? Snakes in tea? Snakes, the aphrodisiac snakes? "Snakes?"

"Yes, snakes."

I made a slithering motion with my hand. Her eyes lit at the revelation of her mistake. She bounced the heels of her palms off her temple and lapsed into laughter so complete and so unabashed that several smiling faces glanced into the room. "Oh no," she said, barely able to get the words out. "Not snakes. Snacks."

She wiped a tear from her face and lifted the lid off the dessert dish, segmented with sugared flakes of ginger, candied lotus, watermelon seeds, and small Thai hard candy. She sampled a piece of ginger and then gave one to me. The flake sizzled a moment like a hot tamale but quickly lost potency.

"Do you feel delicious?" she asked.

I looked at her a moment, wondering whether to correct her English as she'd asked me earlier. "Yes," I said.

A few minutes after Thuy left, Minh barged through the blue and white plastic strips draped across the doorway. Just inside, seeing me at her tea table, she stopped short. Her tongue peeked momentarily at the corner of her mouth.

"Oh, James," she said. She glanced at the side doorway, then craned her neck tortoiselike for a glimpse at the dining table nook. She turned and swept her gaze both ways along the porch, as if to make sure she'd not been followed. "Do you have a moment?"

When I nodded, she hurriedly moved the carousel dish and emptied her backpack on the table. She retrieved several books from a nearby case: a mammoth English-Vietnamese dictionary, an asthick lexicon, a grammar text, a thesaurus, a book of English idioms, and a Streamline English paperback.

Minh was eighteen years old and a "freshman," she'd told me proudly, at the local teacher's training college. A smattering of freckles peppered her cheeks, and her face was pudgy with late adolescence. Her eyes were rounder than her sister's but that might have been traced to the amazement she felt at finding a live tutor at her table. Before sitting she sharpened two pencils and handed me a notebook with a prancing yellow duck on the cover.

"I'll be Tom," she said, glancing at the back doorway, then opening the Streamline book to a dialogue skit we'd covered twice already, "and you be Fred."

Gamely, I plunged in, all enthusiasm and encouragement, des-

perate to reveal myself as a good sport. My hearty laughter carried
out the doorway.

After our lesson about two men on the verge of being released
from prison, Minh placed her finger under the first word in a list
of new vocabulary to review. I said the word aloud, and she repeated
after me. She clearly lacked her sister's facility with enunciation. I
repeated the word again, and she did, once loudly and then softly,
as if to herself, several times, before looking up earnestly to confirm
whether she'd nailed it. We went on endlessly with the one word,
like characters on a Mobius strip, until I lied. She placed her finger
under the next word on the list.

"Wait," I said. I looked up at the picture of her grandfather. "Do
you know much about him?"

"Not much."

"But he's your grandfather?"

She bowed her head toward the vocabulary list, anxious to move
on. "Right. P—"

"Your father's father."

She leaned in the chair and looked through the jailhouse mul-
lions of her window. Her forehead riddled with concern, and her
voice went hush. "My father's father was *quan lai*. Do you know
that word in English?"

I didn't, and she looked it up in her dictionary: *mandarin*. A
member of the elite Vietnamese ruling class who'd ascended to
privilege through a rigorous examination system that had been undone around the time of World War II.

I'd been trying to account for Thuy's poise, the soft edges in her
voice, her unflappable reaction to my presence and the long stories
that scrolled out of me, about Big Sur in California, Paris as viewed
from the deck of a *bateau mouche*, my meeting with Senator John
Kerry in Saigon. Nothing impressed her, at least not on the face

of things. That her grandfather was a mandarin explained some of this refinement.

Minh repeated the word quietly, *mandarin*, and I repeated it, and we went on like that until her sister Oanh arrived, also wearing the *ao dai* under a great coat.

"My fourth sister," Minh said, rising and reaching for her young nephew, nicknamed Rin, after *rin-rin*, a Vietnamese bastardization of the word *original*, which were the kinds of clothes Oanh sold.

Oanh's husband, Dung, looked at Minh's books, at the tea service, at me, and promptly went to a crate and drew two bottles of Huda beer. Thuy's father's cronies retired, and in another moment, the old man joined us at the dining table. Dung poured the beer over ice and held his glass aloft for cheers.

"How many bottles can you drink?" Dung asked me.

"Ten," I answered. It's what I always answered.

"Strong man," Thuy said, setting down a plate of sticky rice on a banquet table. "Bad pronunciation. He asked how many bottles, and you told him 'nose.' *Muoi* is 'ten,' and *mui* is 'nose,' and you said 'nose.'"

Another sister, Nguyet, arrived with her husband, also Dung, and two young sons. Dung-Oanh referred to Nguyet as the second sister. The fifth sister, Vui, arrived, pregnant, with a husband and daughter. And then the first sister, Nga, with two children and a balding husband who was a microbiologist at the Pasteur Institute in Dalat.

"Second sister is most happily married," Thuy told me, sitting back from the romp that had taken over the room as the children began their play. "First sister, Nga, is the best at arguing. She argues very well. You can never win her. Fourth sister, Oanh, is most quiet."

In terms of beauty, humor, luck, and other categories, they all

knew where each stood. They talked unabashedly about the hierarchy but didn't seem to want to climb up or down over one another
to get to a new spot. To check how thorough the rankings were, I
asked Minh where she was on the quiet ladder. "Sixth," she said
without missing a beat. Minh was ranked first in the funny cate-
gory, but she complained that she ranked last in terms of beauty.
They unanimously agreed that fifth sister, Vui, was the most beautiful. As a high-school senior, she'd been chosen to pick the weekly
lottery on the local television station. Although she was the only
sister not to go to college, she nevertheless ranked first in terms of
intelligence and a talent for English, though she'd stopped studying
a long time before. Thuy ranked first in what Minh translated as
"ask-and-answer," or repartee, and a close second to Vui in beauty.
People sometimes asked Thuy why she'd grown her hair out, they
looked that much alike. The big difference between their appearance, Thuy told me, was a matter of interpretation. Vui's looks were
"bright," she said, meaning "incandescent," while her own were
"calm and quiet."

Last to come that evening was third sister, Dieu, who lived clos-
est to their mother and who ranked as the sweetest. She had three
children and was married, but her husband, Phuong, was absent.

Thuy unwrapped banana leaves from a sticky rice cake, then
sliced the tubular loaf into doughnut-sized wheels. The outer rind
was tinged green from the leaves; inside, the glutinous rice was
marbled with pork fat and a generous dollop of bean curd. Dung-
Oanh tipped a wheel of sticky rice onto a small plate of blue china
and slid it before me.

"If you want to drink a nose of beers, it's better you eat a lot of
banh chung," Thuy said.

Dung-Oanh and another brother-in-law made certain my beer

glass was never less than half full. Thuy's sisters pressed boiled pig's ankles on me, and boneless chicken feet. There were pickled banana buds, pickled branches of lotus plants, pickled sea cucumbers, seed meats from squash, sunflowers, and watermelons. Cracking watermelon seeds for the sliver of seed meat inside seemed to be the default occupational activity. To this spread I'd contributed a one-pound bag of M&Ms, bought for six dollars at a shop near the bus station. Thuy's mother filled a bowl with M&Ms for general consumption, but reserved a larger portion for the ancestor altar. Her grandchildren, as soon as the brimming bowl of shiny red, green, and yellow treats was set down, ignored the lotus and ginger candy. When Dieu's husband, Phuong, arrived, he put a halt to his kids' consumption of the M&Ms, a gesture that reminded me of the French language police who were trying to make sure that "hamburger" never infiltrated their dictionaries.

I felt a skittering of regret for having brought the treats. Almost immediately, I saw myself as a Coca-Colonialist, as a microcosmic example of the first American to open a McDonald's in Hanoi. I pictured the inevitable gush of Western goods and businesses that were bound to overwhelm the Vietnamese market as soon as the embargo was lifted. I saw a Sheraton rising on what the Vietnamese called Non Nuoc Beach but what the Americans had called China Beach during the war and was bound to be called China Beach again. I saw the bicycle traffic in Hue making way for more and more Toyota Camrys and Fords again, and perhaps even the minivan of the modern mother. I saw the fate of the *ao dai* in a flash, sloughed away for Laura Ashley dresses. Pretty soon, the T-shirt that Thuy's younger brother Thang was wearing, the one that said HELLO UNCLE FUNNY, would say SHIT HAPPENS.

Phuong's kids stepped back from the snack table, deprived and plainly morose, staring at the fast-vanishing bowlful of foreign snacks. "It would have been better, I guess, if I hadn't brought those," I whispered to Thuy.

"Why?"

"Look at them."

"That's his problem," Thuy said, nodding toward Phuong.

"He doesn't want his kids overwhelmed by foreign temptations," I said. "Nothing wrong with trying to keep things traditional."

She stared back at the table and spoke softly. "You think that's why he won't let them eat the snacks? Not right. His son plays GameBoy. His girls watch American cartoons, no problem. They can't have them because you brought them."

"This is a traditional holiday. It makes sense you wouldn't gunk it up."

"No, no," she said. "It's because of you, because you are an American."

From across the room, Nguyet, who spoke English, shushed Thuy.

I knew that Dung-Oanh's father had been a Viet Cong hero, but Dung didn't seem to harbor any derivative hostility toward me. I didn't know Phuong's background. "His family was for the North?"

"No, for Saigon before 1975," Thuy said more softly. "But that's not it. He made trouble for my sister yesterday. He thinks my family is making a big mistake, letting you into my house."

"What does your family think?"

"We don't think much about what he thinks. About anything. He makes too much trouble for my sister, and we don't like that. We don't respect his ideas about anything."

Phuong hadn't greeted me when he arrived, and I hadn't thought much about that until now.

"He thinks Americans are only interested in one thing from a Vietnamese."

"What's that?" I spoke too soon because as soon as I'd said it, I knew what it was. "Well then, he's a jerk."

"That's what he says, as if he's looking out for me. But that," she stopped and laughed, "is not it at all. He doesn't like me, and he knows I don't like him. Anyway, he's wrong about his idea, even if he is pretending to be concerned about it. Because I know already."

"Know what?"

"Know you're just here to get stuff for your magazine."

Midway through the evening, a young man puttered into the courtyard on a late-model Honda Dream motor scooter. He was my age, or slightly older, and carried himself with the quiet self-assurance of someone who's already achieved success. He was a pilot with Vietnam's fledgling airline, and though educated, he didn't speak English. He spoke Russian. We'd been playing rummy 500, and as he took his seat with us, I dealt him in. Thuy translated my instructions.

A little while later, another young man showed up. His manners were impeccable. Inside the doorway, he nodded perfunctorily at us, then stepped toward the side doorway, hailing Thuy's parents. Thuy's father came to the door and shook his hand. Then, the young man lit three incense sticks, kowtowed at the altar of Thuy's ancestors, and slipped the incense into a cinder pot. None of it seemed artificial, nor did the enthusiasm with which he engaged the pilot.

"They haven't seen each other for a couple of weeks," Thuy told me.

"Who are they?" I asked.

"My boy friends," she said, separating the words.

"Plural," I said.

"What?" she asked.

"More than one boyfriend."

"Of course."

Thuy kept her distance from the latest suitor's animated conversation, focusing instead on the cards, but when she made a gradually rising groan of protest at the new arrival's story, I sensed that none of this was coincidental, that she knew how to juggle. At her protest, he opened his arms appealingly in a demonstration of truth. In shirtsleeves, he had the bulging, well-honed arms of a gymnast.

When the dentist showed up, home from Saigon for the holiday, and the family all turned out for him, I began to feel like a character in a Russian court novel. The dentist also happened to be a grandson of the great Vietnamese nationalist and poet Phan Boi Chau, who had been a predecessor of and inspiration to Ho Chi Minh.

"Do you know his poems, Jim?" Thuy asked.

I told her I didn't, frowning with what I hoped passed for scholarly interest.

Thuy selected a volume from a well-stocked case. "I will read for you one," she said, "first in Vietnamese so you can hear the beautiful sound of his words."

It was a poem about an apricot blossom; and as she read, the others picked up the verse, mumbling it by rote like communicants.

"Wonderful," I said when she finished.

"And how about your Grandpa, Jim?" asked Minh. "What's his job?"

I glanced at the portrait of their grandfather. His dress whites. The medals. The slightly effete look to his face, like a British aristocrat. All I could stack against him and the revolutionary was a tool-and-die maker and a man who worked in newspaper circulation when he wasn't on a binge.

They were snacking again on watermelon seeds, shucking meat from the husks with deft snaps between the teeth but waiting for my answer. "Newspapers," I said. "My grandpa was in newspapers, like me."

After ten o'clock, the explosions of fireworks steadily intensified, the whumphing bursts of cherry bombs, butterfly whirlers, bottle rockets, and Roman candles shrieking colors over the rooftops. On the verandah, Thuy's thirty-five-year-old sister, Nga, sat on the wide, flat banister, staring out at the frenetically lit sky. This evening was the twenty-fifth anniversary of the Tet Offensive, a co-ordinated nationwide assault on the cities and towns of South Vietnam that was no more devastating than it was in Hue. For some minutes I'd resisted giving in to curiosity, but the legacy of that battle was palpable, made redolent by the anniversary and the deafening barrages of noises all over the city.

"Twenty five years ago, terrible," I said, as if offhandedly, though making sure Nga heard me.

Nga got promptly into the story. Back then, the family was living in a house two blocks away, very close to the An Hoa Gate. At midnight, while fireworks crackled all over the city, Nga saw men with weapons crouching along the ramparts of the Citadel walls. She sensed that these soldiers were allied with Hanoi and so hurried inside to tell her father who was home on holiday leave from his ARVN unit. He fled at once. For three days Mrs. Bang and her five daughters hunkered down at home, the Battle of Hue raging around them, while he hid on the roof of an elementary school that Thuy would later attend. He didn't have food, or water, but he survived. The history books say 10,000 others in Hue did not and that many of them had been buried alive by the Viet Cong and North Vietnamese.

"If Ba was home when the VC burst into our house, they would have killed him," Nga said. *"And we would have watched him die."*

During the same battle, an artillery shell exploded on the home of the Nguyen's neighbors. Shrapnel riddled the wall above Nga's bed. Outside, Nga saw the scattered, bloody body parts of her neighbors.

"Did you know this?" I asked Thuy.

"I heard something about this, one time before," she said. But it wasn't part of the family lore, as if anyone would want it there.

A sulfurous white haze rose in the neighborhood, thickening as the fireworks strengthened. The racket surged and ebbed erratically as thousands of families who lived within the Citadel's walls plowed into the New Year. Thang unfurled an eight-foot wheel of firecrackers and cherry bombs and hung it from a tree limb out front.

"We are scaring the ghost-a," Thuy said, adding a suffix to the word. "All over Hue, my neighbors scare ghost-a with firecrackers." She placed her forefingers in her ears as Thang lit her family's string. "So loud, I think next year we don't have any evil my city."

Shortly before midnight, Thuy's father and mother went out into the courtyard, to a table laden with mung bean and lotus pudding, mounds of sticky rice, a skinned chicken and cinder pots for incense. The feet of the chicken had been removed.

"My mother will tie those feet with string peeled from bamboo and hang in our kitchen," Thuy said. "Later, she will take them to the fortune teller, so we can know how will be our luck for the rest of the year."

Up and down the street, the neighbors were turning out likewise, the eldest members of each family, the men and women clad in a ceremonial *ao dai*. Thuy's father wore a mandarin's cap. In the fluorescent porch light, I could see Thuy's mother's teeth glistening black.

Mr. and Mrs. Bang clasped lit sticks of burning joss and bobbed nine times in a prayerful obeisance to *Ong Troi* and *Ba Dat,* Father Sky and Mother Earth. Mr. Bang mumbled prayers first, then Mrs. Bang.

"They are calling on Father Sky and Mother Earth to help us through the year," Thuy whispered to me. "My mother asks for safety for her children . . ." She looked off into the middle distance, meting out the translation in beats as if tuning into a distant signal. "For prosperity. For success in business. For things to go smoothly. We will be thankful and never forget the good fortune you bring to us through the year, Father Sky."

Now, there was no break in the din. It was as if the city had harnessed time, and we were galloping on it. At midnight, we hurtled into the Year of the Rooster on a crescendo. The noise tightened around us, like a noose, running the blood, and we cheered into the deafening offensive against hard luck. Thang, like a line officer, was passing out butterfly whirlers, bottle rockets, and Roman candles. Still in her *ao dai* but heedless of it, Thuy stooped to set off a barrage of bottle rockets, lighting them out of an old drab green cartridge box, stenciled U.S. ARMY on the side. The rear panel of her dress lay over the cement like a train. Her excitement was girlish and skirling as we pumped hallucinatory colors out of the Roman candles.

She emptied her candle before I did mine, and then placed her palm on my forearm for the vicarious thrill of shooting more. Her hand was moist; she gripped with every expulsion.

"Welcome to the New Year," she said joyfully. "It brings good luck to the family if the first visitor is cheerful. So you must smile and laugh a lot."

I nodded

"Begin now," Thuy said.

. . .

Because we had swapped the monkey for the rooster as reigning animal icon for the new year, I wondered whether that transition had licensed Mr. Bang's consumption of the monkey wine. Had we been coming into the Year of the Monkey, perhaps there would have been less interest in imbibing one? Then again, there had been no shortage of chicken on the Nguyen's holiday table—a slight to the rooster if ever there were one. So much for my theorizing. I had a lot to learn.

After the Nguyen's Tet celebration, my sense of Hue as an East Asian idyll, as lost to the wider world as Brigadoon, deepened. The Perfume River spliced the city into a north bank and a south bank, each as thickly settled but each with a different visual feel. On the south bank, the city owed much to France, which after more than two centuries of commercial and evangelical interests in Vietnam, officially consolidated its hold on Vietnam in the late 1880s. The colonizing Europeans had sprawled along the south bank, building a palace for their governor, mansions and villas for administration officials, hotels, Catholic churches, a cathedral, boulevards, and an esplanade, most of which had survived the First Indochina War and the Vietnam War and made coming into Hue a bit like coming into a provincial French city.

But the indulgent European splendors of the south bank were no match for the extravagances on the north bank, where the Nguyen lords had reinforced their hold on all of Vietnam in the late eighteenth century. Here, several miles inland from the South China Sea, the Emperor Gia Long began construction of a mammoth citadel, two and a half kilometers square, twenty feet high, sixty feet thick, and surrounded by a moat. Thuy lived within the walls of this citadel. So had the emperors. Not content with a single walled city, they fixed one eye on the Chinese capital in Peking and built their own Imperial City for their own Son of Heaven. Here, encompassed by a perimeter of interior walls, was the Palace of Supreme Harmony and the monumental Noon Gate, as physically imposing and inspiring as ever despite the two wars that had rolled through Hue. Still, those wars had cost the Imperial City most of its dynastic structures. Hardest hit was the Forbidden Purple City, the walled inner sanctum of gardens, temples, and halls, all modeled on the Forbidden City in Peking and reserved for the exclusive use of Vietnam's Son of Heaven, his wives and concubines, and their attendant eunuchs. In 1992, the foundations of many of the destroyed structures in the Forbidden Purple City served as the borders of gardens for beans and peanuts.

If Hue was the most regal city in Vietnam, it could also lay claim—perhaps more than any other in the country—to the Vietnamese soul. Its landmark pagodas had turned out Vietnam's most renowned Buddhist monks: Thich Quang Duc, who set himself ablaze in a Saigon intersection in 1963, hailed from Thien Mu Pagoda; and Thich Nhat Hanh, the prolific exile who was nominated for the Nobel Peace Prize by Martin Luther King in the 1960s, was reared at Tu Hieu Pagoda.

I had plans for exploring all these places in the coming days, weeks, however long it took. I took note of them in my guidebook, but my guidebook said nothing about a more immediate concern, the protocols of getting to know a young woman here. For guidance, I went to Boi, a cyclo driver I'd befriended outside one of the city's cafés. He advised me to move to a small hotel across the river. "One, maybe two kilometers from her house. That's better."

"No," I said. "I'm just talking for example. What do men typically do in Vietnam?"

"What color *ao dai* did she wear?"

"Who?"

Boi brushed long Ramones-like bangs off his eyes and, clutching his flannel shirt at the unbuttoned throat, flapped out the heat. The shirt went back to Kurt Cobain, and the Mekong whiskey he'd been contemplating in a teacup went back to Axl Rose. Rose, he'd assured me at least twice, was "very good at drinking whiskey." Boi spoke fluent pidgin English, and he was hip to the harder side of American rock music—Guns 'n' Roses, Nirvana, and Pearl Jam—though he had an odd affinity for mushy songs like "Me and You and a Dog Named Boo" and the odd Karen Carpenter number. He was having none of my runaround. "What color?"

Somehow he knew. "White with yellow flowers," I admitted.

He repeated the phrase and mused on that a moment, sucking on a Dalat brand cigarette and then exhaling smoke in a bluish pall. "Okay, okay, very good. *Ao dai* is very difficult to wear. Yellow is no good. You have to ask her to wear purple. Purple means she has the boyfriend."

"I'm not there yet. I'm just asking for an example. I'm curious about the pace. Do you know that word?"

"Pace, right. You must go to her house many times, my friend," he told me. "Every and every day. Go for lunch. Go for dinner. In Saigon, my friend, very different. Go with girl for coffee, listen to music, then make love. Boom-boom. Ooh la la. But in Hue is very different."

"I'm not talking about boom-boom."

"I know, my friend. Only to joke. But cannot live like lonesome monk every night shooting down Hueys and B-52s." His wheezing laughter released enzymes that shot to his knees and elbows, buckling him into a curled-up ball of vibrating mirth.

"What do you mean?"

"Monks wank, my friend. Some nights in bed, have no woman,

shoot down a Huey. Some nights, very good at being alone, very strong, maybe shoot down B-52."

Night after night I biked the same route to Thuy's house, telling myself I was only following Boi's advice as if this was the pace of romance in Vietnam. But it was not the way they did things here, and I knew myself better than that. This was my pace.

In the States, the protocol was clear. The day after a fine first evening together was spent in self-restraint. You hoped that that restraint would be construed as evidence of other interests. No matter how rash the yearning for more contact, you had to pretend your life was going on without her, that you had other friends, plans, and obligations. She might have dazzled you, but she hadn't blinded you. You had another life.

I'd never dated a girl without front-loading the whole affair. From the ecstatically gained summit of a first date, I could see forever, all the way down the road, Walter Mitty with bionic vision: weekends away, heartfelt revelations, the glitter of a diamond. Though I frequently tired first, exhausted from so much castle building, I'd always find myself sprinting off the mark again the next time, as if it weren't a whistle I was hearing but the first note of a glorious love song. Every time it was going to be different this time.

David Relin had returned to Hue the day after I jumped off the train. He'd traveled as far as Danang, the next stop, though it hadn't taken him that long to figure out that we probably wouldn't rendezvous in Saigon, that Koh Pi Pi was out of the question, and that the magazine article we were on together was in jeopardy. Those were the immediate reasons for his coming back, stated as I helped lug his gear toward yet another shared hotel room. But they ran deeper than that.

"I want to see if you can picture yourself outside the movie," he said. "See if you're able to come down off this moat-induced high or if you just float off to la la land."

He was right. There was something cinematic about the way everything was coming together: the lush tropical setting, the exotic local girl, the suite of suitors, the ancient feel of this backwater city, this Brigadoon, this undiscovered starlet behind the soda fountain. Hue was the perfect milieu for a fleeting, illicit romance that might tread the waters of memory for years to come, but I took myself more seriously than this. Everything was at stake. I knew it, and Relin knew it.

One day at a late lunch, we sat with a pair of travelers who'd talked about climbing the limestone cliffs near Krabi. One of the backpackers, an Austrian, was disappointed by the degree of difficulty available over the routes they'd chosen. Too light. "Not satisfactory at all," he'd said.

"For some," Relin said after they left, "if it doesn't come with difficulty, it's not worth having."

"No pain, no gain," I said and looked down at my bicep. "Yeah."

"You start up a route that's five point four or five point five, and even if the view is stunning and the sun is tremendous on your back, and the rock feels right under your fingers, the climb's no good cause it's not *hard* enough. It's not fun unless it's really difficult."

"It's not worth climbing unless it's beyond what you can do." I shook my head a bit ruefully, as if we'd each reached a similar peak and seen the lay of the land as it was.

"And that's fine," Relin went on. "I mean, if we don't push ourselves, if it's all too easy, then boredom sets in. A balance has to be struck. How much of what I'm doing is what I'm doing because I'm truly captivated by this, right down to the essence of who I am and what I've got? How much is that, and how much is the degree of difficulty?"

His tone had wandered from irony to ruminative, and I suddenly realized he wasn't merely talking about rock climbing. He let his question hang, obliging some sort of response.

"Well, yeah, it's a balancing. You got to keep it in perspective," I said.

"I remember that story you told me about that one girl in college, how many times you asked her out. Again and again and again is what you said. She had a boyfriend at the time. The deck was really stacked against you. The more you asked and the more she said no, the harder you tried. You on a campaign?"

I'd told this to Relin during a conversation we'd had about the thin line between winning and losing. I'd seen something noble in my perseverance, even when things did not work out. "At least I tried" was always my out.

"How many times have you asked Thuy out?" he asked.

"Let's talk about the Austrians."

From a nearby pagoda, a group of monks began their four-o'clock incantations, a hypnotic string of prayers punctuated by light raps of a hollow gourd and, sparingly, a brass bell. A monk in Dalat once told me I should count to three and focus on my breathing for three seconds whenever I heard a bell. When I told him I didn't hear bells that often in America, he said I should use the ring of a telephone as a proxy.

"Beautiful," I said after we stopped listening.

Relin nodded. "But not for the height they add to the deck."

I fell into a groove, crossing the river at dusk. Past the Noon Gate, the monumental entrance to Hue's Imperial City, I'd brake at a corner shop to buy cookies, the most expensive kind of coconut-flavored biscuits imported from China, the same kind every night. With my fledgling Vietnamese, I would haggle with the shopkeeper, a mock battle that was a parody of most interactions between the people of Hue and the foreigners who visited. Every night, back and forth in Vietnamese, volleying insistent bids for the shiny silver package of biscuits.

"Eleven thousand dong, and no more!"

"Never. You're American. You pay fourteen thousand."

"I'm a poor American. Lower the price to twelve. That's enough for you!"

"Can never agree. Fourteen thousand, you must pay."

One night, a young couple on a motorbike paused to watch the battle over cookies. The driver nosed the front wheel of his Honda to within a few feet of the woman's display case, and they stared undauntedly, as if they had paid admission. I was getting used to this. For weeks, I'd been waking up in guest houses where, when my room was on the first floor and there was a window, I'd find a bouquet of children's faces keeping vigil over my postdawn sleep.

"Toi ten la Jim," I said at last, telling the couple my name.

"Who asked?" the woman said in English. She had wrapped her arms around the driver's waist and pressed her cheek against his shoulder. Her English was perfect.

"Where you going, Jim?" she asked, as direct as a trial lawyer.

I twisted my hands at my ears, a Vietnamese gesture to communicate incomprehension or finality.

"What's her name?"

"Who?" I hung the bagged cookies from my handlebar.

"Who?" she mimed back.

"Khong nho," I said. I don't remember.

The girl smiled and touched a spot in the air, anointing what could have been prescience if it hadn't really been gossip. "Her name is Thuy," she said.

People knew, and because they knew, Thuy's mother worried. One night, her voice carried out from behind the wardrobe, disembodied and a bit plaintive. I couldn't catch the gist of her message, to which her daughters listened with rapt attention, but I knew the message concerned me.

Thuy left the table as she spoke and returned with a notebook of grid paper. She spoke tentatively. "You come back my house again, my mother, she thinks it's better you get permission."

I nodded as if I understood.

"Do you know why?" Thuy asked.

I shook my head.

"In my country, it's illegal for the foreigner to visit the home of a Vietnamese unless he has special permission."

She turned to a blank page and smoothed it beneath her palm, but Minh took the book and started writing: *Please allow Mr. James D. Sullivan to visit 16 Nguyen Trai in Tay Loc where he is offering English language lessons to Miss*—"I write my name here only," Minh said. "Not Thuy's."

"Why?"

Minh didn't look up. "If I put my sister's name, this may cause jealousy. Because she is beautiful, many people know about my sister."

I glanced at Thuy to see if Minh's reference to her looks had unsettled her. But she betrayed no discomfort; she knew her measure. She held my glance for a moment, raising a forefinger to her lips, shushing any further talk.

At Boi's suggestion, Relin and I moved to a storied old hotel that stretched a city block along the Perfume River. This was the Morin, and when Boi wasn't idling along Le Loi Street, he was here fishing the stream of foreigners exiting the hotel. Shortly after check-in, I opened the door to a woman in a powder-blue negligée and a ghoulish application of white pancake foundation.

"Ma-sah?" she asked in a voice so feathery light it was barely audible.

"Ma-sah?" I called back to Relin.

"No ma-sah," he said.

"No ma-sah," I relayed the word.

She took my wrist and led me to a set of shuttered French windows that gave onto the hotel's interior. Across the courtyard, two women sat on a single stool at a door with a sign overhead that read MASSAGE. "You want ma-sah . . ." She gestured at her friends, who beckoned me with hand flapping.

"Okay. I see. That's where. Okay, thank you."

Ma-sah was a staple service at every hotel. At the rank guest houses, the same woman who brought you tea water and who would take your dirty laundry might also ask if you wanted ma-sah. At the more upscale places, she might wear something flimsy, powder blue or pink, and she might dispense with the pretense altogether. In Nha Trang, the ma-sah girl made room for me on the landing as I squeezed by, carrying my gear. When I nodded my thanks, she pounded the flat of her palm with the butt of her other fist, then hiked her eyebrows in appeal. "You," she said bluntly.

In Bangkok, where the use of makeup and banter was artful, the temptation was dazzling, especially along Patpong, where the go-go girls wore numbers. The prostitution in Bangkok didn't look depraved; it was more like harlotry. The boyfriend-girlfriend artifice of the go-go girls smacked of genuine feeling. You are different, they'd tell you, and then they would tell you about their cats and their little brothers back home. No wonder so much of the tourist traffic in Bangkok, in fact all over Southeast Asia, was voyeuristic.

During the month we'd idled in Thailand, waiting for visas, I quit the nightly jaunts to Patpong. Paying for sex was a threshold I wasn't ready to cross, and that had less to do with politics or ego than it did trepidation; a huge percentage of the women on Patpong were HIV positive. More than that, it was a matter of inertia and perhaps a smidgen of Puritanism.

Relin loved dancing on the threshold. For as long as we were in Bangkok, he was bungee-bound to Patpong. All it took was the nudge of night. "I go bright lights, big city," he'd pidgin, contemplating another audience of a go-go girl boxing extravaganza or a lurid second-floor sex show. Then he'd inflate the rotundity of his eyes, which was what he did instead of rolling them, and shrug his shoulders as if to say this departure for Patpong, this acquiescence, was to something obligatory. But he was careful too. Before going out, he would empty his wallet of any meaningful sum. In the morning, I would find a Polaroid of him and a bar girl. It was what there was instead of a torn condom package.

Hue didn't have bright lights, big city. In the evenings, while I was at Thuy's, Relin hung out in the Rock Café, as Boi dubbed the one place in town that played everyone from Hendrix to Vedder and catered to the disenfranchised sons of former soldiers and officials who had served the government of South Vietnam. One day, Relin mentioned a woman he'd met upstairs at Dong Ba market, a fabric saleswoman Boi knew. Hoa was a political outsider. Most of her family had immigrated to the United States several years earlier, but Hoa and her brother remained behind. Relin couldn't say why—going to America seemed foremost on every Vietnamese wish list—except that Hoa admitted to a kind of distance from others.

"She's a loner?" I asked.

"No, more like a castaway," he said. "She's interesting."

When he mentioned her again, he proposed we meet for lunch or dinner, all of us together, but I shrugged him off, noting Thuy's reluctance to leave the house in my company. I'd proposed a number of trips—to the Forbidden Purple City, Temple of Literature, Linh Mu Pagoda, the tombs of the Nguyen emperors—harmless little forays that could always be cast in the clear light of tourism. She never actually refused, but we never actually went anywhere either. The only saving grace to not leaving her house was not having to meet Relin and Hoa. But even after Thuy cut the tether and we started out into Hue, I used the same excuse.

After we'd visited the Linh Mu Pagoda and Temple of Literature—always in the company of Minh and a retinue of nieces and nephews—Thuy asked whether I wanted to visit the tomb of the Emperor Minh Mang. Most of the Nguyen emperors had built lavish mausoleums in the shallow folds of hills rolling off the Perfume River. No mere crypt or ossuary, Minh Mang's mausoleum was a sprawling walled compound of temples, steles, sepulchres and gardens, streams and piney knolls, all laid out with meticulous regard to classical Chinese tradition.

Together with Minh and Dieu's two daughters, Ni and Na, we launched one morning from the South Bank in a river sampan painted swimming-pool blue. While the skipper tinkered with his diesel engine, his wife poled us away from the landing to deeper water. A troupe of costumed musicians clustered under the boat's wooden canopy and fielded questions from members of two other families that had joined us. On the rear deck, Minh, Ni, and Na were heating a snack of cuttlefish over a flaming Sterno.

"Do you want to ask the captain any questions?" Thuy asked.

"No." I leaned back against the gunwale.

"For example, about the engine or the river?" She was sitting erectly prim beside me with a Hue City guidebook in her lap. She hadn't carried the book before.

"No, I'm fine."

She asked anyway and reported back that the engine was a 22-hp diesel made in China. The river was six feet deep.

Thuy opened her book and read about the geomancers who'd sited the Nguyens' tombs. The royal fortune-tellers had roamed the countryside, using a geomantic compass to locate the most auspicious natural interplay of hills and streams. If the site was good, that emperor's progeny would enjoy success and fortune.

"What happens if a site is not good?" I asked.

"If it's not good, bad things will happen to that family."

"Bad things? For example?"

She looked away for a moment, concentrating. "That place we had lunch, everyone in that family is dumb?"

"Yes."

"They believe that a root grew through the mouth of an ancestor, he's buried. That's why nobody in that family can speak. We believe if the grave of our ancestors is disturbed—for example, it's not in a high place where the floodwaters cannot go—then bad things will happen to that family. It's very and very important we take care the dead."

"Do you believe it?"

My question drew a long wake of silence, and I wondered if I'd offended her. I couldn't be sure. The cadence of our rapport was offbeat; at least, it didn't subscribe to anything in my experience. Sometimes I'd ask a question she wouldn't answer at all. Just because someone asked you something didn't necessarily oblige a response.

"I don't know," she said finally. "But it's been in my culture, I guess, for thousands of years. I don't know whether I believe or not. It's just there."

As we passed beneath the trestled spans of the Truong Tien Bridge, the boat's musicians launched into song. They played a moon-faced lute and a zither. One woman rhythmically clinked tiny porcelain teacups on her fingertips like castanets. They all wore the *ao dai* as they sang traditional songs about Hue, about *banh beo* and *bun bo Hue*, two local delicacies; another song about a black horse that I'd heard before; treacly songs about loss and love, for which the achingly expressive singer would move her hands in slow-motion gesticulation and far-off wonder in her face, pressing home her sentiment.

As we passed Hon Chen Temple, set on a precipitous wooded bluff at a bend in the river, the musicians broke into song about this storied place. More pilgrims visited this site than any other in Hue. The melody dissolved into wild, chaotic noise as the musicians mimicked the sound of a ghost entering the soul of a live body.

"My mother," Thuy said, leaning in whisper toward me. She didn't say any more than that, but I understood her to mean that her mother would respond to this music. She, I was led to believe, did not.

The sampan skipper's wife and eldest daughters prepared lunch on a wood-stoked cookstove. I recognized the chicken, when it came on a platter, and the greens didn't worry me. Two dishes did bother me, and I steered around them with my chopsticks.

"Why you don't try this?" Minh asked, the query fractured, coming up through laughter as if a punch line. She deposited a piece of gristle in my bowl.

I looked back at the platter and its ribbed cartilaginous texture, its haunting curvaceousness not at all mitigated by its sprightly garnish. I'd eaten the wombs of pigs in Vietnam, the stomachs of chickens, dog soup by accident, and I'd been on the lookout for this dish, to avoid it.

Two men in another party looked on and clinked their beer bottles in a cheer when they caught my attention.

"We're lucky to have this dish," Minh went on, gesturing her chopsticks at the men. "Those men, they make a special order for this dish today."

Thuy removed a segment from the rice bowl, and I could hear the small noise as she crunched it down. No part of an animal's anatomy was beyond her appetite. One of her nieces asked whether people like Mr. Popsicle could eat this food.

"It's from the water buffalo," Minh went on, absolutely delighted.

"I know where it's from," I said.

"Water buffalo is good," she said.

I had no problem with water buffalo in general. As often as not, the steak served in restaurants was cut from water buffalo. I took up my morsel and chewed. It had no taste, or I may have been holding my breath.

Ni and Na beamed at me. "He swallowed too fast," Minh reported to Thuy.

Thuy had taken a more sober view of my consideration of the water buffalo penis, as if she'd seen hundreds of foreigners attempt Vietnam's culinary hurdles.

"You really like this?" I asked her.

"We like," she said, removing another choice morsel.

"How about the gall bladders of bears and ground tiger bones? Would you like those too?"

She shook her head dismissively. "Tiger bones are for the man."

· · ·

Our sampan put in at a muddy landing, and one of the boys stretched a gangplank to shore. Up the rutted path of a short rise, we threaded a stretch of bamboo concessions, manned by aggressive saleswomen who stepped into our path like cajoling carnival barkers: *"It's so hot today. You look hot. You look thirsty. Would you like something to drink? We have special drinks here."*

"We're very famous when we're with you," Minh said as we came out of the concessions.

We entered Minh Mang's mausoleum at a nondescript entrance to the right of the Great Red Gate—shut since the emperor's coffin passed through in the 1840s—and passed into a vast, landscaped park bounded by an undulating ten-foot wall. Pines towered at the perimeter, and clipped, potted shrubbery bordered promenades tiled in squares of clay. We moved naturally toward the mausoleum's main axis, stretched out between two lobes of a man-made lake. Here was the emperor's Courtyard of Honor, his commemorative stele and cult temple, ornate porticoes and columns swirling with dragons and flowering vines rendered in bas-relief. Open-air pavilions stood upon layers of plinths mounted by wide stairways that looked ready to crumble under step. It had been decades, really, since the mausoleum had been tended to, but all that decay emitted an intoxicating stimulant. It was a parkscape that compelled strolling and generated its own soundtrack, of zithers and lutes that could be heard if only you listened.

From the heights of the stele that commemorated Minh Mang's reign, we could see all of the mausoleum's grounds, its groves of bared frangipani trees and the emperor's tumulus, all of it working 150 years later to manufacture the kind of serenity that Minh Mang hoped to enjoy eternally. As I traced the grounds' perimeter wall, the cement facade fallen away to reveal the brick in many places, I glimpsed Relin and Hoa, sitting on a knoll just inside the enclosure. She was wearing the *ao dai* and cat's eye sunglasses.

"Let's go this way," I said, veering off the mainstream we'd flowed on to the stele.

In a nook beside the Huu Tung Tu Temple, we peeled longans and jackfruit. The nieces played a game like horseshoes with their sandals, and Thuy continued to translate out of her paperback. She detailed the thousands of coolie laborers required to build the temple and referenced the legend of a massacre of the king's grave diggers so no one, including robbers, would know where he was actually interred. She'd been unusually committed to getting out the word on Minh Mang. If it had been her sister, it would have been characteristic, but with Thuy it was off-kilter.

"But in 1885, the French soldiers, they robbed Minh Mang's Temple," she said.

"Amazing to think about your family at that time," I said, "where they were, what they were doing."

"Right," she said.

"Maybe they had something to do with this place."

She didn't follow my lead but went back to the paperback to tell about the Temple of Infinite Grace, and beyond the Pavilion of Light where Minh Mang used to relax when he came out to watch the construction.

After a while, we continued on to Minh Mang's alleged burial site, then back along the axis to the Courtyard of Honor, where life-size stone statues of military and scholarly mandarins flanked either side of a large parade ground. Minh boosted Ni and Na onto the stone back of a *ky lan*, a mythical Sino-Vietnamese dragon horse. The girls looked at me with forlorn hope. They knew I hadn't brought a camera, but perhaps the desirability of such a photograph might conjure one.

I saluted the military mandarins and marched past, barking for each to snap to, look alive, and buck up. Minh wondered aloud whether I'd ever served as a soldier. I told her no, the CIA. She gasped and went back to her nieces, taking my joke as fact.

"Hey," I said to Thuy, "look at this guy." I advanced on the expressionless face of the mandarin. A long, pointed beard fell from his chin, and his left hand held a long sword against his side. "He looks like your grandfather."

"I don't think so."

"Maybe your grandfather's grandfather." *Mandarins beget mandarins*, I thought.

She didn't say anything. I jotted a description of the statue in my notebook.

Minh gasped again. "It's better you don't do so; everyone can see," she called.

I raised a finger to my lips, shushing her, and her eyes widened in alarm.

"Okay," Thuy said, opening her paperback. "Do you know why these statues are here? No," she answered before I had time to. "Because they protect and serve the emperor in his next life. Do you know why they're made of stone? No. Because in the old day, they buried soldiers alive with the king. This is better."

"Maybe I know enough history now," I said casually, hoping to somehow crack the slightly pedantic tone that had crept into her speech since we'd set out today.

She strode away to the statuary mandarins, then stopped and placed her palms on either cheek of a Minh Mang guard. She stared into his eyes.

"Do you have enough for your magazine article now? Does David?" she asked. "I don't know whether his friend has this book, but if you want, I can let her borrow so he can take information."

I looked back toward the knoll, but David and Hoa were gone. Except for that brief distant glimpse, I'd not seen them again, and hadn't thought Thuy had. I didn't think Thuy had known about Hoa, but it seemed obvious now that the gossip mills in Hue had spewed some of this her way.

"It's not like that," I said.

"What did you write in your book?"

I showed her, and she started through the rest of my notebook. I pulled it back, chuckling to cover my embarrassment and the awkwardness of the gesture. I'd written things in there, images, mostly about her and mostly overwrought flights of description—the way the amber cast to her skin resembled the coloring of a woman's face simmered by candlelight, about the peculiar ascent of her hairline from left to right—things you don't want anybody to see.

"I see," she said.

"I didn't bring a camera. I scribble it down here instead. And it's not like that. I don't know what David's doing with that woman. It's not serious. It's not real for him, I'm sure about that."

"And how about you?"

"It's real. This is real. It shouldn't be, but it is. I don't know why."

She stepped under the *ky lan*'s pavilion and stared into the dragon's face. "He never eats the grass when it's green," she said, a fact she knew already, no guidebook necessary. "He only wanders into this world when the times are good. He is good."

She petted his head and stepped out from under the roof. She looked at me and then made another grammatical mistake that I wouldn't correct. "I don't know too."

All through the Tet New Year, the suitors showed up every night. We drank tea. We ate sticky rice and cracked watermelon seeds between our teeth. I continued to bring cookies, and though Thuy served them on a plate, she and I were the only ones to touch them. Cookies were for children and women, I found out later, not men and certainly not suitors.

Within an hour the other men would leave. The regularity of their visits, not the length, was a measure of the seriousness of their suit; brevity was customary. I pretended not to know. I stayed and stayed. I bid them farewell from the door, standing beside Thuy, waving while they smoldered into the dark, handicapped by custom, undone by the ignorance of a guy who wore a Day-Glo yellow rain jacket and shorts in a country where only children wore shorts.

Although I'd planned to act on the note Minh had written and had started pedaling toward the police station a couple of times, I couldn't bring myself to complete the trip, hat in hand, seeking permission. When it came to the authorities, asking for anything was asking for trouble.

One night, I was sitting with the pilot and the guitar player when an unusually deep guttering of a motorbike sounded in the courtyard. "Be Nho," Thuy said sharply, using the family name for her young sister.

Minh grabbed the massive Vietnamese-English dictionary she'd bought with her scholarship money and opened it on the tea table.

"Ahh, Jim, do you know this word, bas . . ."

Thuy started talking to the dentist.

I leaned over Minh's dictionary. "Basidium," I said. "It's very seldom used. Better to say 'mushroom.'"

Minh began repeating the word *mushroom* as the new motor-cyclist stepped through the windstrips. He was a slender man, even for a Vietnamese. A weak mustache struggled for credibility, and several long hairs grew from a mole on his cheek. He gave me a plastered-on smile as we shook hands and room was made for him at the table.

Thuy returned with a fresh pot, and the newcomer, Dich, rinsed everybody's cup and poured a fresh serving. He then passed around a basket of bananas, as if none had dared touch them until his arrival.

"So where are you from?" Dich asked me, all the words sliding together as if it were one word.

"*My,*" I said, answering him in Vietnamese.

He smiled and strained for comprehension. "Again, please?"

"*My,*" I said. "*Hoa Ky.*"

I knew I could make myself understood with these words, but Dich blinked at me, then glanced at the pilot and the guitar player to see if it was him. "In English, please?" he asked.

I nodded and sipped from my teacup, irked by his posturing.

"What country you live?" he asked.

"I'm sorry," I said. If he couldn't understand me, then perhaps I couldn't understand him.

"America," Thuy said flatly.

"And why have you come my country?"

"Curiosity," I said.

"About what?"

"This country." I smiled and looked at him with as much forced pleasantry as I could muster.

He lit a cigarette and made a sucking noise as he took a breath through his nostrils. "May I see your passport?" he asked.

"My what?"

"Passport? Do you have it?"

"No, do you have yours?"

He dragged off his cigarette, then chuckled.

Thuy studied a water stain on the poured concrete floor.

"Why do you ask about my passport?" I asked.

"It's my business."

"What's your business?"

He looked at me with a deliberately flaccid expression, letting that pass for an answer.

"Police," Thuy said.

Until then, I hadn't noticed his olive green trousers with red piping. My thoughts ricocheted from the notice that Minh had written, to the niche where Mrs. Bang was sitting. She had asked me to obtain permission to be here, and I'd ignored the request. Now she had an unregistered visitor in her house, and who knew the consequences?

"And where did you get your travel permit?" he asked.

"Ho Chi Minh City," I said. No Saigon, no chances.

Outside, a bread peddler bicycled down the street, calling out his wares, *"My, banh my,"* in a weak ancient dirge of sound hearkening back to the age of inquisitions, dungeon racks, and carts of piled dead. Minh selected a new word from her dictionary and promptly bungled the pronunciation.

"Acuity," I corrected her. I leaned over the dictionary, suddenly absorbed in our student-teacher relationship.

"Ush . . ." Minh tried to say it.

"Uk . . ."

"Uttts . . ."

"No, uk—"

"And where did you get your visa?" the cop asked.

"In Bangkok. At the embassy."

"And your extension."

"A-cu-i-ty," Minh said, jumping back in.

"How do you know I have an extension?"

"My job is to know."

"Then you should know where I got it." I could feel my grip slipping.

"Right," he said, "I should know. I know the law my country."

He took a pack of Souvenir-brand cigarettes from his pocket and shook several from the top. Though I'd never seen the guitar player or the pilot smoke, they each took one and lit up. He tilted the pack in my direction and held it there, cocked. I ignored the offer and let him continue to hold the pack. He couldn't let it down without a demurring gesture from me. The seconds unraveled, and Thuy was now anxiously massaging the skin above her temple. I couldn't do this to her, and I knew as well that I shouldn't be doing this to myself. I held no cards here.

"Khong hut thuoc," I said. I don't smoke.

In my peripheral vision, I could see his brow clamp in a frown. He was going to feign comprehension. The pack idled at my shoulder.

"No smoking," Thuy said in English, pressing the words, obviously exasperated.

"Oh no smoking. Healthy man. You go by bicycle, all the way from Ho Chi Minh to Hanoi. Maybe you are very strong."

He squeezed my bicep, and I stood up fast. His grin was a short distance from my elbow, and in a nanosecond, the jerk sprinted out of a place in my head. I could picture the concussion of knobby bone on his upper cheek, the pivot of his head, the follow-through of my weight, and his collapse to the floor. Everything would collapse, I knew, and I managed to contain my jumping up to standing only.

"You're going?" Dich asked. His brows lifted slightly.

"To the bathroom, yes," I said.

"If you can bring your passport back with you," he said, "that's better. It's very difficult go around my country no passport."

Dusk fell upon us like stage drapery, curtailing the end of our excursions to the tombs of the Nguyen emperors and pagodas nestled into the valleys of gentle nearby hills. The decision to "go back" was always abrupt, precipitated by a certain slant of sunlight that tunneled through ancient passageways and opened up secret chambers. I began to recognize that exact moment, a non sequitur of silence and stillness that always made me wonder whether Thuy had heard or seen something I had not.

"What is it?" I asked.

She shook off my question but then one day answered, "Mulberries."

"I don't understand."

She leaned across the space between us and her fingers darted to one of my gear levers. Nearly all Vietnamese bicycles were one-speeds, and she'd noticed that I was very protective of those gear levers when little kids swarmed my bicycle. She cranked the lever back and forth, as if to strip the gears. "Tell me when you do," she said.

We bicycled back through gauzy droves of insects that we couldn't see and couldn't duck. She spoke to me in Vietnamese and would not translate her side of the dialogue or let me fall back on English. Though I hadn't met anyone in Vietnam who enunciated English as well, she believed her grasp of the language was unwieldy and bumbling. And so, if only to remind herself, she turned me at least once a day into a caricature.

We never talked about my departure, and I kept from thinking about it, putting it off, waiting for an epiphany that wouldn't come. It shifted beyond us, sliding by overhead, glinting off the silver underbellies of the rare passing plane, in the odd snatch of mellifluent English we heard evenings as her father tuned in the BBC. But it remained unspoken, a fiction to our nonfiction.

Gradually, I exhausted my finances. Though I might have arranged a remittance between a Hue bank and my bank, where I had money pooling from a fellowship, instead I fixed a date for my departure, and we began to move toward it.

One evening shortly before I was to leave, it was just getting dark when Thuy came to the front room of her house. She glanced around quickly, then hurried to the door, flapping her hand for me to follow. "Quickly," she said.

"Wait," I said. "Your mother doesn't know we're going out."

"No problem."

She unlocked her bike, an imported, sky-blue model from Thailand with a plush, square saddle seat and a deep white wire basket below the handlebars. She eased it off its kickstand, grimacing as the spring snapped. We wheeled our bikes toward the gate. I was anxious to break free of our evening routine at her house, but wary too. I'd established honorable credentials in my repeated visits to her home, and this seemed to put that in jeopardy.

But there was more to it than that. As I watched Thuy lift a leg over the sloping top tube and watched her hair swing against her back, I had a feeling there would be no turning back, not from this, not from any of it. As she pressed down on her pedal, her mother came to the door and called. I couldn't turn around. If I did, I was afraid I'd see disgust written all over Mrs. Bang's face, that I'd be found out as a foreigner who only wanted one thing.

"Wait for me one minute," Thuy said.

Several minutes later she came out of the house with her hair in a long French braid.

"What happened?" I asked.

She shrugged and brushed one of her cheeks off a shoulder, an admission of shyness that she hoped would do for an answer. We rode in silence for some time, and I asked again.

"Your hair is braided now?"

"Ah," she said, reaching back in mock surprise. "Is it true?" Her hand felt for the braid. "Yes, *troi oi.*"

She pulled over near the Noon Gate, and removed the rubber band from her hair. She turned away and combed through it slowly with her fingers, lifting and pulling, again and again, as if I were privy to none of it. We still hadn't touched. Thuy had let that buffer between us when she'd declined to shake hands, and I observed it. Now, weeks later, my longing had mutated to illness. I was yearning like a boy, held at bay by the sureness of Thuy's decisiveness and by these extraordinary surroundings. Touching it might make it go away, and I hadn't wanted to risk that. It had its own leavening.

"It's because the ghost."

"What is?"

"Why my mother wants my hair to be in the braid. And why she doesn't want me to wear the light shirt at night. If my hair is loose, maybe a ghost can fly in there to live. If my shirt is light, the ghost can see me."

We pedaled slowly. As young people veered around us, bunched three and four on the long saddle of a motorbike, their heads swung back to take us in.

"This tree," Thuy said, gesturing at the long, dappled trunk of a tamarind, "if it doesn't grow fruit, maybe it's because a ghost lives up there. You see? Another example, some days ago, you asked why did my mother make a dirty mark with her thumb on the face my nephew, he is the baby? It's so he looks ugly, so the ghost doesn't want him."

"You told me it was a mistake."

"Yeah. Right." She acknowledged her diversionary response, which she seemed to believe she had as much right to as the truth.

"I didn't know Buddhists believed in ghosts."

"Not Buddhist," she said. "Something else. Most Vietnamese, they believe many things, not just about the Buddha. For example, we often think the monks, they are lazy."

"So you believe in the ghost," I said. My tone carried the weight of judgment, and she picked up on it.

Her eyes narrowed, and she shook her finger at me. "You are Catholic?"

"As a boy."

"My old aunt is Catholic, so I know."

"Know what?"

"You believe in the ghost, he is holy. *You* believe in the ghost."

I told her I was raised as a Catholic but didn't know what I was now. I didn't know what I believed.

"Like me. We don't know there are ghosts or not, but it's better we avoid them."

After crossing a bridge into the Gia Hoi subdistrict, we pedaled two more kilometers until the space between the buildings loosened and the shops and homes fronting the street petered out. Larger, gabled homes sat deeper in spacious lots. Between them, a longer view opened over the river to a large riverbank hotel, lit like an ocean liner.

Thuy stopped pedaling at the gateposts of a French villa. A shingle hung from a tree branch, identifying the home as 242 Café. She didn't say anything. She just stopped, and it took me a moment to realize that here, for propriety's sake, it was my job to usher us over the threshold.

"Do you want some lime juice?" I asked.

"It's up to you."

We wheeled our bikes over a courtyard of packed dirt while pop music floated from the villa's windows. Out back the garden was a thin forest of low pruned trees, the boughs twined with blinking holiday lights. A half dozen couples sat at bamboo tea tables scattered among the trees, facing the river.

"I'm coming here with my girlfriends," Thuy said, distancing herself from couples on the garden's fringe, holding each other in the dark.

We took a table on the bluff, six or eight feet above the river. While our waitress went for cane juice, a fisherman worked the bank below. A lantern dangled from a bracket jutting from the bow, and he leaned over into the light, tilting the stern of a long thin canoe.

"Those mulberries," I said, "you didn't hear them this evening."

"I hear them."

"What do they sound like?"

She didn't answer, and I dangled for several moments in the silence.

"Why do you like me?" she asked. The question emerged in a whisper, as loud as normal speech but spoken from another place.

"I don't know." I looked at her, but her sight remained fixed across the river at the sampan of a water gypsy gliding downstream on the tide. Her profile was cast in a stew of changing light, greens and reds and blues, a whole spectrum of light and possibility.

"My neighbors think you are CIA," she said. It was a confession, not suspicion.

I nodded.

"And my father says Americans are very good at leaving."

I pictured him at the window of their house, looking outside, hands clasped at the small of his back, imparting what he knew about those people.

"That was before," I said.

"And now," she said, turning to look at me.

"But I'm coming back in two months." I hadn't ever said this out loud before, not to her, and not to myself. We'd understood this to be true, that I would be back, but I had never vowed this much explicitly before. I reached into her lap and took one of her hands in mine, feeling all those weeks pour through the fingers. Our hands turned eagerly over each other.

"Is it true?" she asked.

"Yes."

She whispered, "I want you to stay in Vietnam forever."

I raised my palm to her cheek and leaned close, gently measuring the buoyancy of her lips with my own. A tiny gasp escaped between us. It might have been her; it might have been me. Her hand curled around the nape of my neck and pulled me deeper. We sunk against our chairs.

For hours we wandered around this new threshold, like teenagers, oblivious and indefatigable. From time to time, I sensed that we had lost purchase on the evening; there were chronological markers to honor, tolls that wanted heeding. We were heedless. Only after the music ceased and I heard murmurs from the café staff, wondering no doubt, about those two over by the river, did I pull away.

I whispered the hour to her, but she didn't respond. There was dream in her face, something untethered, drifting on the medley of light that played across her face. She stared numbly into the middle distance, as if chemically affected. For minutes, I waited for her to emerge from this torpor. When she didn't, I placed my hand beneath her arm and ushered her up.

She leaned against me, and I guided her through the empty café. Sight of the bicycles pushed her partway out of it, and she managed to get on and get under way. She pedaled weakly beside me, then grasped my wrist and stopped pedaling entirely. I was able to pedal for both of us.

For weeks, she'd dictated the pace of our relationship with a firm hand, but now her willfulness had deserted her. Her languor worried me. I looked for an antidote in mundane questions. How often did they tar the roads in Hue? Why were so many homes in Hue painted ocher? She didn't answer.

The streets were deserted and quiet but for the women in conical hats and scarves who swept up clouds of dust with long-handled whisk brooms. I knew the way back, but near the market, I deliberately turned wrong.

"Another way," she said.

She pedaled on her own for awhile, coming out of it, but then grabbed my wrist again as we approached one of the Citadel's gates.

"If you come back—" she said, suddenly sober.

"I am coming back."

She stopped her bike on the other side of the moat. "If you come back," she said again in the same tone, dismissing my interruption, "and if you and I—if anything can happen—you must stay in my country for one year, minimum."

"Why?"

She leaned over the stone railing and stared for a moment at the water's moonlit surface. "Because I have to know your temper."

I'd run into Dich several times after the Tet New Year. He would come by the house, check my passport and visa and then, because Thuy would have fled at the sound of his motorbike, I'd listen to him ramble through a discourse on the perseverance of the Vietnamese soldier and the iron will of a man on his home turf. Dich was several years older than me and a northerner whose family had migrated south, like thousands of other northern families, to take a privileged place in the new postwar South. If I had been one of those right-wing hawks who still argued that we, the United States, had been justified to prosecute our war in Vietnam, I might have taken offense at Dich's harangues. The content of his speeches didn't bother me, but the subtext did, and a couple of times I felt compelled to play devil's advocate.

"Some would call 1975 a Pyrrhic victory for the Vietnamese," I said once, more bored than roused.

"Yes, a great great victory."

Usually, however, Thuy and I slid through those evenings on our own, perched on the verandah. We stretched them as far as we could, through the hour that brought out the peddlers who roamed the neighborhood by bicycle, droning the words for bread—*myy, banh myyyy*—in a cry that seemed to hail from another age. Beyond the lullabies of a neighbor. Past Minh's return from her nightly study group. The mosquitoes were merciless.

"In the summer," Thuy said, scooping her open palm into a fist, "one hundred every time."

"We'll see."

"Right, we'll see."

After that night at 242 Café, she never once mentioned my return to Vietnam. She would not plan for it and refused to allow that it would happen. But as the mornings, afternoons, and evenings skipped inexorably toward my departure, she and I held on to each other with as much strength as possible. It's what I had from her instead of a spoken promise, and for a long time afterward, I could feel the exact pressure of her embrace like an echo.

At ten o'clock, the city's one television station signed off, turning the background soundscape over to the crickets, to the susurrations of the neighborhood's street sweepers, and to an inevitable murmur from Thuy's mother, calling her daughter in.

One night as I stood to go, Thuy's mother spoke again. She asked if it bothered me to ride home when the streets were deserted and the power had failed, as it did regularly. I told her it didn't.

Thuy translated my answer, then returned her mother's response. "She says it should."

"Ghosts?" I asked.

"It's better we avoid them," Thuy reminded me.

I could have changed my route, or varied it; there were any number of ways home from her house. But I loved my route. Some nights, when lucky, I would trail a bread peddler through the blacked-out streets, finding my way by crumbs of light that fell from his ember-filled warming trays. Most nights, I passed a gang of street sweepers, all women, scarfed like Bedouins against the swept dust. They knew my name and sometimes chirped it, *"Chim, chim,"* also the word for "bird" in Vietnamese, flapping their arms as I sped by. I reveled in the familiarity of my landmarks, especially the Noon Gate entrance to the Imperial City, with its winged belvederes and porticos, its fan-shaped windows and tiers of roofs with flying eaves. I had never actually passed through the gate itself, to the palace buildings that lay beyond, but as I bicycled home each night, the architecture of this dynastic vestige began to resemble the threshold I believed I was on the verge of crossing myself. And I knew that's why I was going home too. Because I didn't trust myself. Because I was going over a moat every night to visit the granddaughter of a mandarin, and because I couldn't straighten out the line between what was real and what was storybook.

Two nights before my departure, the headlights of two motorbikes lit my path through the blacked-out streets of the Tay Loc neighborhood, turning where I turned, slowing as I slowed, accelerating as I did. Maybe it was a measure of my exhilaration that I suspected nothing for so long, that I chalked up their presence on my tail through these deserted streets to coincidence, and even luck, for their light enabled my reckless speed. I felt triumphant and had no other way to celebrate but to blaze my way home, fast.

On the long straightaway that paralleled the southwest wall of the Imperial City, still in ruins from a battle the U.S. Marines fought here a generation before, it occurred to me that I should have been overtaken. Those lights should have passed. A wing beat of fear flapped in my chest. I didn't make much of it. There was bitterness out there, I supposed, among the living and maybe even the dead, but I believed then that I was protected from it. Like a lot of Americans traveling abroad, I believed that I was, for political reasons, invincible.

As the seconds stretched by and the trailing motorbikes didn't pick up their pace, I picked up mine. I pumped harder and flicked the gear levers with my thumbs. The chain ratcheted from the middle sprocket to the larger ring above, and stepped down the smaller rings off the rear wheel hub, increasing resistance and my speed. I mumbled an aimless prayer, striving to feel the distance lengthen between their pace and my own, but their engines whined after me, closing the gap.

I braked hard at the next corner, skidding off balance until I released the levers and the bike righted itself. By then, the motor-bikes had gained on me. Ahead was a half-kilometer straightaway, past the Noon Gate, to one more right turn, and a 300-yard sprint to the gate that would take me out of the Citadel and into the relative security of thicker traffic.

I stood off my bike saddle and bore down on the pedals. The motorbikes redlined their rpms, deepening the light before me. I had nowhere to turn. Flame trees lined either side of the road, like the quaint plane trees of provincial France but dreadful here. Their barren branches intertwined overhead, tunneling me in.

The motorbikes roared past, giving me a wide berth. Not until I saw the olive-green trousers of their uniforms and the red piping along the side seams did it occur to me that they were cops. Relief bubbled up my throat in light laughter.

The motorbikes' tail made perfect sense to me now. They'd spotted a strange-looking bicycle outside the areas of Hue haunted by foreigners at this hour, and they'd followed it. They'd checked it out. Now they were going back.

At the Noon Gate, the motorbikes braked and made a tight turn in the narrow roadway. Coming back, they accelerated up the center of the road. Their engines screamed through high rpms, providing maximum acceleration. As I veered right to make way, one motorbike veered with me, intending collision like a kamikaze. I jerked my handlebars. My front tire slapped the curb, and I was pitched forward as the wheel jammed.

For a moment, I felt myself completely and uncontrollably airborne. My shoulder hit ground first. My head whacked off new sidewalk tiles, and I skidded through grout to stop in the moonshadow of the Noon Gate.

The motorbikes had stopped too. Their brake lights were bleeding into the darkness, and I kept still. I couldn't tell how badly I was hurt. My instinct was to play dead, but even my throbbing head knew that kind of consequence was too outlandish, and not at all what was required. Better to play injured, scared and injured. I let out a groan, which is maybe all he wanted.

CHAPTER THREE

Driving home from the airport, my mother unburdened herself with uncharacteristic candor, confessing to the list of nightmares that had plagued her during my five months in Southeast Asia. I couldn't head her off course or change the subject. With morbid indulgence, she insisted on peeling each strand from the nauseating ball of worry that had built up in her stomach while I was gone, and holding each to the light: the tidal waves, shark attacks, and kidnappings, especially kidnappings. No threat was as terrifying to her as that, even if as a twenty-seven-year-old I no longer qualified as a target for pederasts and as the penniless son of a hard-luck subcontractor I was hardly prey for extortionists.

"Hostage is what I meant," she said. "Abduction."

It hadn't mattered, I realized now, that I'd spent all that time before my departure reassuring her, painting Vietnam as a safe travel destination and the Vietnamese as an unresentful people, attributes I'd gleaned from a guidebook and that turned out, largely, to be true. She figured they were still pissed, more than pissed—vengeful. They would be lying in wait. She saw them in her dreams, smoldering, crouching in bushes, camouflaged, and armed to the teeth.

"Remember those Japanese soldiers after World War II who were stranded on those islands in the Pacific?" she said. "How they still thought the war was going on twenty and thirty years after it ended? That's what I'd been thinking."

I was surprised and discouraged at the depth of her relief, though I understood. She could worry about perils that defied the laws of physics—air conditioners that spewed carbon-monoxide emissions, televisions and stoves that were subject to spontaneous combustion—and defied the passage of time. She had become a mother just two months after the first U.S. combat troops waded ashore in Danang. For the next ten years, a blitzkrieg of televised and photographic images transmogrified Vietnam from the name of a vague place near China to the name of an unrelenting catastrophe. Meanwhile, she watched scores of kids from our neighborhood graduate from high school to rice paddies. They included her classmates. She was a young mother who'd graduated from high school in 1962 and could tick off the names of guys she had sat next to in homeroom and history who had made a tour of Vietnam in the mid-1960s. Growing up, we knew one of her classmates, a guy named Dennis who'd been voted cutest in the 1962 North Quincy High yearbook but who was a haunted wreck now, the bearded face ravaged by alcohol, a perpetual vacancy in the eyes, a mutterer who chain-smoked cigarettes and stalked our sidewalks with a determined sense of mission but no destination as far as we could see.

Before I left, my mother had said little about my going. She'd had to work at her reticence. She always had. She'd put no argument to my revelation, years earlier, that I no longer considered myself Catholic. She was trying hard to be as liberal-minded and progressive as her own mother was not, an effort that grated against the mettle of our neighborhood, whose mothers preferred their children to settle inside the circumference of a local phone call.

My grandmother, for one, hadn't understood my plans. To graduate with a master's degree and then fly off to Vietnam on a bicycle trip was lunacy. "You should put your foot down," Bernice told her daughter after I announced my plans in the spring of 1992.

"Where am I going to put it?" my mother wanted to know. "He's twenty-seven."

"All the more reason, Joanie," she said. "He doesn't *have* to go."

Over the Neponset River Bridge, we drove through Norfolk Downs, the modest commercial district of my boyhood. Balducci's was still making pizzas and subs on the corner. The barber's candy-stripe pole still revolved outside Frank's shop. But more of the signs carried Chinese characters. The plate glass of one shop was stenciled with the cartoon head and shoulders of a glamorous model, beautifully coifed and brandishing a perfectly manicured hand. This was Truong's Nail Shop, and Truong was a Vietnamese name.

For more than a decade, the part of Quincy that borders the Boston neighborhood of Dorchester had slowly absorbed Chinese immigrants, whether from abroad or from Chinatown no one really knew.

"People don't mind? All these Asians moving in?" I asked.

"Doesn't affect property values," my father said. "Bottom line."

"Kids get along at the high school?" I asked.

"North Quincy has the best math team in the state," he said.

"Kids are dating probably," I said.

My father said nothing. My mother shrugged.

"The changing face of America," I said, not knowing what else to say.

As we turned onto our street, she mentioned that she'd run into Bobby Leonard, my oldest friend, and she said he was trying to make some decisions about my room in his place. I hadn't had any correspondence with Bob since I'd written him from the dingy bowels of my first Saigon hotel, telling him I would be moving in when I got back. Count on it, I'd told him.

Among the letters waiting for me at home were two new deadlines for our *Bicycling* article. Since finishing the trip, and failing to file our story from Hanoi as promised, Relin and I continued to spin our wheels on the piece. But the most recent extension and deadline were unequivocal. Evenings I retired to my mother's spare room and burned joss that Thuy had given me, filling the house with the scent of jasmine. My brother, one night, explained to a friend that the scent was coming from my room, where I was trying to get in the mood to write an article about the bike trip. The joss didn't help. Nor did the books I read in the crammed old wing of the city's library. The monograph published in the 1960s about village life in Vietnam. The translation of *The Tale of Kieu*, a long, lyrical poem that I'd heard Thuy quote from several times and that the Vietnamese leaned on the way people in the West leaned on Shakespeare. And a history of the Nguyen Empire and the Chinese roots of Hue's imperial system, from the construction of the Noon Gate to the examinations that culled mandarins from the rank and file.

"What's a mandarin?" my sister asked one evening, going through my pictures from the trip. The preceding question had asked who the girl was, in so many pictures, and I'd answered that she was from Hue and that she was the granddaughter of a mandarin.

"Like a baron, a duke, an earl," I said.

Later, telling Bob about Thuy, I rolled out the same European touchstones, supplementing the little I had on her grandfather with information I'd gleaned about the mandarin class from a scholarly history and from old black-and-white images of aristocrats carried to work through the Noon Gate on hammocks borne by coolies. That meant less to him than the answers to a couple of other questions he'd asked. He nodded through the pictures I drew for him about these old scholars and their long wispy beards, the two propellerlike appendages jutting from their hats, and hurried back to more relevant information.

"No phone?" he asked again. "Did you really tell me she's got no phone?" I told him I had, and then he asked me if her house was made of grass.

Long after I could blame my sleeplessness on jet lag, I kept waking up every morning an hour or so before subway cars started through the neighborhood. I listened to noises that were indiscriminate but familiar, sounds that had been inaudible to me as a kid but as warm as a blanket, a weaving of distant sirens; faulty, sputtering street lamps; men in trucks gearing up to work, to haul the night's casualties on their wreckers, to deliver donuts to coffee shops on the corners. They haunted me now, as if testaments to the fact that we lived our lives in circles, that eventually, no matter how far we roamed or how much we believed that our lives graduated from stage to stage, we always returned.

One morning, though we'd come into spring officially, snow was trickling from low-lying cloud cover, exhausting a front that had dumped two cruel inches on us in a bitter last act of winter. My boots squeaked down the driveway, and I stepped lightly past my father's bedroom window, open now as it was every night.

"Can't sleep," he said.

I stopped and said nothing, not certain whether he'd asked a question or just acknowledged the fact of his own wakefulness. Though they had divorced when I was a freshman in college, my father had recently moved into the first floor of my mother's two-family. The mechanical insulation business he'd launched when I was a boy had collapsed, and he'd fallen from great heights and fast, without safety nets, everything leveraged. If his own troubles were keeping him up, that would have made sense to me.

The springs of his mattress heaved as he turned over. He took it for granted that I was listening. "I've been hearing you go out every night. Where the hell you going?"

"Nowhere." I'd thought I'd been stealthy, that no one had known I'd been getting up nights to walk around North Quincy in the dark.

"Your mother's worried about you taking off at night," he said.

My mother slept with a fan on and couldn't possibly have known that I went out, unless he'd told her.

"You're up worrying about that article, aren't you?" he asked.

Overhead the clouds were breaking up, and I stared into them for a moment, letting his question hang. A few stars shined between the clouds.

"It's the deadline, isn't it?" he asked.

"Yeah."

"It's good to worry," he said, rolling back over. "It's good to feel that pressure. That's how stuff gets done."

Another night, several blocks from home, I came upon an apparition—a man striding down the street with a shoulder pole—that made me wonder whether I'd actually risen from bed and come into the streets, or was I just dreaming, or did I miss Thuy so badly that I was actually conjuring her neighbors as my own? And if I followed him further would he lead me, like the White Rabbit, back into the world I'd only just emerged from? Or had that all just been a dream: a girl who lived in a city on the banks of the Perfume River, who lived over a moat and inside the walls of an East Asian citadel.

The man turned out of my sight, and when I turned after him, I found him up ahead, rummaging through trash barrels with a pair of thin dowels, working them like chopsticks. He picked out several returnables and dropped them one by one like specimens, into his pails. The buckets clattered with cans as he straightened under his yoke and cut diagonally through the snow for the next heap of trash.

His yoke was actually a Cooper hockey stick. His face was sallow, the eyes set deep, and he had a scar across one cheekbone as if someone had snapped barbed wire there. He smiled at my approach but looked quickly from side to side, measuring possible means of escape.

I couldn't tell whether this man was Vietnamese or Chinese. Our neighborhood was mostly Chinese, according to my father. *"Chao Ong?"* I said. Hello, sir.

His face flickered with incomprehension, but that was not conclusive. Most people I addressed in Vietnam, in Vietnamese, twisted their open palms at me with incomprehension, stunned by the fact that a foreigner was actually trying to communicate with them. When I asked this man how he was and he twisted his palm at me, I felt a huge surge of relief. He couldn't understand me, but he was Vietnamese.

"It's very cold," he said. He squeezed his eyes shut and shook his face.

"Vang, lanh qua," I said, agreeing that it was very cold.

"Ahhh," he said, walking away, flattering me to cover his tracks. "You speak Vietnamee very goose."

· · ·

Sunday mornings, I showed up at my father's table for breakfast, big fatty spreads that made no concessions. Not only bacon, but links of sausage and corned beef hash too. Home fries crisped golden brown in a vatlike well of vegetable oil. Buttered white-bread toast. Eggs, which I'd never taken to and he tried to serve me anyway. He always thought my dislike for eggs, when I waved them off, was affectation, symptomatic of new-fangled ideas I'd picked up at college, from a new girlfriend, or liberal friends. This time he blamed it on Vietnam.

"What, they don't eat eggs over there?" he asked.

One morning at breakfast, propped on a banana, there was a sheaf of mimeographed papers, prepared 20 April 1945, about Lieutenant John Edward Sullivan, U.S. Navy. "The grandfather," my father said, meaning his, not mine. "His service jacket. I got it in the mail yesterday."

My father often invoked the name of this man, as if we had bedrock beneath us, an ancestor of stature, a man capable of launching another Boston Irish dynasty. He'd never known his grandfather, but we heard stories as if he had—of a man who could, even in his fifties, do a standing backflip, who had won the "Big E" as the chief engineer on a navy ship, who would take his dog out for a walk at night and send the dog home in a cab if a thirst came on. Stories of a smart, tough old son of an Irish immigrant who "didn't take shit from anybody," which always seemed to be the highest measure of a man in my father's book.

According to the typewritten summary of his grandfather's service, John Edward had enlisted in 1907 and was commissioned in 1914. He'd sailed on the USS *Rhode Island*, the USS *Brooklyn*, the

USS *Wilmington*. And he'd spent time in the Far East, in the Philippines, for which he received the Asiatic Clasp.

My father stood over my shoulder and turned the pages, showing how John Edward had called at ports all over the world. "So where's it going to be next, James?" he asked. "South America? The Serengeti? The Middle East?" He'd loved that I'd traveled to Southeast Asia, just as he'd once delighted in my decision to study French and learn to ski, pursuits that he believed engendered class and raised the bar on achievement for the next generation.

"I guess I don't know."

"Move into Bobby's for a short time, but I wouldn't stay there that long."

"I don't know if I'm moving in there."

He went to the coffee pot and filled both our cups, then sat down across from me. "You're not still thinking about that girl, are you?" His tone was arch.

"I think about her."

"Right, right, you're going to think about her. That means you had a great trip. You didn't just go over there and look around. You got involved. You got to know people. That's what you want to happen. You go out. You have these adventures, then you come back, and you go out again."

He started to tell me about a girl he'd met in England when he was in the navy in the fifties. She'd sold him a set of *Encyclopedia Americana* in Southampton, and then they went out dancing. I'd heard the story many times before and so only half-listened to how he was late getting back to the ship and how he sneaked back on board.

"The point is that I'd thought about going back to see her. In fact, I'd told her I would."

"I don't remember that part of the story."

"Yeah, I told her. I was going to go back, and we were going to see what happened. And she was brilliant too. And English."

I didn't believe him. Yes, about dancing with the English girl, but not the part about his wanting to go back. I guessed that that was for my benefit, this postscript to the stale old set piece.

"And it's a good thing I didn't go back. If I did, where would you be today?"

I kept the Vietnamese man to myself, as if he'd been a hallucination, for days, until my youngest brother talked at dinner about a prank some of the kids on our street had played on Truck.

"Who?"

"Truck. The old Vietnamese guy. You'll see him."

The kids had tied clear monofilament line to a plastic juice bottle, placed it in the gutter, and waited for Truck. When he stooped, they yanked it from his grasp. It was a prank I would have reveled in as a boy when we enjoyed a kind of ownership in the eccentrics who roamed our neighborhood, one of whom we used to taunt until we'd get him stumbling after us in great flights of anger. No doubt, the kids on our street hoped for the same reaction from Truck. Instead, the old Vietnamese man laughed at their pranks, so heartily as the baited bottle tottered over the curbstones and sidewalks that the fun quickly wore off.

In the same way that it had been important for me to know that he was Vietnamese, it became doubly imperative for me to see him again. I had nothing to say to him, but I wanted the contact, to essay the language and climb over the bridge of his voice to a place that was receding further everyday.

Outside Charlie's market, I ran into him one day. *"Chao Ong,"* I said.

"Ohhhhhh," he said, suddenly and surprised, an exclamation that seemed distinctly Vietnamese, that so many cyclo drivers used when I corrected them and told them I was American, not Russian.

"Em di du lich Vietnam," I told him. I travel in Vietnam.

"Oh, you speak Vietnamee very goose," he told me again. "When do you go?"

I meant to tell him I had traveled to Vietnam already, but I'd made a mistake with my tense. I corrected myself, and he asked in English when I planned to go back.

"I don't know."

I took out my picture of Thuy then. He stepped into the delivery lot behind Charlie's and squatted on his haunches. I tried to do the same, but I lacked the flexibility in my hams. Instead, I turned over a milk crate and sat on that.

"Girl of Hue?" he asked, not looking up from the photo. I looked over his shoulder.

"How do you know?"

"Of course," he said. "I am from Vietnam." He drew the picture closer, scrutinizing. "You gotch married?"

"No."

"Future?"

"No, I just met her and we got along."

"Why you don't know? Love or not?"

Behind Charlie's, sitting on a milk crate, I couldn't say. I didn't know whether what I felt was love or intoxication. A "moat-induced high," as Relin, sounding an unusually frank note of caution, had put it.

"Some other men also visit her house," he said.

"Oh," I said, unconsciously mimicking his exclamation. I stood up. "How do you know?"

"I'm Vietnamee."

He'd guessed right. I told him about them, and he nodded gravely.

"When you go back," he said, "much better you beware the shrinking bird."

The Harp was a local bar, the watering hole we'd come of age in and that still catered to a working-class crowd, men who carried their names in embroidered stitches over the breast pocket, who draped brown UPS jackets over captain's chairs, and whose arms were dusted with calcium silicate from work in crawl spaces and boiler rooms. Chunks of street tar fell from the folds of clothes of guys who worked on paving crews, to ding the brass-coated bar rail at their feet and puddle about the legs of their bar stools. Most of them drank beer, either draft or in bottles, and tipped well, a buck a beer. I met Bob there one night.

"Bud?" I asked, pulling out my wallet as he approached the bar.

He looked at me curiously a moment, measuring something, then propped his elbow on the bar and hung his hand limply at the wrist, doing a languid eenie-meenie-miney-mo over the bottles on a shelf behind me. He wore a kelly green nylon shell that zipped up one shoulder and featured a shamrock on the other. "Make it a wine cooler," he said.

I looked at the selection. "They got Seagram's, they got—"

"Yeah, I'll have the penis piss," he said.

"What?"

"What do you think, you go away five months and the world changes? Just make it a Bud."

I'd ducked several of his phone calls recently, and I knew why he was here: to ask when I planned to move in. Bob was the kind of guy who, if you said something once, he was going to hold you to it for the rest of your life. Though I'd told him about Thuy, he had not made the connection between her and my hesitation or didn't think it was necessary to. When I'd first mentioned to him that Thuy was Vietnamese, he asked, "What, like Ned McDonagh?"

McDonagh was a guy we'd grown up with who was a loner and who only dated foreign women, especially Asian women. "No, not Ned McDonagh," I told him.

We watched the Bruins for fifteen minutes, saying little, until his wife, Kristin, came in and slid a dollar into the jukebox. The B-52s came on, then Madonna, then Melanie, singing "Candles in the Rain." She still wore the sea-green hospital outfit of a nurse, just in from work.

"Did you tell Sull yet?" she asked as soon as the music started.

"Not yet."

"I'll tell him. We have someone we want you to meet," she said, turning to me. "I work with her at the hospital."

I looked at Bob. He was staring up into the television, frowning at the Bruins.

"She's our age and doing her residency at the hospital," Kristin said. "The other day I was walking by her office, and I heard that music you kept drumming into us last summer."

"Gretzky," Bobby said, coming down from the TV.

I looked back up, but the B's weren't playing the Oilers.

"That symphony," Kristin said.

"You mean Gorecki," I said.

"That's what I said," Bob said. He went on, "You said that music was . . ." and here he altered his tone, "the single greatest piece of music written in the latter half of the twentieth century."

"A signal work," Kristin said teasingly, quoting me. I could tell they'd talked about this afterward.

The previous summer, I'd obsessed for weeks over Gorecki's "Third Symphony, of Sorrowful Songs," the strings that rose in layers through the first movement to an aching solo soprano by a woman grieving over the loss of her son.

"It's a great piece," I said.

"Ah, but no longer the greatest?" he asked.

"There's other great music," I said.

"There always will be," he said. "That's my point."

"I didn't know you were trying to make one."

Kristin twirled her fork at her ear. "She was listening to it and loving it, the intern was. So I told her about you, how you'd forced us to listen to that music every day of our vacation last summer."

Kristin had told the intern about my bicycle trip, about my graduate-school education, about the fellowship I had received. The intern wanted to meet me. "She's gorgeous, Sull, and your type."

I'd asked Bob not to say anything to anyone about Thuy, and from what Kristin had to say about the intern, it appeared he hadn't, not even to his wife. In fact, it was as if he hadn't heard what I'd said at all.

"Isaac," I said when Kristin left for the rest room, "I'm trying to remember. Did you not sit down with me in this very bar a couple of nights after I got back?"

"I did."

"And I told you something."

"You did."

"So what's this?"

"A big favor."

It was spring, and wedding invitations arrived in the mail. For my mother, invites from the children of cousins and friends on heavy cream-colored card stock, scripted in calligraphy, heralding big, sumptuous Catholic affairs; "Ave Maria," Wagner's "Wedding March," tuxedos, taffeta, and receptions at the Knights of Columbus. Over the previous few years, I'd managed to dodge a fair number of weddings, usually by excuse of geography but sometimes just by checking the "will not attend" box on the RSVP, a gesture that endeared me to no one. I sometimes worried that my reluctance to attend was borne of penury, and that was part of it, I suppose, but it also sprung from disappointment too, that people I knew who hadn't ever made room for religion in their lives were making room for it now so they could put on a big show. I was cranky on the subject, and a bore, and people didn't like me for it.

One of my college friends who was getting married phoned the night after his invitation showed up in my mail. The script on his was professionally printed, but the handwriting was his fiancée's. Around the borders of the card were a series of icons, denoting symbols of relevance to their shared past: a patch of moss, an aardvark for all the aardvarks they'd seen on vacation one year, an old Pullman train car to remember their first trip together.

"The invitation was honest?" Miller asked on the phone.

"Very."

"Then I'll see you here."

I drove north through Boston over the Mystic River Bridge, now renamed and better known as the Tobin Bridge, after a politician. As children we'd come north this way on summer vacation every year, a week away that held much more promise when we knew we were leaving the city by spanning this river. And not only a river, but a river that rose and twisted through places so fantastic that they'd had to name it the Mystic. It was not really a river—it was more an inlet of the sea fed by a creek—but I hadn't known that then. And when my father would take Interstate 93 to avoid traffic, thus avoiding the Mystic River, our vacation was somehow compromised.

Route 1 made big sweeping turns you had to slow down for and then straightened out in Saugus, where the fever pitch we had for summer vacation piqued at the landmark orange dinosaur, a prop in a mini golf course on the southbound side of the highway. Heading north out of Chelsea, my brothers and sister and I jockeyed for position in the backseat and way-back of our station wagon. Whoever sighted the orange dinosaur first was the winner, of what we never knew. Going home we had no interest in the dinosaur; he was more ominous then, portending school and even winter, and we were so dispirited by the sight of him. But he was an altogether different creature going up, and once, miraculously, my father turned around and stopped so we could play a round of mini golf through the legs of the standing *T rex*. My mother shared an ice cream cone with the baby that late afternoon while the rest of us made our way over the plastic green carpets with dented putters and a feeling of such permanence in the world that even today I'm sometimes frightened by the magnitude of that loss.

Up Route 1, many of the landmarks endured from the 1970s: the giant neon saguaro cactus of the Hilltop Steak House, as if the desert should serve as a beacon for quality beef; the drab, flat-roofed motels from an era when people could venture this far from the city, park their cars, and believe they'd landed some place worthy of a vacation. For years, these tawdry little roadside attractions worked magic inside me, until one year I didn't see them at all. That year, all I could see was the rear end of my family's trailer, our Shasta, and the cheap little map of America that my father had rigged to the back and started filling in with decals of the various states we'd visited, stretching from Maine to Maryland. When he'd hung it there, he told me he hoped we'd eventually see them all. And maybe we would, but individually, not together as a family. He was driving the Shasta, with my brother and sister that year, while my mother and I and my youngest brother followed in the Bobcat. The Bobcat had been a Christmas present from my father months earlier, and for a while I had thought it was a guarantee of continuity. Now, driving north in separate cars, I knew that's exactly what it was not. It was part of the means by which he and my mother could disengage from each other. He would drive our trailer north and set us up for our two weeks, and then he would return to Quincy alone. They hadn't told us that separation was imminent, but as I stared at that vast, empty map, at the faintly colored outlines of the Midwest, the Plains States, all the way west to California, I knew we wouldn't see them, that Maryland was as far as we'd go together.

My parents' marriage ended not much later. My father's father's marriage, too, had ended in divorce, and I had seen, leafing through my great-grandfather's service record, that his marriage had also ended in separation.

"Look out for the Y chromosome," my father had warned me once, a warning I never forgot because it carried the authority of genetics. He'd had a few in him when he told me this, which was when he told me all the stuff I never wanted to know. "Sullivan men don't make the right proteins."

It was past dark when I finally arrived at the wedding hotel. The night was crisp, and my classmates had gathered at the pit of a lobster bake held earlier and restoked now as a large campfire. For a few moments, I stood beyond the circle's fringe, picking faces out of the firelight. Most of those I didn't know came from Middlebury College, where the bride had gone to school, but I recognized them anyway: The women in simple yoke dresses and gingham shells;

the men in linen, seersucker, and bow ties. As my eyes adjusted to the dark, I found myself standing beside a fieldstone shelf that ran away in either direction, like a stone wall except stouter and held together by mortar. I followed it, watching where the wall made right angles, until I realized it wasn't a wall but the foundation of an old home, the bride's summer place, destroyed by fire shortly after World War II.

Miller had told me about this fire two years earlier in Bar Harbor, where I'd spent the summer bartending. She has a summer place, he'd said. Her father worked for Westinghouse. He'd nursed a pint of Samuel Adams that night and went over what he called her papers. "Papers" was what he'd wanted to know of any new girl any of his friends had begun dating after college. Where had she gone to school? What did her father do? The questions came masked in irony that was only thinly disguised because it was a genuine consideration for him.

Once he knew he had bedrock beneath him, he never talked about her papers again. I'd asked about them, half teasing, and he brushed the question off as if it no longer mattered. What did matter was something that I would overhear the bride tell one of her own friends about meeting Miller, about how they'd met at a poetry reading and come together over Theodore Roethke; that was why there would be a reading of "Moss-Gathering" at the service. But it went deeper than that, to Dexter Gordon and a mutual interest in vanished civilizations and so many other things in common.

This was how it happened with these classmates. They married within station. They married the scions of families who'd made millions selling medical equipment. And attended the right schools. They shared a love of Roethke and ethnic cooking. They were married in fields or on islands. And it did make a kind of sense. Their conversation was robust. They were friends first, best friends, they said. That was the prerequisite, and still delivered with a pinch of disbelief, as if the fact that they had managed to make a friend first of the man or woman they loved was a rare and special gift. "I guess I'd have to say my wife's my best friend." Even when it wasn't true, it's what was said, and it was always said.

The group around the fire finally prevailed upon a guy to break out his guitar, and pretty soon there were the opening chords to Dylan's "Tangled Up in Blue." By the fourth verse, people had put down their beers; they were craning forward, half-shouting lyrics that renounced the safe, predictable life that everyone in the fire-light agreed was so greatly to be desired.

On the porch of a long Dutch colonial, older couples came to the railing. Illuminated by the soft red light of Chinese lanterns, I looked at them, so many pairs of matching middle-aged couples. The women who still wore their shoulder-length gray hair in po-nytails. And men who still wore summer-weight sport jackets. I wondered if they knew something that my parents had not, that you had to be guided by not only the heart and the moment but by the head as well.

My exposure to *this* world, of summer people on the coast of Maine, so far from his own roots in South Boston, was my father's doing. I hadn't understood him when I was a senior in high school and he told me that the most important thing about college would not be the education I received there; that I could get anywhere. It was the people I'd meet. And that's why he'd wanted a small, prestigious college for me. It's where people knew the words to Dylan, not Pat Benatar, though he wouldn't have put it quite that way.

"Your mother's roots are Gaelic," he'd said once, "but you'll do better. If you're lucky, she'll be Anglo-Irish, and maybe she'll have a hyphen in her name."

• • •

After Miller's wedding, I saw Truck, or Truc as his name was truly spelled, several times and by daylight now, walking a leashed dog, sometimes a little girl. His route went by my mother's house at unpredictable parts of the day but always, it seemed, when I was in the yard, turning the earth for a vegetable garden she wanted put in. One afternoon, she caught me.

"What are you doing?" she asked.

I was pressed against the clapboards of the garage, hidden from the street, as the Vietnamese man walked by. I told her it was an itch, and then I told her that the twelve-by-twenty-foot garden plot she wanted was too big. She'd spent all winter reading about gardens and mapping layouts on sheets of blank white paper. Straight, x-ed out lines denoted her root crops—the carrots and potatoes and onions—while rows and columns of small circular blossoms, one for each plant, symbolized the tomatoes and lettuces she would put in.

She didn't want the earth rototilled; instead, she wanted the sod skimmed off and the ground turned, spade by spade. For several days, I worked the spade out back and kept a lookout for the Vietnamese man. When I'd finished turning the earth, I sifted the dirt for rocks and roots and shaped it, smoothing the sides and surface until I had a beautifully rectangular bed. I was sitting in a lawn chair beside it and a dozen bags of unemptied manure when my mother came out onto the porch steps and sat down.

"When you leaving?"

"Tomorrow, I guess."

I'd already told her that I planned to move into Bobby's, and she greeted this news, and the implicit revelation that I would not be going back to Vietnam, in a way that surprised me. The possibility of my returning filled her with dread, I knew. She couldn't help that. But when I'd relieved her of that, mentioning plans to live in Quincy, she'd merely nodded.

"You didn't rake the manure in," she said.

It was a statement but lifted like a question.

"Because you don't know if you've combed through the dirt enough, and fished out all the rocks?" she asked.

"Yeah."

"You could have turned this all in one afternoon. Instead, you've been here four days, ducking that Vietnamese guy."

"I'm doing it right," I said.

"You should just spread it." She stood up and lifted her face into the sun for a moment, the way people will after a long winter. "I think you're making a big mistake," she said, "moving into Bobby's."

Then she went back into the house.

I had a theory about attraction: that we are drawn repeatedly to women who resemble the first girl to reject us. In that primal snub, for better or worse, she sets the archetype. She determines what we will desire in other women's hair, in the cast of their skin, in the degree of focus they bring to the present, whether to regard it with insouciance or astonishment. In eighth grade, I'd fallen for a girl who played soccer and made no apologies for her involvement in the Girl Scouts. She could name both the northern and the southern termini of the Appalachian Trail, and it showed in the kind of boots she wore to school, black chocolate hikers from Italy, rubbed to a sheen with beeswax, I'd found out, and bear fat too. She wore no makeup and no earrings, and her hair was always darker in the morning, damp from showering, no blow-dryer, no spray, no poof.

After weeks of thinking about it, I finally called her one evening from Bobby's basement and invited her to the Trailside Museum, a zoo that penned animals indigenous to the Blue Hills just outside Boston: whitetail deer, bobcats, otters, red fox. I made a big deal out of the bobcat; although there was always a pen for a bobcat, they didn't always have one in residence. Now they did. She pressed me about the exhibits, and the Hills in general, before she delivered a crushing tinkle of a laugh, a sound like spilled pennies, and said, "Thanks but I don't think so." No explanation, just no.

Over the next year, I called her a few times to chat and ask her to the movies and for ice cream, but the answer was always the same. The last time I phoned, a boy's voice identified itself as her brother's and then humiliated me. "She's got a boyfriend. Now stop calling."

She receded from me after that, but I never stopped looking for someone like her. And neither did my friends. We knew the kinds of girls each other liked. When we went out together, at twenty and twenty-one years old, into Copperfield's and the bars at Faneuil Hall, we could identify who would try to talk to whom, and we would cede the initiative to each other, as if individually we held patents to certain tastes. When my day came, I'd always supposed she'd look like the kind of woman I'd tended toward, with unfettered shoulder-length hair, the residual traces of a freckled girlhood, a lot of soccer in her past, someone who vaguely looked like me. I knew you could run, but I believed you couldn't run far. None of us had a penchant for foreign women. They were off our radar screen and blipped, largely we believed, for those guys who couldn't cut it with American women. They were out there, we knew, guys who were socially inept, bereft of friends, loners with weird ideas who could hide all their quirks in the culture gap. They were the guys who had fixed ideas about Asian women, that they were submissive, they'd never talk back, their only job was to minister to their husbands. Ned McDonagh was one of those guys, a guy you could barely hold a conversation with, who believed that all American women were argumentative and bitchy, who thought everything had gone south since June Cleaver.

Since Bob had raised the specter of Ned McDonagh, I'd begun to wonder whether my motivation in any way resembled Ned's. It didn't matter that Thuy was the first foreign woman I'd dated or that I had a history of running from women in general. McDonagh's failings were suddenly mine, and I was smart to recognize it.

The blind date that Kristin arranged for me looked like my eighth-grade crush: the freckles, hair that fell to her shoulders and parted on the side like a movie actress from the 1940s. She wore running shoes and pants that stopped two inches above the ankles. Her only piece of jewelry was a Native American ring of hammered silver and turquoise stone.

Pease apologized for being late; she'd been tied up at work. She fell into a chair with exaggerated exhaustion and said she was always tied up at work, so much so that lately she'd been revisiting her decision to become a doctor. "I mean, I haven't been to India, and I've been wanting to see the Taj Mahal since before I wanted to become a doctor."

We were sitting on the patio of a bookstore café on Newbury Street, a black iron fence dividing us from couples and shoppers strolling the sidewalk. Pease asked for a glass of pinot noir, which the bookstore didn't have. Neither merlot or Chianti would do, so she ordered a beer.

"So," she said, pouring the beer into a pilsner glass, twisting it as she went along. "Quincy man rides the cycle of history."

It took a moment to remember that the line was actually a headline that had appeared in the Boston Herald. They'd written a story on my trip, and Pease, evidently, had found it.

"A great trip," I said.

"They left a lot out," she said.

"They did."

"So tell me."

I'd told the story dozens of times since I'd been back, refining it as I went along, playing with the rhythm and chronology so that it flowed seamlessly from Saigon to Hanoi. A story that provided pathos and enlightenment. Children maimed by dormant, unexploded ordnance. The spiritual victory of the Vietnamese people, who'd moved beyond bitterness and vengeance. I said nothing about Hue.

As she listened, she massaged the underside of her chin with the side of her forefinger. Her face reflected the drama that inhered in my story, wrinkling in smiles when charmed by one anecdote, wincing and shaking her head over the bomb craters that people were now using as fish farms. She listened attentively and drilled deeper with smart questions.

When the waiter asked whether she wanted another beer, she declined. "It was a voyage," she said.

"A super trip."

"No, a voyage, a real journey. You've got to do something with it. Do you have anything in mind?"

"No."

She interpreted more profundity in that than I'd intended. She gazed off a while, thinking. "You just went there to see it? No objectives? No other motives? Just travel?"

I opened my palms and shrugged.

Again she made a revelation of this. "Sometimes, I keep forgetting that not everything is a building block. I know it on one level."

She tapped the back of her head. "I know we're supposed to let things happen, or make space for that kind of spontaneity in our lives. But every time I try, something trips me. I once had this six-month opportunity to let India happen. And it didn't because I looked down the road and pictured people—decision makers (she applied air quotes around this word)—looking at my résumé. I heard them asking, *What happened here these six months?* And I didn't want to hear that question. As if going to India would have been irresponsible. Evidence of equivocation. 'She says she wants to be a doctor, but here she is with a backpack on the subcontinent.' So I took an internship instead." She squeezed her hands into fists and cringed.

"Look where you are today. The best hospital in the world."

She frowned. "The question is 'Where else might I be?' " She seemed to be finding her way toward something. Her tone changed then, becoming flat and businesslike as she told me that even three months ago, she would not have agreed to meet me.

Something in me stiffened, and everything went quiet for a moment. The cheerful clink of glasses. The piano concerto on the café's speakers. And a huge memory yanked me back three months, when I never would have agreed to meet her. I was sitting with Thuy, at the tea table in her mother's house. What had changed between then and now?

"I don't know what triggered it," Pease went on, "but I realized that unless I changed, I was going to have the world's best résumé. I had to feel the wind on my cheeks. I started taking sailing lessons. The wind decides where I want to go. It's important, I think, to just follow the wind."

I nodded.

"Look where you can land," she said. She held up her glass and I met her toast. "That day, when Kristin heard me listening to the

Gorecki, and she told me about you. . . ." She paused a moment and placed her fingers on my forearm. "Isn't it funny, if it hadn't been for Gorecki, we wouldn't be sitting here right now."

I knew exactly what she meant. She was right. The ties that bind can be no more substantial than gossamer. People's lives pivot off accidents. If it hadn't rained for three days straight, and if that rain hadn't soaked all my clothes, I probably wouldn't have walked into Thuy's older sister's clothing shop that first day. And if Thuy and her sister hadn't ridden out into the rain that evening and found Relin and me, I wouldn't have showed up at her house for tea that night and probably wouldn't have returned to that house the way I had, insistently, running on instinct and feeling, no map, no papers, no flashlight, but an abiding sense that I was in the right place, at the right time, with the right person.

"If Gorecki had been run over by a train forty years ago, you'd never have played that symphony for Kristin, and she wouldn't have walked into my office that day." I was half-listening to Pease then, when she said something about meeting me again, the following Tuesday. An art opening. A friend's gallery. Did I want to go? Would I meet her?

But I was half-listening to myself, subject to the grip of something that felt a little bit like betrayal and a little bit like revelation. I'd been demanding a lot from the ties I had to Thuy. I'd been thinking that they had to be cables, bound by similar backgrounds, interests, grooming, personalities. That they had to resonate with the chords of guitar songs, if that was what you liked.

Pease said something else about the opening, and then she stared at me waiting.

"What?"

"The opening. Can you make it?"

"I don't think so."

. . .

In Boston's Chinatown, I shopped for a return ticket to Vietnam at several different agencies. The trade embargo prohibited flights to Vietnam by American airlines, so I bought a ticket on an Asian carrier.

"Return date?" the agent asked.

"I don't know," I said.

"When will you come back?" the agent asked again, thinking I'd misunderstood her question. She was a middle-aged Vietnamese woman who'd permed her naturally straight hair into a helmet that had all the play of foam rubber. Her nails were long and painted in a colorful seashell motif.

"Maybe next year," I said, remembering the year that Thuy had talked about, like a prerequisite.

So I can know your temper, she'd explained, *meaning "temperament."*

And I can get to know yours, I'd said.

No need, she'd said. *My temper is good.*

"Can you leave the ticket open?" I asked the agent.

Her face wrinkled in disapproval. Beyond her, hung from the cornice, were the red stripes and yellow field of the flag of old South Vietnam. In the soup place I'd taken lunch, I'd watched "Paris by Night" videos of young Vietnamese women singing dreamy, sorrowful songs about soldiers gone away to war. There was a poster of Ho Chi Minh on the wall, but his profile was circled and banned by an X. "You stay too long," the agent told me.

That night, Bobby asked for another look at the photo of Thuy. "One thing I really can't tell from this picture is what the shape of her nostrils is like."

Remember that girl you were with for a while, you didn't like the shape of her nostrils. Like diamonds, right?"

I shook my head.

"And how about this girl's fingers. Too short, maybe, like that other girl's? What about her upper body? Out of scale with the rest of her body. Isn't that what you said?"

"I'm not going there with you."

"Or maybe it'll be her voice, too much like a cartoon character's. I know you better than anybody, including you. I've got more perspective. You meet women; you go out with women; and then you find something. The thing, remember, capital T. You look for the fucking thing. Some grating little detail that gives you a reason to walk away."

"That's natural."

"That's not natural. That's fucked up. And look at you. You got a million Things. You walk like a goddamned duck. And your nose? Before we know it, people are going to start mistaking you for Tip O'Neill." He stopped and looked at everybody else in the Harp, everybody like us. "I never knew you liked Asian women."

I hadn't either, and didn't think I did. In my mind, it wasn't about her being Asian, not the way it was for guys who decide to only date those women or black women or Latinos.

"I've known you a long time, Sull. What, since we were three? And in all that time, I never once heard you say anything about an Oriental girl. I know you better than anybody, and I *know* you're a weirdo. You go golfing by yourself and hiking, camping. You go to the movies alone. Nobody does that. We stick around here for school; you go somewhere you don't know anybody. Then you graduate and get on an old ten-speed and start pedaling to California."

"I never finished that trip."

He banged his Bud bottle on the bar, prefacing a revelation. "You've never held the same job for four months." This was it, his tone seemed to say. This was who I was. We could read from this and know what would ultimately happen to me and Thuy.

"I was at the *Kennebec Journal* for six months."

"Okay, six. You've never had a girlfriend for more than three months. You don't stick to anything, a month here, a month there, and now you're telling me you're going to Vietnam to marry some girl from a village. It just doesn't make sense."

I packed for a year, if that's how long I'd have to be gone. I took a small library: histories of Vietnam and thick paperbacks I'd always meant to read; *Bleak House,* all of Shakespeare, and the Bible. Cassette tapes of music I'd never have access to in Hue. The typewriter my father had bought to send me off to college.

"That's a lot of gear for traveling," he said.

"Well," I said, "I'm only thinking about going back to the one place."

He drew a palm down his face, kneading deeply. "Not the same place, I hope."

I was only partly surprised by his question. He knew where I was going, but he was hoping that I'd only scratched the surface.

"Hue," I said.

"What about China, if you're going that far? The Philippines where the grandfather spent some time?"

And Philadelphia, I was tempted to say, where the grandfather was court-martialed for drunkenness and fighting. Or Brooklyn, where he was demoted for an incident that included insubordination to a superior officer. Or wherever it was that he'd picked up syphilis. There were plenty of places to avoid. I understood the wellspring beneath my father's remarks. It came from the same place that financed my college education, the same place that encouraged my pursuit of fluency in French and alternative sports, the kind that engendered class and reflected breeding. He wanted to see a quantum leap in the generation that succeeded him, and in some way that's what I believed I was doing.

I said good-bye to my Quincy friends at the Harp. They were mostly married, embarked upon mortgages and pension plans. They could talk about day care and disparaged the notion that you couldn't use a microwave to heat a baby's formula. All evening, as we roamed the bar, shooting small basketballs through a plastic net, throwing darts, they were tethered to the games at play on the Harp's half a dozen television sets suspended from the ceiling. Everyone had had too much to drink, and at one point I saw DiCarlo tightening the laces of his high-top basketball sneakers.

"You got to be kidding me, he's doing that," I said to my friend Vinny.

"Some guy just told him ZZ Top sucked. Dave's ripped."

"So there's a fight coming cause of that?"

I could feel my own adrenaline ramping up. DiCarlo tightening the laces of his shoes always meant trouble. When we were younger, loose laces meant no traction, which was terrible for throwing a punch and terrible for keeping sneakers. Once he'd lost an expensive sneaker in a fight, and the bar wouldn't give it back to him. Ever since, he tightened up when he knew trouble was coming.

"Sull," he called me over.

"You got to be shitting me, Dave. ZZ Top? ZZ Top does suck."

"Sull," he said, throwing an arm over my shoulder. "Sull. Sull. Joke's on you."

After hours, Bob and I walked back through the deserted commercial part of Billings Road, called Norfolk Downs, past Frank's, whose eponymous owner was the first barber to cut our hair and who was still cutting hair. McClellan's, the old five-and-dime, was gone now, made obsolete by Bradlees and now Wal-Mart on the fringe of the city. There were video stores here, that nail salon, a cheap Chinese gift shop—stores that no longer carried the staples but trafficked in heartless trifles.

The commercial district gave way to stately but worn homes that we once thought were mansions, inhabited by doctors and lawyers. The spotty front lawns still sloped down to low stone retaining walls that we'd walked along as four- and five-year-olds, traveling to the Downs in the late morning with our mothers, brothers, and sisters, the babies in prams. Drunk, Bobby hopped onto one of the walls and extended his arms, exaggerating his need for balance. I followed him, and we walked each two-foot wall in succession until we reached the last, one block up from the three-decker home he'd lived in as a boy and was living in again now. His arms dropped suddenly to his side, and he stared at his place a moment, the porch light burning. His three-decker was changeless, the pale green as-bestos shingles, the tier of solid front porches and trim painted yellow, as was my old home, also a three-decker, standing beside his, the width of a driveway distant. It was slightly shorter and less stout than Bob's, an architectural liability that had once wounded my pride, though our yard had been redemptively large. Today, the yard was a parking lot.

As I looked at my old place, not more than a few miles from South Boston, where my family had lived until the 1960s and where they had lived since crossing after the potato famine, I thought of how remarkable it was that we really hadn't budged off the spot where we'd landed. My line was so full of Irish blood. My mother was a Gallagher; my other grandparents were Meehans from Galway and Martins from Wexford; and so on all the way back through our tenure in America: Clancys and Crowleys, another line of Sullivans, Barrys and Kelleys, and Heanues. One of the lines was Gilmore, but that was Northern Irish. *Thoroughbreds* was a word I'd heard my father use to describe my brothers and sister and I, each of whom bore the map of Ireland on his face, and the map of this neighborhood in his genes, it would seem. In the past, I'd faulted my ancestors for staying put. "Slow," I'd called them. "Loyal," was how my father corrected me.

From the same place, I could see the recently vinyl-clad two-family where my mother's parents had lived for decades. There'd never been a question of elsewhere, of plunging deeper into the suburbs, after that initial move out of the city, for less clamor, a bigger yard, a few apple trees, or a view. It wasn't necessary. My grandfather had literally married the girl next door; he didn't have a career but a job; and he was absolutely joyous in the orbit his life was making around the place he was from.

"Isn't there a lesson in Charlie Gallagher?" Bobby had asked me a few days earlier. "The guy sits tight his whole life, pleased as punch. Never feeling the need to reach out for more and more. You been yapping about Buddha this, Buddha that, eight rules here, four more there, how they got things figured out over there. He figured it out, Charlie did, and he's right here."

His point had been a good one, and a rebuttal to some of the things I'd been saying, but as soon as he'd voiced it, I dodged and kept moving. I hadn't yet been able to articulate why Thuy made as much sense to me as she did. If I had, perhaps I'd at least have been able to answer Bobby.

A salt-filled breeze freshened the night air and dinged the halyard clip against the hollow flagpole behind us, a mournful dent of noise in an otherwise balmy night.

"I used to have this fear when I was kid that I'd get stuck inside here." Bobby said, gesturing with his thumb at the Parker School behind us. "The summer recess bell would ring, and everybody'd be streaming out of the school except for me. I'd get snagged on something and be stuck inside. I wouldn't be able to free myself, and while everyone else was going off into the summer, off to the beaches and lakes and all these other fantastic places, I'd be trying to get out of Parker. But it'd be too late. I'd be trapped."

He stared across the street at his house, at the light burning off the third-floor porch. The first-floor porch light was out. "You ever feel that way?" he asked.

"I always knew I'd get out."

"I was thinking earlier, you know, that any place you've ever lived, I've come out to visit. When you went over to Ireland. All those places up to Maine. Down the Vineyard. Out in Iowa, Kristin and I drove out that time."

"California. You never made it there." We were all going out together, me and him and Vinny Barry, the summer after I graduated college. We'd schemed over the plan for months, California first, then up to Seattle. But things happened, and that fall I drove out alone.

"But I've been to California. I've seen those trees." He leaned back on his elbows and looked up. "I'm probably not going to make it over to Vietnam."

"That's all right. I release you."

"I don't need to. I don't have to check it out." In his voice was the resolution of someone who'd figured out some things about himself, who knew which doors would open for him and, more importantly, which he'd want to open.

"Of course you don't."

"You on the other hand . . ." He hopped off the retaining wall and stepped across the sidewalk to the curbstone before turning. He raised his arms and stretched, arching back and to the side, a gesture that struck me as one that wanted a La-Z-Boy lounge chair in it, a clock that's just struck ten, and a long day on the job tomorrow. His bed was only up this flight of stairs. "You, Sonny, you probably do."

I left Bob at his three-decker and walked through the Parker schoolyard, past the square of spray paint that marked our stickball batter's box, the basketball hoop where the price I'd paid for losing a one-on-one to DiCarlo in the late 1970s was a crew-cut haircut, the unmarked spot of blacktop where we'd watched the O'Hare brothers fistfight each other like strangers, where we'd ringed them in unrooting silence, knowing that each would remember later who had been against his brother. I'd made all my first friends here, at recess, choosing from among a multitude of kids. Those friendships had endured. They'd been the right choices. But how had we known that then?

At the corner, I peered through the plateglass windows of an adult day-care center where, as a boy, my father had taken me to drawing class on Saturday mornings. He'd inherited an aptitude for drawing and for painting. He sharpened his talent in the odd night-school class but failed to pursue and make of it what might have been. I demonstrated no talent for drawing and dropped the Saturday morning class after several weeks. That was okay with him. There would be other places for me to go.

The streets were quiet now, a weeknight, the silent cushion between when the second-shift workers drove home and the construction workers started their 6:00 A.M. commute in town to beat the traffic. In the near distance was the hydraulic hiss of something going up and down, and an even fainter pounding, like men at excavation. A dog stole out of a side street with a shred of garbage hanging from his lips, stared at me a moment, then turned and fled back the way he'd come.

Truc saw me first. "Still cannot to sleep," he said.

"Just having a last look around," I told him.

"Now you come back to Vietnam."

I told him I was leaving in two days. He nodded and turned over his empty five-gallon buckets. "Sit down, please." He offered me a cigarette and when I declined lit one for himself. "I know your brother, Jeff," he said.

"Everybody knows Jeff."

"He told me many times about your trip my country. When you were in my country and when you come back."

Jeff liked to talk, and like our father, he liked to tell all, as if not revealing personal business compromised the stability of the bridge he was always trying to build between himself and everybody else.

"He tell me about that police in Hue, one night he drove his motorbike into you."

"I don't know if he was police or not."

"Jeff said to me, two motorbikes and a sidecar. He also said you saw uniforms on those guys."

"I did. But I don't think it was a big deal." A sudden bolt of fear shot through me. If Jeff had told Truc about that night, would he have told our mother?

"Maybe it's a big deal, some police, they crash into you on a dark night in Hue." He sucked through his teeth sharply, recognizing the brisk night air. "That's why I told you already about the shrinking bird, why you have to be too careful you go back Vietnam."

"Shrinking bird?" I'd assumed that the shrinking bird had to do with losing interest.

"Same same before 1975," he went on. "Many American, they come to Vietnam. So many Vietnamee girl love them, you know Vietnamee man he is like second class now. Sometime he see the American, and," he gestured toward his crotch, "he has the shrinking bird. That was before 1975, but I think maybe the Vietnamee man can still have that feeling."

After the motorbikes had run me off the road that night, I'd tried to believe it had been an accident and that Dich, the cop who visited Thuy's house, had had nothing to do with it. Even as I lay still on the ground, feeling the fire in my shoulder and the warm seep of blood at my temple, watching their brake lights glow in the darkness, Pollyannas were streaming into my head like coagulants. It had not been deliberate. I hadn't crashed. I'd lost my balance in the dark. I walked my bike back to the hotel that night, persuaded that to make more of the incident than accident was absurd.

Truc turned over his lower lip in disgust. "Much better to be careful with *bo doi*," he said, referring to northerners like Dich. "Most Vietnamee, they don't think much about before 1975. But some, they remember."

At the Hibernia Bank, my mother and I signed for a joint account, and I wrote a letter to the administrators of my fellowship, asking them to deposit my monthly disbursements there. In turn, my mother gave me a lump-sum advance, and I converted it to traveler's checks.

We walked then to lunch at Brigham's, an ice cream shop that advertised its sandwiches in colorful, laminated photographs. At the window counter, we watched lunchtime addicts churn through the doors of Dot's Smoke Shop and a man on a ladder change the marquee at the Wollaston Theater. The marquee's white paint was flaked so badly you'd have thought the cinema was abandoned, but the house hung on, playing revivals and films that had already pe-tered out at the multiplex. Several doors down was the site of the old Mug 'n' Muffin, where my mother had worked weekend morn-ings, wearing a striped apron and a funny, pinned cap. My father rarely took us to visit because, inevitably, leaving without her was always a tearful undertaking.

When the waitress delivered lunch, my mother looked down at my plate with mock solemnity and said, "Your last hamburger."

"I could be back in a month," I said quickly.

She grinned to let me know she knew why I'd said that. "Oh, then if that's the case, you pay for the hamburgers."

I spent all of lunch detonating the latent fears that would even-tually rise to the surface of her worry. When a police car passed, I told her that one of the really great things about a police state—which was what Vietnam was, as far as I could see, for communism there looked more like window dressing—was that the rate of vi-olent crime was extremely low, especially if you were a foreigner. Poor countries that are trying to build tourist traffic fear one thing more than any other, I told her. They'll do anything to keep tourists out of harm's way.

"What about those men who drove you off the road that night?" she asked.

"What?"

"Jeff told me."

"Jeff is an exaggerator, and he can't keep anything to himself."

She recounted what he'd told her, and it was exactly as I'd told him. He didn't stretch the truth at all, but I chuckled—persuasively, I hoped—all the way through my mother's version of the story.

"Ma, you know Jeff. He's just like Dad that way."

"I know."

"And besides, that guy was transferred. That I know for sure."

"You know what, Jame?" she said, finishing her hamburger. She waited a moment, chewing the rest of her food. Then she made a dumb face and nodded. "You suck at lying."

Outside, we started down Hancock Street. A waterfall tumbled out of a grotto at Johnson's Funeral Home, and I noticed a small replica of a pagoda propped on the rocks halfway up. The Johnsons still owned the parlor, but a sign in Chinese characters showed that they were responding to Quincy's changing demographics.

Up Hancock Street, we walked past a liquor mart that I still thought of as the Purity Supreme supermarket. I saw the old names for all of the businesses that had evolved into other less essential businesses. Liquor marts replaced supermarkets. Dollar shops took over for five-and-dimes. Video stores in the place of old pharmacies. Once, we'd been able to walk for all of our staples; now we'd been hollowed out.

My mother motioned us into a picture shop just below Balducci's. Inside, I roamed the gallery while a clerk retrieved her order. There was the picture of a lighthouse being smashed by a towering wave, posters of whales breaching and calving icebergs. Original oils pictured Quincy's icons: the birthplaces of Presidents John Adams and John Quincy Adams, the Quincy granite quarries, and the original Howard Johnson's and Dunkin' Donuts, which had both been founded in Quincy.

"Interesting," I heard a clerk say.

"He looks like an Amerasian, doesn't he?" my mother said back.

I went back to the counter, where my mother held a portrait of a boy on canvas. A two-year-old boy with one leg stretched out and one angled in. An open-mouthed smile, hair that couldn't quite part on the side, and eyes that, for the lack of folds in the skin, looked faintly Asian. It was me. Nineteen sixty-seven.

"Remember this?" my mother asked.

"Vaguely."

"Paul had it painted from a Sears photo Dad sent over to him in Vietnam. You can see that the artist couldn't quite get the eyes right. They look Asian, no question about that."

I held the portrait and looked at it, remembering it on the wall of the hallway on Billings Road. It had hung there for years, until we'd moved out of the three-decker in 1971.

"It was in the hope chest, scrolled up," my mother said, "and I found it by accident."

She took the photo from me and walked over to the broad plateglass window. She studied the picture and then looked out at the sidewalks of Norfolk Downs where I'd been that boy, my hand in hers, ambling up to the soda fountain stools of Baker's Drug for Peggy Lawton brownies. "It's funny," she said, "how things come around again."

I paid for the framing, and the clerk gave me a small, flat paper bag. "Hers?" I asked.

"Yours, I think," he said.

I stepped away from the counter and moved slowly toward my mother. I pulled a piece of laminated cardstock from the bag. The paper was stained from a spill long ago, and creased with a fold line. I read the information about my birth weight and length, the time, the name of the doctor, the hospital.

"You laminated my birth certificate?" I asked.

"It's rainy in Vietnam."

I laughed a little. "I know, but you know, my passport's all set. I don't really need the birth certificate for traveling."

She looked at me again and smiled, the same knowing grin I'd seen at Brigham's earlier. "Just keep it."

CHAPTER FOUR

Saigon, when I returned that spring of 1993, was in tumult. A vast jostling throng of Vietnamese pressed on the gateways to the departure terminal, as rapt as gamblers, held in check by strings of baton-wielding, uniformed cops. The heat hung in the mid-nineties, and the air, even beyond the runways and Plexiglas distortions of fuselage windows, retained the shimmery texture of vapors. As I watched the crowd, a horde of taxi drivers buzzed around me, quoting fares. I hesitated, persuaded that the crowd's surges were the preface to some imminent spectacle.

A taxi driver gauged my interest. "Same same every day," he said, "but nothing to do."

The urgency didn't go away. The road in from the airport ran heavy with all kinds of traffic, all subject to a peculiar hierarchy of vehicular respect. The oxcarts made way for the small tractor-trailers, the bicycles for the motorbikes, the few automobiles for the few minivans, and everything for the long-haul buses, painted in a circus of primary colors and jammed to the gills with passengers. At intersections with traffic signals, no one paid attention to red lights unless there was a policeman present. The motorbikes hurtled into cross-traffic and avoided collision with skills that seemed more derivative of sonar and faith than sight. Miraculously, the system seemed to work, except for when it didn't. Two days later, still in Saigon, I watched a man's body thump grotesquely against the pavement, as if energized by electricity, while blood spilled out of his head and pooled beside a baseball hat whose foam front read CALIFORNIA. Nearby a drab green Honda Cub and an off-white Vespa scooter lay crossed like mangled swords. Four people died like that every day in Saigon, according to my guest house's proprietor.

My first suspicion—that I'd arrived on the brink of a momentous event—wore off after several hours, replaced by a more sober appreciation of where I'd been and where I was now. In Saigon, most of the living was done on the outside. The cooking, the commuting, the selling, the relaxing for the most part lacked the shields of house walls and car doors. No doubt, the city was as naked and raw when I'd first passed through, but I hadn't been. Traveling with Relin gave me a buffer against it all. Now, everything looked meaner.

One night in Saigon, a man in a doorway asked whether I had any interest in buying a match from him for 1,000 dong. For as long as the match burned, I could look at a naked Vietnamese woman in a room upstairs. The children who used to hail me as a *Lien Xo*, now called out SIDA, the French acronym for AIDS, when they saw me. Some little boys smiled and told me to "fuck off." *Fuck* was a strange word to them, a word that carried weight with foreigners, they knew, and they were having fun with it, tossing it around and watching the turbulence it created in the increasing numbers of white faces they found on their sidewalks. The more crazy the foreigner became in response to it, the more they laughed.

One night, my sleep was interrupted several times by the peel of a cat that sounded like a wounded baby. At daybreak, when I threw back my louvered shutters, I found a mosquito net tent pitched against the side of the building across the street. Inside, a mother was pressing her reluctant infant against one breast and then the other. When a little bit of the child's resistance came out in a cry, this was the sound I'd been hearing all night.

The impression of Saigon, and all of Vietnam, that I'd carried back to America was of a buoyant city, submerged for years beneath the weight of communism, but rising now, zigzagging past silly bureaucratic hassles that couldn't stem the inexorable tide of the free market. It was grooming itself as the next East Asian little tiger economy. The streets had been rampant with expectation. Old friends. More dollars. The launch of joint U.S.-Vietnamese ventures. I'd thought I was coming back to a Rodgers and Hammerstein musical, but it was as if while I was gone someone had moved in the props from some dark drama.

In the letter I'd faxed to Thuy about my return, I'd asked her to fax me back, ostensibly, to let me know what kind of medicine— antibiotics, lotions, over-the-counter pain relief—to bring back for her older relatives. I'd sunk that request in there like a barb, obliging a response. And then I waited.

In the mornings, I started following my mother to work, not literally, but from a seat beside the phone, timing her down Freeman to right on Vassal to left on Oxenbridge to right on Willet, a hard left on Willow, then right again on Elm Avenue, where she worked for three doctors who had a fax machine. I would imagine the time it took for her to unlock the door, hang up her jacket, and shuffle through the faxes that had come in overnight. But in that last week, the phone never rang between 8:50 and 9:00 A.M. because Thuy hadn't sent a fax.

I couldn't phone; there was no phone. And so, that last week all the resolve I'd sensed that evening with Pease began gradually to go rickety until, getting on the plane, I kept wondering whether I was incapable of governing myself.

As the plane sailed west, I rationalized the absence of a fax from her: From the post office in Hue, it cost more than seven dollars to send one. That was too much money. That, or she was reluctant to make public her relationship with a guy in the United States, which a fax would most certainly do.

That explanation was solace for a little while, but only until I remembered that I'd received just three letters from her in all the time we'd been apart. They were great letters with enthusiastic salutations—*Dear James oi!*—and promising closures—*See you in the next letter!* But the fact remained. There were only three. I had posted a dozen envelopes for her, but she'd acted on only twenty-five percent. I'd tried not to read too much from so little, but airborne, thinking of how little contact we'd had gave me vertigo.

En route to New York, to Anchorage and Seoul, the vertigo worsened. My mind worked on explanations like a factory. Until I had known for sure that I was on my way back to Vietnam, the questions had been mine, all mine, as if Thuy, halfway around the world, sat like a bedrock of resolve. I had taken her own commitment for granted, as if I had only to decide for myself and she would be there.

Although I'd arrived in Saigon without incident, my luggage hadn't. After an hour of looking and asking, I got to the appropriate airport official. Instead of a receptive audience, I found a man who wouldn't look me in the eye and who nodded prematurely at the descriptions of my luggage and my best guess as to where things might have gone wrong.

He'd led me to a stand-up desk in a secluded corner, where he met my eyes for the first time, smiling faintly. I got the message.

This was my opportunity, but the prospect of bribing him turned my stomach; he should have paid me for the inconvenience. His window of interest closed quickly as he sensed my unwillingness, and he passed several forms across the desk for me to fill out.

"We call you when we find," he'd said.

"But you don't know where I'm staying."

He laughed, more at me than his own mistake. "Okay, you call us."

That evening I woke from a nap I'd tried to avoid taking, showered, and dressed in the same clothes I'd been wearing since my departure. The coming of night hadn't done much to raise the city's comfort level, and the sweat I'd washed off was on me again by the time I reached the desk of my guest house and asked for my passport. Several of the proprietor's children sat clumped on a wooden bench, nursing infectious low-grade giggles while they waited for Charlie Chaplin to perform another antic on the TV screen before them.

"Do you like Charlot?" the man asked, pronouncing the word *Shaht-ler*. When I told him I didn't know Charlot, he pointed at the TV.

"Oh, Charlie Chaplin. I don't know him very well."

"We love Charlot, and Sherlock Ohm." He leaned over the high desk and settled his gaze on the screen.

I asked for my passport again, and he told me it would be safe with him. I hadn't liked surrendering it earlier, but it was impossible to check into a hotel or guest house without leaving your passport at reception. The proprietors cited Vietnamese law as the reason why, and several times I'd cited U.S. law back, as if there were one, arguing to keep it. They usually won. When the rack rate was right, they held all the cards.

I trumped my proprietor's hand by telling him I needed the

identification in order to change money. He bid me wait and made a phone call. A short time later, a policeman braked his motor scooter out front and strode through the guest house reception area, which doubled as the owner's family room, and passed a folder across the reception desk. Coming in and going out, the cop didn't deign to glance at me or the TV, or to acknowledge the proprietor's fawning gratitude.

"Okay," the proprietor said, handing me my passport. "Number one."

Downtown, vendors filled the little parks in front of the old French opera house and city hall. Small replicas of U.S. helicopters cut from the cans of Budweiser, and fighter jets cut from Heineken dangled for sale from the spokes of bamboo poles. T-shirts urged the U.S. to LIFT THE EMBARGO, NOW and provided a canvas for a portrait of a beaming Ho Chi Minh. For fifteen minutes, a too-thin man shouldering the hull of a model sailing ship ambled after me, hoping to parlay my cursory interest in the hemp rigging and crimson sails into a purchase. His price dropped precipitously from more than $100 to less than $30 before he finally quit on me. On the park's fringes, in the baylike bottom stories of bleak five- and six-story blocks of apartments and offices, more dubious vendors trafficked in what were reputed to be the dog tags of U.S. soldiers. I browsed through several batches, stored on giant key rings, noting misspellings in soldier's names and religious affiliations. A jaded Aussie traveler had told me once that that was how to know the dog tags were fake. They can't even get the spellings right, I remembered him telling me. But according to an American I'd met in Hanoi, who worked for the U.S. delegation charged with locating missing U.S. servicemen in Vietnam, that was exactly why they were not fake. Whenever the guys who cut the tags made a mistake, they'd toss them in the base sump. Eventually, after the bases had been salvaged by postwar scavengers, the dog tags wound up in the most likely place for sale, which was here, among the light tourist traffic making its way through Vietnam.

At Dong Khoi Street, I heard "Satisfaction" by the Rolling Stones and followed it, indulging a desire for familiarity and accessibility on a day that, so far, had defined itself by the loss of my luggage. The music was coming from the Apocalypse Now bar, just up the street from the Good Morning, Vietnam bar. Inside the Apocalypse, the paddle blades of the ceiling fans doubled as the rotors of helicopters painted upside down on the ceiling. The namesake movie poster was plastered on a blood-red wall. The patrons, mostly, were foreign, young people on *wandrejahre*, wearing the indigenous peasant garb of the countries they'd traveled through like stickers on a steamer trunk: *camàs* from Cambodia, tasseled batik sarongs from Indonesia or Thailand, *longyis* skirts from Burma. Some looked like they were going native, or trying to, the hair tangling to dreadlocks or bound in head dressings, as if on some personal *Heart of Darkness* journey. Some had this eyes-wide-open way of looking at you, this studious commitment to the present tense, as if the mindfulness of Buddhism had withered the preoccupations and anxieties of their Judeo-Christian roots. Among them, I sometimes sensed a competitive desire to be moved so completely by a place that they would lose their bearings and in that waywardness and alienation, gain a kind of hegemony over fellow travelers. Anybody's upper hand was having been somewhere five years before you, before it all went to ruin, which meant popularity. I'd stopped at the Apocalypse the previous year, and it didn't look any different to me.

As soon as I'd settled in a stool by the entrance, a shoeshine boy caught my eye from across the bar. I shook him off, but he made his way toward me, anyway, only to be undone by my flip-flops.

He gazed mournfully for a moment, as if I were playing unfair, then, half-consciously, laid his arm across the shoulders of a middle-aged foreign man seated nearby. I had nothing to dissuade the next saleskid, who carried a cigarette tray of Wrigley's chewing gum, postcards, wall maps of Indochina, coins of the imperial realm, poorly pirated versions of Graham Greene's *The Quiet American*, the Lonely Planet's guide to Vietnam, Vietnamese phrase books, and a token smattering of dog tags. He didn't ask me to buy anything. He just stood there, smiling while he repeated the refrain to a song he knew from the bar's repertoire: "Rollin . . . rollin' . . . rollin' on a reevuh." When I bought a pack of postcards, at the price he named, he called me number one and hustled his tray toward another new customer.

I passed a 5,000 dong note to the bartender and requested a selection from U2 or R.E.M., if he had any. As soon as U2 cranked up, a guy about my age who wore a camouflage-green bush hat stepped to the bar and offered up his own dong note. When Jimi Hendrix kicked in, the guy drummed the long neck of his bottle in time, then looked at me. "The 'Nam," he said. "The fuckin' Nam. This is it."

During the bicycle trip, I'd made a rule for myself: I wouldn't use any of the GI-speak from the war, no matter how common the currency among the Vietnamese I met. I refused to refer to the son of a man we'd hired as a guide for several days as Babysan, as he did. No references to boom-boom or things that were number one or number ten. And no 'Nam, especially not that. Partly, I suppose, I was haunted by the memory of a man who'd come to my bar on Martha's Vineyard, where, toward the end of that summer, I'd talked with patrons about my winter plans for travel in Vietnam. He was old enough to be a veteran of the war, and he seemed to be holding on to something from the era. He wore a ponytail that had more hair below the rubber band than above, and he sat brooding for a while after I'd told him about my plans to travel up Highway 1 from Saigon to Hanoi. "You got no problems that way," he told me. "About the 'Nam." Later, he told me I ought to go to Nicaragua if I wanted to go some place that really meant something to my generation. He was an islander, and later I found out from my cousin's husband, also an islander, that this guy hadn't gone to Vietnam either. When the young American at the Apocalypse raised his empty bottle of 333 beer at the bartender and said, "Same-same," I moved to one of the tables on the sidewalk.

Outside, the stars burned in a sky whose depth was made accessible by the city's weak lighting. If not for the encroachment of buildings, it would have been possible to make out constellations. During another break in the music, I could hear the faint musical clopping of hoofs coming from one of the homes across the street, either from a television or radio, a piece of folk music I thought I could identify as "The Song of the Black Horse." Across from the bar, a tailor wheeled his motor scooter up a thin concrete ramp, then drew an accordion grate across the entrance and padlocked it. From inside, he swung paneled doors against the grate. Up and down the street, grates fortified the bay entrances to scores of homes and shops.

Beggars had been working the bar's fringes all night. Legless men who dragged themselves along the sidewalk belly down on the kind of dollies that mechanics slide under a chassis. Stooped, older women whose eyes were white with cataracts and who were led to the shoulders of possible benefactors by children. I watched several people pass on a younger woman who was cradling a sleeping baby who was wearing only a shift that fell as far as his knees. His legs hung limply from the woman's palm. I gave her some money when she came to me.

"You know," said an Aussie, leaning toward me from a neighboring table. "These beggars will rent those babies and drug them to sleep."

I regarded him blankly for a moment, as if mystified by his language, then lifted my beer bottle in a toast. *"Na Zdroviya."*

He looked at me for a moment, then down to the B.C. HIGH letters on the front of my T-shirt. His lips tightened, and he made to say something else, then turned back to the two young Vietnamese women at his table.

The women were wearing the *ao dai* and shared a single seat, though there was another vacant one at the table. The less attractive woman was anchored to her friend with both arms, and stared back and forth between a pubescent bar girl perched in the lap of an ungainly foreigner and the nostril ring of an androgynous young person playing a thumb game with a friend. There was nothing clandestine about her interest. It was as direct and unapologetic as the sun. Even as she whispered commentary to her friend, she continued to gawk, sometimes pointing. The other woman was sophisticated by comparison. She wore a dark shade of lipstick. Sunglasses dangled from her neck.

It was on her that the Aussie lavished his enthusiastic attention. He strived to communicate with her in Vietnamese, working out of both a Vietnamese phrase book and a *Viet-Anh* pocket-sized dictionary. The attractive woman complimented his pronunciation. Occasionally, she corrected him and put him through a short drill, during which they volleyed the same syllable until she'd decided that his version was good enough.

I gathered from their digressions in English that the women were guides with SaigonTourist, a government-run agency, and that he'd hired them for the day, perhaps the evening. Eventually, he asked whether she was available the next day. She told him she was busy. They both were.

"I'll be here several days," he said then. "Perhaps, there's another day you're free."

"For example?" she asked, raising her eyebrows.

"The day after tomorrow, for example."

"We're busy." Her tone was flat and definite. "If we cannot see you again, maybe you can leave us your address. Maybe we can be pen pals."

Inside the bar, I watched one of the dreadlocked guys press his body against the slight figure of a Vietnamese girl who had leaned over the pool table and was sighting along the length of a cue. He took control of the stick, and she laid her small hands on top of his. He closed his forefinger over the cue and slid it back and forth through the aperture, delighting his friends and the guy in the bush hat, who probably couldn't believe his good fortune. *And bar girls too! Just like China dolls.*

The gesture was lost on the girl. Her face kept up its mask of bemusement, as pitifully worn as the blue mascara now smeared around her eyes. For an unwieldy moment, I felt like hurling my beer bottle and smacking off that bush hat. Righteousness was doing funny things to my face. I kept trying to catch one of their eyes, to cut them with contempt. They never looked my way.

When I left the bar, a group of beggars and street kids shambled after me. My stride was brisk and angry, and I outpaced them by the next corner. A pair of cyclo drivers was more tenacious, pitched forward over the handlebars and seat backs of their berths, touting their availability in pidgin. Beyond the glow of light and music shed by the Apocalypse, I could hear the raspy revolutions of their chains.

"You go boom-boom?" one of the men asked.

How many times had I fielded this question? "No."

"Very good, the boom-boom. Very beautiful," said the other driver.

"No boom-boom. No ma-sah," I said. "I have a wife."

"That okay," the first man said.

"Is it?" I asked. I stopped and looked at him. "Do you have a wife?"

The man nodded. His T-shirt was threadbare and gashed from shoulder to sternum. "Four baby," he said, holding the fingers out of a fist. He raised two fingers out of the other fist and waved them at me before drawing one of them to his lips, admonishing me to silence. "And two wife."

In the morning, I woke up with the same torturous shame that afflicts people who've had too much to drink the night before, and too much to say. But I hadn't had too much to drink, and if anything, I'd heard too much.

In the downtown post office, I replayed the Aussie's invitation to the Vietnamese woman the previous evening and her more haunting reply: *I'm busy.* The insistence and enthusiasm of his interest in the young Vietnamese woman kept knocking on a door I'd been trying to keep closed inside my own head for weeks if not months. I saw clearly in him, and in the woman's response to him, indications of deeper meanings that I'd been blind to in myself: She wanted a pen pal.

Thuy's reluctance to talk much about my return, I decided then, had less to do with a celebration of the present moment, as I'd thought, and more to do with doubt. Her father had warned her that Americans were very good at leaving. Once a soldier of the

Army of South Vietnam, he knew that about Americans. He also knew they were not very good about coming back.

It occurred to me now that in the weeks I'd been away the suitors had never stopped coming to her house. The dentist. The pilot. Dich, the cop. And the neighbors had never ceased their gossip. They'd wondered out loud if I were CIA, a suspicion held of every American in Vietnam then. I knew Thuy didn't put any stock in this sort of gossip, but other, more damaging gossip was at large. I knew what they wanted to know. Why was a young American visiting a Vietnamese girl? What was wrong with the girls in his own country? More to the point, what was wrong with him? Unlike the motivations of a tubby, balding middle-aged European, looking for an Asian Lolita, my motivations were unclear. Something's wrong, they'd told her. Watch out.

After phoning the airport and learning that my luggage had been located and rerouted—it would arrive the next day—I addressed another fax to the post office near Thuy's house, telling of my delay and again asking her to fax me back at the post office.

On the wall above me was an enormous old wall map of Vietnam, plastered there by the French when this had been a Bureau de Postes and the country had been divided into the provinces of Cochin China, Annam, and Tonkin. The paper had wrinkled from humidity and decades, and some of the place names had changed since the French had left. Tourane was now Danang. Cap-St.-Jacques was now Vung Tau. If I didn't see a fax from her the next day, I decided, I would not go on to Hue. As soon as I'd decided this, I went through my litany of excuses for why she hadn't faxed me back before, reciting them in my head like push-ups. But every time I lowered myself to come up with another excuse, the floor hit me in the face: since when did pen pals send faxes?

CHAPTER FIVE

No fax arrived. I got on the train anyway, propelled by the momentum of having come this far and the determination to see it through. As the Reunification Express started out of the station in Saigon, the only other passenger in my four-berth roomette was a middle-aged Vietnamese man who wondered if I was fluent in Polish. He'd assembled cars in communist Poland for a few years in the early 1980s. Because I had a decent nose, he told me he thought I might have grown up in Gdansk.

"Lech Walesa!" the autoworker said.

I seconded his enthusiasm with a thumbs-up.

"Ah American!" he said. "Okay."

The introduction of my nationality seemed to reflexively spark a desire in him for a cigarette. Cause and effect: American—cigarette. He offered me one, rising partway out of his seat to lean forward with the pack extended. I didn't smoke, but the show of his generosity was too much for me to decline. I took one. He deftly shucked another from the pack (another for later), and I slid both into my breast pocket.

He lit his cigarette with a Zippo lighter, the kind GIs used during the war and were today sold in souvenir shops. While he steadied the flame at the tip of his cigarette, I made out the script engraved on one face of his Zippo: *I'm an American advisor. Let me into your hearts and minds or I'll burn down your fuck'n hooch.*

He pulled two drags off his cigarette, then, sufficiently primed, put one to me. "So why you come my country?"

I gave him the usual: Vietnam was a beautiful country; it was relatively inexpensive for me to travel here. Then, because it's easy to bare your heart to a stranger, I told him I was going to Hue because of a girl.

"Ohhhhh," the autoworker drawled, promptly rubbing out his cigarette on the windowsill. He looked from my knees to my chin to my hands, my hair, as if reappraising me in a new light. He seemed alarmed. I regretted saying anything.

"I know one Vietnamee," he said. "Gotch married with th'American many year ago." She was a Saigon woman who'd married an Army sergeant in the early 1970s. She returned to the States with the sergeant after his tour was up, but the marriage fell apart not much later. According to gossip the autoworker gathered, it seems the Army sergeant was a great—the autoworker didn't have the word for this in English, but he drew a pyramid of balls on his palm, a single ball positioned further away—pool player.

"Not pool," he said, shaking his head over the billiards entry in my English-Vietnamese dictionary.

He drew lane lines on his palm—bowling. The sergeant was in a men's league. He took inordinate pride in his ability. But his Vietnamese wife didn't appreciate that talent. This, the autoworker said, busted up their marriage.

I came away from his story, wondering whether he was trying to advise me to make sure Thuy had it in her to appreciate the skills of good bowling or, if I was serious about a Vietnamese and a great one for bowling myself, to think twice.

The autoworker remained oddly quiet after his story (maybe he considered it a parable), but I was just as happy. He'd more than made up for his lack of fluency in English with decibels. By the time he raised his brows over the end of the sergeant's abandonment of his acquaintance, my ears were ringing.

Midway through his story, two more passengers entered our compartment. They were burly men, truck drivers from Danang who'd sold one of their vehicles in Saigon. Under normal circumstances, they wouldn't have shelled out the twenty-four dollars it cost a Vietnamese for a first-class berth on the overnighter to Danang, but they had got a great price for their truck. One of the men shouldered a wooden crate of BCI beer. They had no other luggage.

All morning, the train clattered through the unarable littoral of the south-central coast. The highlands rose not too distantly in the west, hemming the railway into a parallel run along the sea's edge. I read about the landscape in one book of the portable library I'd assembled for my time in Hue. Until soldiers of the Vietnamese Le Loi Dynasty sacked its capital, Indrapura, in 1471, this land had been the territory of the Kingdom of Champa, a country as extinct now as Hibernia or the Cherokee Nation, its people for the most part annihilated or assimilated. What was visibly left of the kingdom were the ruinous brick towers of their 800-year-old temples, rising off swells of ground, as forlorn as old castle walls trying to hold up a memory in a pasture.

All afternoon, the gang of beer bottles rattled in their crate like whispered threats. I kept wishing my compartment mates would get on with it and get it over with, but when during lunch they drank tea I knew we were in for a beer bash come dark. It began at dusk, not long after the train porters scooped our rice dinner out of a massive cauldron that took two men to carry. A half dozen friends of the truckers congregated in our compartment, every one of them a chain smoker. I shared two beers with them, then retired to an upper bunk for the night.

Their ensuing conversation was din to my ears, but at some point in the evening it coalesced around whether it was more grammatically appropriate to say in English, "too much money" or "too many moneys." The discussion of the matter seemed interminable, with each man sounding each phrase repeatedly until I drifted into a dream of someone holding a dripping bag of water over my forehead.

Since leaving the States, I'd tried to avoid thinking about Thuy's mother's teeth. But as our train crawled through a crossing south of Hue, and I looked at halted traffic that included an antique bulbous-fendered, long-hooded Citroen, the story nudged itself into the open again.

Her mother's two oldest sisters hadn't lacquered their teeth, so it wasn't a consequence of custom. It was something else. Nga broached the subject apropos of nothing one day, asking did I want to know why.

"To protect her teeth," I said. Thuy translated. Lacquered teeth were virtually impervious to rot.

"Khong phai," Nga said. Not right.

In the early 1950s, after Thuy's mother had betrothed herself to Mr. Bang and he'd been conscripted by the Viet Minh, her grandmother's wine business attracted the attention of a colonial French official. He was broad-shouldered and bearded. His own family, he'd told them, lived in a walled city like Hue. He had a chauffeur, a dark-skinned man who wore an odd hat. Thuy looked up the word in the dictionary: *turban.*

After a while, it became obvious to Thuy's mother and her family that the official was more interested in the youngest daughter than the family's wine. If she wasn't at home, his purchases were brisk. When she was home, he lingered over small talk.

"This is not true," I said.

Nga fixed her eyes on me a moment, then without breaking her gaze beckoned her mother, *"Ma oi, Ma."*

"St. Ma-Lo, I remember the name of the place he came from," Thuy's mother said. Until then I hadn't known she was in the room with us, ensconced in the nook behind the wardrobe. *"He used to talk about how strong the ocean was there."*

"One day, the French man brought a Vietnamese interpreter, who asked our mother if she had a desire to learn French. The administrator, according to the interpreter, believed our mother was very beautiful. He wanted to know her better. That news caused a lot of confusion in our family. People still remembered the days when the emperors adopted beautiful women as concubines. The French were now as powerful as the emperors of Vietnam had been, and there was no telling what he might do, even though our mother was already betrothed to our father. Finally, they hit upon a solution. On three successive days, an old woman in the village applied black tree sap to our mother's teeth. Our father, he wouldn't care about that because he's Vietnamese. But the French, the first time he visited mother's house after that was the last time."

I looked at Thuy. She was leaning over her lap, staring at her hands, clasped and bouncing slightly before her knees. Not until later did I begin to wonder whether she had known Nga was going to tell this story, and perhaps whether she had asked for the story to be told. As the train neared Hue, I felt certain that there was a message in this story for me.

When the conductor announced our arrival in Hue, I was standing between two of the cars, looking out as the train curved slowly into the station, a great green arc of railroad cars sliding toward a lavender dock, and the same platform on which I'd said good-bye to Thuy three months earlier. I remembered her then, wearing a purple, short-sleeved polo shirt and jeans from China. My chest was pumping hard, as if to will her back onto this platform now, in that same outfit, bearing the same desire I believed we'd had for each other then and that smoldered in me now. I remembered the way the heat had shined her face and how luminous her smile was as she waved good-bye. I'd thought that the smile had been a brave response to what, in me anyway, was a wrenching, bittersweet parting. But as my heart picked up the pace of its beating, I wondered how brightly pen pals smiled for each other when they said good-bye.

I looked at the faces of the people on the platform, some waiting to board, others waiting for friends and families. She wasn't among them. I stayed there between the cars, looking as new passengers began to board. A drowsy conductor asked for my ticket, and then straightened up and opened his eyes on me to explain that we'd reached Hue. He reached toward my elbow, and there was nothing to do but lug my baggage off the train.

I waddled down the steps into the track rock, across another set of rails, and onto the station deck. On intuition, I moved toward the station gate where Thuy and I had parted weeks earlier. On each side of the gate was raised lettering and numerals marking the distance south to Saigon, 1,088 kilometers, and to another city, Hanoi, 688 kilometers, whose letters had been chipped away.

The debarked passengers and their greeters poured through a single exit in the old French railway station. I was swept among them, so burdened by my bags that I had to rock from side to side to keep everything in balance. Beyond, temporary corral fencing restrained the circus outside the station: the horde of cyclo drivers, clumped together waiting for fares; the motor-scooter taxi guys; the bicycle taxi guys; several guttering Lambro 550 three-wheelers; a half dozen bread carts; ice cream vendors blaring radio cartoons; a circle of idle men juggling a shuttlecock with their feet. My eyes jumped from place to place, snagging momentarily on long black hair and the willowy figures of young women, until finally I spotted her.

She held my glance for a moment before turning and blending back into the crowd. As she handed her ticket to a station offi- cial, I called her name, but she didn't look back. A dozen other people nearby did. They gazed on me, on this foreigner in their midst who'd just shouted the name of a Vietnamese woman— Xuan Thuy. Ordinarily, I wouldn't have shouted for her. I knew better than to draw attention. But the sight of her there after these weeks, months, and the anxiety that had been rising in me like a temperature over the previous three days left me no alter- native.

That she was inside the gated area meant that she had purchased a station ticket. Meant she got my faxes. But what did this flight mean? Outside the gate, she stood a moment, searching in the crowd until she fixed me again, then she turned and fled through the circus toward the An Cuu Canal and Le Loi Street.

I worked my way through the bottleneck until I reached the gate attendant, then genuflected to let down my baggage and rummage for my ticket. The attendant, a woman in a tottering military cap, watched me with a hurt, almost angry expression, as if I'd insulted her.

"*Khong co,*" I told her. I don't have it. I winked and barged forward. Ahead, Thuy had reached the far side of the bridge, striding purposefully away, not looking back. She'd seen what she had come to see, I believed then, realizing that none of everything she'd tried had worked to deter me. Neither the revelation of her insistence that I come back to Hue and stay for a year. Nor the trickle of pen-palish letters, written, no doubt, from a sense of inherent goodness, never thinking that anyone would interpret such little contact as a summons. Nor—and this one hit hard as I saw her heading toward two cops on motorbikes, parked by the side of the road—the suite of able suitors. The attendant braced her legs to bar my way. *"Dung,"* she said. Stop.

"I don't have them." I hadn't bothered to say this in Vietnamese. The woman glanced at several station officials nearby, and I quickly dove back into the pockets of my bags, muttering, barely in control.

I glanced ahead again, to get bearings should I need them, should I decide against chucking the whole thing as I felt myself on the verge of doing, and I saw that Thuy had stopped, not beside the cops but beyond them, next to a vendor's tier of dry goods. When she saw that she had my attention, she lifted a package of Chinese cookies off the shelf. The briefest gesture. The package was displayed at shoulder level, and her hand raised them overhead quickly before she put them down. But the gesture was a kind of semaphore, for those cookies in their distinctive metallic silver-and-blue wrapping were the coconut-flavored snacks that I'd always brought to tea. The only cookies I liked in Vietnam, the summons I'd been waiting for.

As a fare, I was worth five or six times as much as a savvy local rider, and with all my baggage, there was work for two men at least. Like sharks feeding on fresh game, the cyclo drivers circled, importuning me to go to this hotel or that hotel, "my friend." I shuffled toward Thuy like a ball in rugby scrum, retardedly, a little bit this way, a little bit that way, as drivers tried steering me toward their own vehicles.

By the time I reached her, some had peeled away, but there were still a half dozen glommed on, grumbling no doubt about what they considered my penurious resistance. But then, my stopping at Thuy introduced a new factor into the equation. The drivers backed off some, mildly bewildered about what kind of truck the foreigner had with the local girl.

Thuy's cat-and-mouse play was clear to me now; this was exactly what she had been hoping to avoid. One of the first words she'd used to describe herself to me was *discreet*, and now she wasn't getting to be that way. I was desperate to hold on to her, briefly, if only to confirm with touch that there had been light at the end of the tunnel, but I didn't dare.

"Tour guide," I said, turning partway to address the cyclo drivers.

Two of the men had lit cigarettes. They regarded me skeptically, as if I'd have to do better than that. Fifty yards back, a disgruntled driver who'd fallen off the chase grabbed my attention. He'd raised his hands overhead, fingers clasped, and knocked the heels of his palms together three times, a gesture for boom-boom.

"Jim," Thuy said, "Minh is waiting for us over there."

She'd seen what the driver had done, and I felt miserable for her. She'd never been considered ill-reputably before. She had good standing in Hue, but now I'd returned, and that reputation was wilting.

I wanted to ask her to say something else. The sound of her voice lent another kind of credulity to this reunion, but unsettled as we were, we were drawing an audience. Better to get somewhere fast.

Thuy took two smaller bags, and we walked across the street to a small café. Minh was sitting in a low rattan table in the shade of a lychee tree. Three beaded glasses of cold sugarcane juice awaited our arrival.

"Jim," Minh said, clapping once and half-standing. "It is my pleasure to welcome back to my country, you. On behalf my family, I'm delighted . . ." Her tongue peeked out the corner of her mouth, and, frowning, she lifted her eyes into the bower of the lychee tree, struggling to retrieve the rest of what she'd memorized. She went on. ". . . hospitality . . . the life . . . your constitution is commendable . . ."

Thuy said something sharply to her. Minh smiled at her and looked at me, smiling still. In English, Minh had developed a tick. She was overly formal about things. Thuy wanted her to stop.

I sat down beside Thuy. Two more cyclo drivers had bailed on my prospect, but three others were still in play. They'd followed us slowly along the sidewalk and were now sitting on their high saddles, waiting as sullenly as seagulls.

Except for the white socks painted on the rows of trees lining either side of Le Loi Street, the city looked as I'd left it. And Thuy too, though she claimed to have gotten thinner. Together, they agreed that I was *map*, fat, which people take as a compliment in Vietnam. It was as hard to get fat in Vietnam as it was to get thin in America.

After a glass of rich yellow cane juice, we hired three cyclos, and together traveled slowly down Le Loi Street. Towering tamarinds lined the avenue and sometimes locked branches overhead, dappling the road in sunlight. It disappointed me that the base of every trunk carried a fresh sock of white paint, as if the city fathers had lost the war against the pests. I complained to Thuy and Minh.

"It's not right, Jim," Minh said, meaning that I had it wrong. It wasn't pests. "Because the power often goes out in my city at night, we want the tree trunks to be white at the bottom so we don't . . ."

She consulted with Thuy for a moment, and Thuy gave her the word she was looking for: "bump into them."

Both Minh and Thuy, like most of the women bicycling Le Loi Street, wore wide-brim hats. Thuy's hat looked like it had come right off a Merchant and Ivory movie set in Edwardian England. The crown was softly rounded, like a bowler's, and wrapped with a scarf whose colorful decorative scheme borrowed from abstract art. The scarf was new, but the hat was the one I remembered and was a persistent part of the image I'd formed of her over the weeks we'd been apart. I loved the hat for its classical overtones and for the honesty of purpose that it carried. Deeply tanned women wore such hats in the West, but as accessories. Here it was a shield against the sun.

"So how is Dich doing these days?" I asked, trying to sound off-the-cuff.

"You know," Minh said with an alacrity that made me think she'd been waiting to tell me just this, "he come to my house more and more and more often now. And when my sister sees him come to my house, she runs to my kitchen until he is gone."

"I never want that," Thuy said with a look of resolved distaste. "You know, Jim, I have an interesting story about Mr. Dich."

"About what?" I asked.

"Do you know how I met Mr. Dich?"

"No."

"He was a friend of a friend my old sister. After I met him, he began to bring film to my old sister's shop very and very often. We laughed many times because we imagined that he offered to make pictures for all his friends. It's very expensive to make the picture."

"Very good friend," Minh said.

"One day, he invited me to go to a birthday party at the home of a beautiful girl, so beautiful. But you know, I only smiled. I didn't say anything. But the day of that party, Dich asked that girl to come to my house and carry me to that party. She did so. So amazing, can you imagine?"

"Did you go?"

"Of course.

"Bien sur," Minh said.

"After that, Dich used to visit my house very often. Not alone. He was shy about that, I always think that, so he invited an older friend go with him."

"He didn't desire a younger, more attractive friend to visit my sister," added Minh.

"Dich's old friend was a guitar player," said Thuy. "A very romantic man. His head was always in the clouds."

"I met him," I said.

"No," Thuy said, shaking her head over a sip of cane juice. "Another guitar player."

"That old guitar player," said Minh, "he began to like my old sister."

"Nga?" I asked, remembering her name.

"No," Minh said, nodding toward Thuy.

"You mean older then," I said.

"Oh yes, forget! Older."

"It's true," Thuy said. "He began to like me." Her voice lowered clandestinely then, and she squeezed her eyes at a point in space as she remembered the next part.

"Dich had to go Danang many times overnight. One time Dich is gone, the guitar player visited my house alone."

"So terrible," Minh squealed.

"Yes, he didn't come into my house, but he called me from outside like this: *Thuy oi, Thuy oi, Thuy oi.* Just so. He came because I told him I liked music very much. And he thought, because I like music very much I can also like him very much. But you know he dressed . . ." She consulted Minh here for a translation.

"Slovenly," Minh said.

"Slovenly, yes, and I told you about his head. He offered me guitar lessons and one day, he drew a map to his house. I always hate that," she said, as if men were always drawing her maps to their homes.

"Why do you hate that?" I asked.

"It's difficult for me to say in English, but how can he imagine that I would go to his house. I am a girl."

"I see."

"Dich found out what the guitar player was doing," said Minh. "My city is very small. And many people talk."

"I know," I said.

Thuy lifted her index finger in the air for emphasis and shook it gently. It was apparent that the presumptuousness of the guitar player had miffed her. "Guitar player, he never came to my house after that. I think Dich, he did something with that man."

"Did something like what?" I asked.

"Not sure. You see, before he liked me," Thuy said, "Dich, he liked another girl."

"And she liked him too," Minh said. "Very much."

"I think maybe Dich was going to marry that girl," Thuy said. "But then, you know, a *Viet Kieu* from America, he came back Hue. A very rich man, he fell in love that girl, and they got married each other. Now she is living in America."

"You're joking," I said.

"No. And you know, some weeks before I met you, I got a letter from Dich. He wrote, 'If that ever happened to you, I am laying myself on the ground in front of the plane that will carry you away to America.' "

"You're making this up."

"Minh?" Thuy said.

Minh was giggling hysterically, but she managed to confirm her sister's story. "Yes, it's true. Sure."

I flashed to an image of Dich at the airport in Hue, lying sacrificially on the runway as Thuy's plane accelerated to take off for America. "And how has he been lately? Dich?"

"He is fine," Minh said joyfully. "Last time he came my house he told me, he got a big promotion at work."

CHAPTER SIX

THE PAPERS, WHEN I RETURNED, were full of deadly elephant rampages in provinces further south. In one month, a herd of six killed seven people. The deaths were gruesome. One elephant bulldozed the hut of a twenty-six-year-old woman, grabbed her with its trunk, and slapped her to death against a tree. The herd then ground her body into the dirt.

"This is a joke," I said, looking up from *Politics & Society*, a Vietnamese-language newspaper I'd begun to puzzle through with Boi every morning. "Elephants don't do this."

"The next day," Boi said, reading on himself, "all they found about that woman was her hand. See—*tay*."

More, equally gruesome accounts made the press: of a child picked up and tossed twenty meters, of one man's corpse bandied about like a soccer ball, of villagers hearing a neighbor's bones snapped by a rogue that came in the night. The elephants' rage was fueled by the encroachment of farmers and loggers. But by bombs too. One story was about a pair of elephants that had tripped ordnance left over from the war. Another detailed the story of two elephants that had stumbled into a bomb crater. After some local villagers helped them out, the pair ran amok, mauling croplands nearby. Not until the police showed up with M-79 grenade launchers did the elephants disperse. The newspaper editorialized that elephants were capable of connecting bombs, and even bomb craters, with humans.

"Elephants remember," Boi said.

Since the *International Herald-Tribune* rarely made it up or down the coast from Saigon or Hanoi, I bought a shortwave radio to round out the news coverage provided by *Politics & Society*. Mornings and evenings, I tuned in the BBC World Service and listened to those small transcendent voices, arcing over intervening space that seemed fraught with peril, over war zones and disasters. At night, I listened to ballroom music that seemed to come not only from a great distance but, amid the fading in and out of frequency, across time itself. The connections were always tenuous. The slightest twist of the dial sent me reeling into a void of pandemonium, as aurally horrible as the image of an untethered astronaut drifting away from his capsule.

Hue had seemed less remote when I was traveling with Relin, when we had each other's familiarity and the momentum of our bike trip to sustain us. It was a different story now, a gloomy one, especially as I looked down the long stretch of a year that lay between my return and whatever Thuy said might come of us.

I was sure it would pass, that my malaise was some sort of normal psychic rebellion to dislocation, something everybody felt. The term for it was *culture shock*. Persuading myself I was in the grip of culture shock was ennobling, but it was also like trying to persuade myself that I'd gone to college in Europe, not Ireland. Homesick is what I was, and I was maudlin with it, lying in bed, going through that lunch I had with my mother at Brigham's, bite by bite, my father and his big breakfasts. Constitutionally, I wondered whether I could bear up against the challenge of spending a year overseas.

Thuy had begun to notice my listlessness. She didn't address it, but it was there, in the tentative way she glanced at me sometimes and the surprise she elicited when I pedaled into her courtyard one evening.

"Ah, still here," she'd said.

I hadn't known it was that bad. "Just wait," I promised. "It'll pass, I know."

Despite the little contact we'd had during the months I was away, I believed those months belonged to the romance. I counted them. Thuy didn't. Soon after I got back, I'd made an oblique reference to her stipulation that I be around for at least a year and mentioned December as the end of that year. We'd met in December.

We were walking our bikes through the old French district near the Morin. I loved this old neighborhood and its hundreds of colonial villas and public buildings. Their provenance was obvious in the quoins that climbed their corners, the elevated first floors and broad stairways, in the pediments, bas-relief columns, and window balconies. Even when you had no sympathy for the French and their *missione civilatrice*, with which they'd tried to justify the colonization of Vietnam, you couldn't help but feel a pinch of nostalgia in Hue. Looking up the half-moon driveways where they'd once parked their Citroens, I sometimes imagined I could hear a gramophone scratching Debussy and Chopin against the itch of homesickness.

Thuy stopped outside the gated entrance to an old colonial villa compound on Ly Thuong Kiet Street. "You're bad at math," she said.

I looked at a plaque on one of the gate's pillars. This was the local station for *Medecins Sans Frontieres,* or Doctors Without Borders.

"I'm good at math. I can do square roots in my head," I said.

"Then you must know a year from now is not December."

Later, she explained her reticence during my absence, at first, on how busy she was. But I knew now that the word was the translation of a perfectly legitimate means of skirting the truth, or an expression that concealed indecision. I had written faithfully, every few days, even in the midst of my own wavering.

"Nobody in Vietnam is as busy as they say," I told her. "Busy I don't accept."

"Some of your letters, I didn't want to accept."

She went into the back of her house, a place I'd begun to think of as a labyrinth since I was never allowed back there, and returned with a sheaf of my letters. She waved them at me. "How many times did you write me?" she asked.

"Many."

She placed them on the tea table. "First, I don't get any handwriting from you. Always by the typewriter. And then . . ." She picked up one of my letters and read from it: " 'It is about 1:30 P.M. now, and I have just eaten lunch. I ate two hot dogs, a peanut butter sandwich, and I drank a glass of root beer.' "

She let that page fall from her hands, then picked up another: " 'Yesterday I tried to cut my hair in the mirror. Not all of it. Just the hair that hangs down over the forehead, what we call bangs.' "

"Any letter," she said, letting that one fall from her fingers. She read more excerpts about the weather and news, various international incidents, flashbacks to my weeks at summer camp as a boy. "Sometimes, reading your letters, I became angry." She spoke more loudly. "You know, so much about the news, news, news, news, news."

"Yes," Minh called joyfully and knowingly from the labyrinth. "The news."

By comparison, her letters to me had been handwritten and full of sentiment, resurrections of moments we'd shared, at Tet, at the tombs, and how ardently she was looking forward to my return. It seemed preposterous that I could have read them en route to Vietnam and still wondered about my reception in Hue.

"Sometimes I had to doubt about your feeling," she said. She placed a finger under my chin and lifted my face to hers. The furrows in her forehead relaxed gradually as I looked at her, but before they were gone altogether, she bit her bottom lip sharply to reemphasize her gripe.

"That's why you didn't write," I said.

She gathered the letters and reorganized them, carefully, I noticed. "Not the main reason," she said casually. "The real reason is because every time Minh read my letter to you, she criticized my grammar strongly."

At six o'clock in the morning, every morning, a man swung a solid iron bar against a short section of train track rail hung from the limb of an apricot tree in the courtyard of the Morin Hotel. He let that first bracing clang resonate for a moment, like the shimmer of a bell, before he whacked the rail again, and again, shortening the interval between beats until a harsh metallic tattoo stitched the morning. And then he'd do it again, and again.

My first morning at the hotel, I jumped out of bed nervously, wondering whether the alarm was general. In the corridor, I threw open the shutters, but by then the man was gone. The garden was in shadow, but a line of dawn had descended beneath the tiled eaves of the interior wall opposite mine. Below, a row of bare-chested men were squatting on the sloped sills of the corridor windows, as uniformly set as pigeons on a wire, having a first cigarette of the day. Their faces glowed out of the shadow with each inhalation, and for a brief groggy moment, as the reverberation of the alarm played within me, I could see them focusing in my direction.

They were part of a construction crew that was repairing the Truong Tien Bridge, the charming old French-built trestle near the Morin's main entrance. The alarm was for them, and no, it didn't bother any of the other guests, Mr. Hue, the hotel manager, told me later. Nor did it bother the hotel's neighbors, for whom all kinds of racket were the ingredients of a morning's porridge. A café on Hung Vuong Street that blared pop tunes at dawn. A motorbike repair shack, whose owners thought nothing of revving engines while the roosters crowed.

The Morin was an old hotel, dating back to the turn of the century, when the French were consolidating their hold over Indochina. On one of the hotel's exterior facades, just under the bracketed eaves of the tiled roof, was the name of the colonial proprietors, ESTABLISHMENTE FRERES MORIN, as faint as an advertisement for crockery or bread on the upper reaches of old brick buildings in American cities. Under French administration, the hotel's seventy rooms catered to guests of the Nguyen dynasty and the *superieur general*, whose palace, before demolition, had sat across Hung Vuong Street.

"Do you know Marshal Joffre?" Mr. Hue had asked on the day I moved in. His name was spelled like the city's, but only foreigners, deaf to the distinctions of the five tones, would confuse the two.

"I don't."

"He stay here."

I'd asked Mr. Hue how much a room cost, but he'd skirted the question with this about Joffre. And not only Joffre, he went on, leading me into the hotel's courtyard garden, but Andre Malraux, Norodom Sihanouk, Somerset Maugham, and Charlie Chaplin, whom he'd referred to as "the clown king."

"Charlie Chaplin stayed here?"

"He drank coffee over there." Mr. Hue gestured toward several empty café tables, scattered over a lawn of thick-bladed grass. "Very good, the coffee here."

Mr. Hue's over-the-top enthusiasm was thematically mirrored in the hotel's courtyard, where a crew of gardeners was trimming shrubs that had been sculpted to look like elephants and elk. Candy-colored birds twittered in rattan cages hung from the garden's frangipani trees. A stork tethered to a stake in the ground hopped onto a grotto made of poured concrete as we passed by.

"Many years ago, our guests watched films from Paris this garden," Mr. Hue said. "For example, Renoir."

Tables spilled out of the hotel restaurant onto a terrace, roofed over by steeply pitched terra-cotta tiles. Around the second floor, large arched windows opened onto a breezeway corridor. At the bottom of a black hardwood stairway, rising in four right angles to the second floor, Mr. Hue stopped. He pointed at the treads, sunk with the footsteps of a hundred years, and crossed his arms to linger over them like a man in a gallery.

"You know I'm not French," I said to him then.

"I'm sorry I don't speak French," he said.

"But I'm not French."

"Ah." This was a revelation. "Not French."

I appreciated his *Indochine* sales pitch anyway. It's what I'd liked about the Morin when I'd first visited. It's what I'd liked about this side of the river, the familiar European dimensions of its architec-

ture, a middle ground between home and the classical Chinese
flourishes that prevailed on the north bank.

"English?"

"American."

"Right."

Up the stairs, Mr. Hue launched his Namstalgia pitch, part of
which I'd read about already. In the Battle of Hue in 1968, the
Morin, then a university building, served as a command post for
the U.S. Marines' house-by-house assault to retake the city from
the North Vietnamese and Viet Cong. Mr. Hue pointed out the
bullet holes in the hotel's facade as he led me through a corridor
to an unrenovated wing of the hotel. He ducked into several doors,
urgently mindful and half-muttering to himself, before he found
the right one.

Inside, the room was long and narrow but high-ceilinged. The
floor tiles were cracked, and there was construction debris piled in
the center of the room. Mr. Hue opened the bathroom door, checking, then closed it again and looked back at me again, grinning.
"Okay," he said. "Have a look."

I looked into the bathroom. An old tub, a pedestal sink, and
more debris—nothing special. Mr. Hue knocked on the door,
and as I turned I saw why we'd come. In a black magic marker,
drawn on the cracked white paint of the door, was the inverted y
and circle of the runic peace symbol. Underneath was the word
LOVE.

My room cost eight dollars per night. The view faced south, beyond the canopies of a tropical almond tree, over the terra-cotta
tile roofs of the French district to the distant spire of a Catholic
church. Across the street and below was a beauty shop, and the

toddler son of the woman who ran it, a boy who rarely wore bottoms and who arched his back dramatically to pee in the gutter. His world was bounded by the sidewalk before his mother's shop, and since my tea table was set there, below the window, I became intimate with the career of his play: his regular friends and the older girl who liked to hoist him on her hip and take him for walks; the crickets he squatted to play with, almost daily, at the feet of an older brother. One day, he raced back and forth along the sidewalk with a tiny kite made of newspapers that wouldn't fly. Quitting, frustrated, he whipped the kite under the wheels of a passing minibus, then looked up at me. "SIDA," he yelled, then turned tail and ran into the shop.

The first couple of nights, I clasped the outside shutters against the decorative iron mullion that filled my window space. But the shutters cut down on the ventilation between my one window and the air vents cut over my doorway. Leaving the shutters open, and a reading light on, attracted mosquitoes, since there was no screen. The mosquitoes attracted bats, who'd crash through my mullion and swoop overhead, from one side of the room to the other, like balls in a bowl, until they finally crashed out again.

The cyclo driver who'd taken me here and who'd tried to deter me from the Morin had been right about one thing: My bathroom had a resident rat whose midnight ramblings scattered my toiletries like bowling pins. I could see that the shelf above my sink was a landing pad for its jump from the bathroom windowsill, and for several nights, I refused to cede him the space. Yelling didn't bother the rat. I had to get up and throw things before it scampered up the plumbing and out an air vent. When I asked Mr. Hue for a trap, he produced a ubiquitous red-white-and-blue tarpaulin shopping bag.

"How?" I asked.

He opened its mouth wide and held it up. "Same same the wind."

The rat won. I moved my toiletries to the top shelf of my wardrobe.

There was little to do about most invasions. Long, wavering trails of ants marched across the walls of my room, like banners undulating in slow motion. The occasional cockroach would sortie out of the bathroom, as if to wonder what else. When I killed them, I nudged them beneath my door, into the corridor. In the morning, I'd find their shells hollowed out by the ants.

A mosquito net hung from prongs that swung out over my headboard, and I quickly learned to take a flashlight to bed and inspect the corners of my tent before sleep; otherwise the mosquitoes would feast. They would also feast from the outside if my shoulder, or any part of bare skin, pressed against the mesh. My allies against mosquitoes were a flock of geckos, large wall salamanders that congregated near light sources and darted like vectors after their prey. They chirruped with victory, and that sound gradually became a comforting reminder of the work being done on my behalf, like the deflection of raindrops on window glass.

When it became clear that occupancy was a challenge at the Morin, I tried to cut a long-term deal with Mr. Hue. He reckoned my proposal to pay 450,000 dong per week on his calculator, converting it first to dollars at the current rate of exchange and then dividing by seven. Two female desk clerks hovered over his computations, whispering back and forth, and when the result showed on the tiny LCD screen, it plagued their faces like an upset stomach.

"But per night," I said, "that's still much more than you charge a Vietnamese to stay in the same room—"

Mr. Hue started to interject, no doubt to reference the fact that I was a foreigner and, per the politically sanctioned double standard, must pay more, as foreigners did at hotels and in restaurants all over Vietnam, but I didn't let him go on.

"—and I am going to guarantee cash flow."

I let the phrase hang in the air a moment, but the promise of guaranteed cash flow didn't resonate with Mr. Hue. He went back to his calculator.

"You want to pay by Vietnamese dong?" he asked, looking up. "Is it right?" He turned the calculator on me. "I can offer you this price."

It was 86,000 dong. Divided by 10,750 dong per dollar, that worked out to be $8 per night. "But you haven't offered me anything," I said. "That's the same price."

"Same same but different," one of the clerks insisted.

Mr. Hue's cheerfulness deflated under my tone. His two assistants, who seemed to think he'd been particularly generous, busied themselves with front-desk side work while Mr. Hue and I each occupied a bulwark of silence, waiting for the other to give. When it became obvious that Mr. Hue wasn't about to budge, I rubbed my palms and then held them up at my shoulders. "Maybe it's better if I shop for another hotel."

"Maybe it's better," he agreed.

As I walked toward the door that led into the Morin's courtyard, I waited for Mr. Hue to call me back. He did not, and because I didn't want to live any place but the Morin, I didn't go shopping.

CHAPTER SEVEN

Evenings, long after the shops had closed, after the bread salesmen had peddled their rounds and the street traffic had subsided to the occasional cyclo and motorbike, the café at 3 Le Loi was a beacon of fluorescent light and taped Western music. After visiting Thuy, I stopped here, partly for the ice-cold beer and partly for the exposure to the café's foreign clientele. Mostly, they were young and mostly French, but Brits and Aussies too and a smattering from across northern Europe. Everyone had at least a couple of fantastic stories, about close calls on the Burmese border or climbing karsts in the Andamann Sea, stories of great vitality that left me feeling, if anything, more despondent, as though being left behind again and again and again.

Gradually, a handful of expats in Hue resolved out of the light traffic of foreign backpackers passing through the city. There was an American teacher named Steve Boswell, who was on the verge of leaving after two years in the city; three French doctors attached to the MSF station and a Swiss doctor who was trying to build a house on the south side of the river; a French accountant; a Dane who helped run the joint-venture brewery that produced Huda beer; and Marian Cadogan.

Marian was director of the European Commission's Refugee Resettlement program in Hue. She was Irish, from near Skibbereen. Though she'd been abroad since graduation from university in 1976, all those years away from home had barely altered a brush stroke in her appearance or her no-nonsense, frank Irish demeanor. Like one of Maugham's characters, and unlike the backpackers, Marian made no surrenders to native customs. She wore tiny claddaghs in her ears, and her wardrobe was completely European. She was an aid worker but brusque. There was no fawning New Age empathy about her; her efforts to learn Vietnamese, though she'd lived here for three years, were slight. At restaurants, she ate with forks, not chopsticks. When people addressed her as Miss Marian, adding the honorific, she asked them not to. The only concession she might have made to Vietnam were the flats she wore, as if to mitigate her height advantage over local males. I sometimes thought of her as the accidental aid worker, a woman who'd been uprooted from a lovely life in Ireland for an unavoidable one-year hardship post overseas. She herself said that she would prefer to live and work in Ireland, but the budgets for the kind of work she did in small-business development were too small.

Finding an Irish woman living next door to the Morin was part of the antidote to my homesickness. Her home, like her self, defied the inherent alienation of being faraway. Though her household decor was indigenous to Vietnam—the conical hats she'd had cut as lamp shades, the shellacked rattan living-room furniture— somehow in that living room, her appointments had acquired the refinement of objects carried by a specialty import shop in the States, rattan you might have picked up at Bombay West, lamp shades that would set you back $100 apiece. The glass-topped coffee table was heaped with oversized picture books, the lower shelf strewn with magazines. A real oasis.

She had a firm grip on the number of expats in Hue: She counted eleven, not including me and not including Steve, but including one other American I'd missed. Gary.

"I haven't met Gary," I told her.

"Right, but you've heard him?"

"No."

"Heard about him?"

"No."

"Right so."

She gave me a book then that Gary had given to her, a book about the Battle of Hue, written by a fledgling eighteen-year-old military historian, and read that way. "Gary calls it, and let me quote him here, 'a singular work of the highest literary achievement.' That'll tell you more about Gary than the book'll tell you about Hue."

To keep the gangrene of boredom from nibbling my commitment, especially after Thuy went back to work at the boutique, I worked up a daily routine. Reading. Coffee. A reasonable nap. News via the shortwave. Language lessons. A trip with Steve, out to see the ruins of an 800-year-old Cham wall or to a forgotten temple he'd read about in the archives of the French priests who'd worked in Hue in the early part of the century.

Like fog lifting, the homesickness dissipated after a few weeks, and when it did, I asked Thuy to marry me. We were standing in the crumbled mirador above the An Cuu Gate, along the ramparts of the Citadel, near her house. I hadn't planned to. The proposal had naturally flooded out of a depth of feeling that wasn't malaise but a sudden and sheer joy.

She laughed lightly, then took my hand and led me down the stairway and along the wall. She walked with purpose, uncharacteristically brisk, past the house of her older sister Dieu and along the edge of a small body of water that, in our previous walk along this route, she had called a lake. On the far side of the lake was the Citadel wall with the dimly lit, feathery crowns of palm trees over the ramparts. At the end of the lake, she stopped at a small hut made of wattles and thatch. The moonlight glowed on a courtyard of swept dirt, and while we stood there, looking at it, a chicken squeezed out of a break in the wattle.

We stared at the hut for a little while, and then she looked up at me. "I was born in that house," she said.

Thanh was twenty-eight years old, and he ran 3 Le Loi's fledgling travel agency. He was, to all appearances, a successful entrepreneur. But business success had yet to translate into the kind of tangible benefit that Thanh pined after.

"You are lucky," he told me one evening. "You are from America. You come to Hue and have the girlfriend. I am from Hue . . ." he smiled, as if this were irony, "but I don't have the girlfriend."

Part of Thanh's problem, I thought, was a matter of style. He couldn't sit in a chair without sinking in it, like a boy in the wake of a dinner table reprimand. And while his family looked to be making great money at the café, and Thanh at his travel business, he still pedaled a black bike with a tire pump rigged beneath the top tube and a blow horn on the handlebar.

His sister, Kim Anh, was engaged to an older Australian, named Graeme, whose arrival in Hue was expected any day now. One night, while I tried to persuade Thanh that his bicycle might be part of his problem, I glanced occasionally at the man I suspected was Graeme. His hair was cut as short as a drill sergeant's, and he looked to be older, in his early forties, not his mid-thirties as Thanh had mentioned. He had a bristle-short blond mustache, and his lips, when I glanced in his direction, were clamped shut.

"Not Graeme," Thanh said. "That Gary."

"American?"

"Of course." Thanh dropped his voice. "Gary, he say he pay my sister for six Huda beer last night, but she say no, he pay only five. A big disagreement, so Gary, he give 5,000 dong my sister, but he throw it."

He gestured, and I looked at the crumpled 5,000-dong note on the floor near his sister's food-prep counter. It was irretrievable.

An Israeli couple at the table neighboring ours asked Thanh if he had a tour going up to the DMZ the next day. Thanh's DMZ business was booming. His trips were going up three times a week now, to the Con Thien firebase, the Witch's Tit, the Rockpile, the Lang Ve Special Forces camp, and the Khe Sanh combat base.

Thanh nodded, and the Israelis asked him to save two seats for them. Thanh collected their money and wrote receipts from a businessman's ledger. When he was done and had resumed his seat at my table, a Brit turned his chair toward the Israelis. It was late, the café had just about emptied out, and Elvis was crooning softly on the cassette deck.

"It's a real bodge job, this Khe Sanh excursion," the Brit told the Israelis. "You drive hours in a foul minivan only to be dumped at some old military installations where you're supposed to gawk over a piece of aluminum revetment or a rusty metal cot." His voice was oddly resonant, not loud but capable of carrying.

Thanh winced, then giggled softly. "My business," he said to me.

I glanced at Gary, who'd moved suddenly in my peripheral vision.

"It's a fleecing is what it is," the Brit went on. "They whisk you from one place to the next. The guide can barely speak English. There Camp Carroll. Then LZ Stud. All these places you've never heard of, and even the ones you have—Khe Sanh, Khe Sanh, look there Khe Sanh—there's nothing up there, that's what."

"What did you expect to find?" Gary called across several tables. He planted his elbows on the table and clasped his hands piously beneath his chin. The warped paddle blades of an overhead ceiling fan riffled the loose fabric of his mustard-colored T-shirt.

An older sister stopped cleaving at her workstation and looked at Gary. The café's other foreigners hardly noticed the Brit's high-toned voice, but Gary's question made a deep silence in the café. Elvis was making his Las Vegas comeback on the tape deck.

"Have you been up to the DMZed?" the Brit asked, pronouncing the z as "zed." There was a civil lilt in his voice.

Gary made a dopey face. "DMZed? What the hell's the DMZed?"

The Brit heaved a sigh and turned back to the Israelis. "Save your money. That's my two cents, as it were." He returned to the people at his table.

But Gary was standing now. "What did you expect to find up there?" he asked, striding across the café. He was a big man, a couple of inches over six foot. The Brit ignored him. He was small, physically no match for Gary.

"What the fuck do you know about the DMZ?" Gary asked. In one swift motion, he overturned the Brit's table. The bottles clattered and smashed on the cement floor. Several of the 3 Le Loi brothers ran into the café from their home out back.

The Brit scrambled out of his chair, and for a moment, stood his ground against the American. But Gary took one giant step across the wreckage, and the Brit started jogging away.

"What's at Dunkirk?" Gary shouted after him. "Tell me that. What the fuck's at Dunkirk?"

Within a few days, perhaps hours, of my arrival at the Morin, most of the staff knew I was seeing a Vietnamese woman. The cleaners, the clerks, the guards, the waiters, the three women who ran a shady massage service off the courtyard—they all knew about Thuy, and they all referred to her as my wife. I corrected their use of the word *vo*, when referring to Thuy, insisting instead on *con gai*, which meant "friend." They insisted on *vo*.

"Vo o'day," a humorless guard told me one early afternoon, rousing me from a nap.

From the windows opening onto the courtyard, I could see Thuy below, sitting on a cement bench beside the stork. Her arms were crossed. Though the stork was a few steps away and looking at her like a loving pet, she paid it no mind and continued to gaze across the garden where several foreigners were having lunch on the terrace.

She hadn't visited my hotel yet, and I hadn't expected to see her until later, at her family's house for dinner. In my room, I put on a shirt and went down to meet her.

"I'm not going to visit your room," she said as I sat down.

"I wouldn't think so."

"I think your hotel is not good." She clamped her lips and kept from turning toward me.

I looked at the diners, quietly tended to by as many white-aproned staff, and beyond to the massage room entrance, where one of the women sat on a stool outside, fanning herself with a laminated menu. A pale blue minibus operated by SaigonTourist circled the driveway that ran around the courtyard's perimeter.

"I know the restaurant is not good," I said.

She made no response. Underneath her thigh was a folded newspaper.

"Did something happen?" I asked.

She heaved a breath and exhaled it over her shoulder. When she looked at me, her eyes were shining with emotion. "I will never go to your room," she said, removing the newspaper. "I just want to say that to you now."

Something had happened. I pleaded with her to tell me. I suspected someone from the hotel staff, but her resolve was staunch. She waved my questions off. Finally she shook open the newspaper. "You said you want to learn to read Vietnamese newspapers, so I want to introduce you to this paper."

She turned to the page she wanted, folded the paper at the seam, again at the fold, and again vertically, leaving a single-image cartoon prominent. The sketch pictured a foreign man, a *tay ba lo*, which literally means "foreign backpacker" but was also pejorative for "budget traveler." The foreigner had a ponytail, earrings, and two-day-old whiskers; a knapsack hung loosely from one shoulder as he aimed his camera at a statue of the bodhisattva. All eighty-eight helping hands of the Buddhist icon were covering its eyes.

"Why do you think?" Thuy asked.

I laughed. "He's lazy to shave."

"Right, and what else?"

I looked back at the cartoon. "His ponytail, the earring. He dresses poorly in the pagoda."

"Continue it."

I looked down into my lap, at the *tay ba lo*'s shorts and the bare legs beneath the hem of my own shorts, a pair of khakis I'd planned to wear that evening—until now. Vietnamese men never wore shorts in public. Since I was a foreigner, I'd thought I had the license.

"The shorts?"

"Okay," Thuy said, taking the paper from me and standing. "The lesson is over. See you tonight."

That evening, as the sisters and their families arrived, they lit incense at the family altar, kowtowed, and retired to the kitchen. Each of the children greeted me in turn, as much from politeness as to give voice to the name of Mr. Popsicle. Gradually, a parade of platters and bowls, carried by the nieces and nephews, marched into the living room, where Thuy's father arranged them on the altar. Each dish was exquisitely prepared—the tomato garnishes cut into rose blooms, thin strips of cucumber curled into the shape of a lotus flower, scallions cut like lilies—as if they were coming out of the pages of a gourmet magazine rather than a kitchen. There were saucers of curry, thick with chunks of chicken and potato; platters of beef wrapped in grape leaves, radiating away from the center of the dish; tureens of soup, steaming and bulging with whitefish and squid. They set up two smaller tables beside the altar and crowded them with mounds of sticky rice, tiny saucers of pastes and other dressings. In the midst of the parade, I made a move through the side door, toward the kitchen, the source of it all, and two nieces shrieked. Thuy hurried out from the back room with a wooden spoon held threateningly aloft. "Back," she said.

The living room was pungent with the feast, but there didn't seem to be an equation between the temperature of the food and consumption. As the dishes cooled, relatives arrived, adults mostly, some pedaling bicycles, some by motorbike, some by cyclo, none by car. The older women wore *ao dai* dresses with the velvety texture and rich hues of Victorian wallpaper. Thuy introduced me to one very elderly man as her grandfather. One of his eyes was cloudy with cataract, and the other wandered. As he sat, he slowly dragged a beret off his head and smoothed a few strands of white hair over his blotched pate.

"I thought he was dead," I said glancing at the picture on the wall.

"Not this grandfather."

"Oh, he is your mother's father?"

"No," she said, oblivious to my surprise.

I looked at the photo on the wall, of Thuy's grandfather in military regalia, a man I'd thought for so long was dead, and tried to remember why I'd thought that he had passed away. Had they told me? Or, as I thought now, had I just assumed so because the photo was so old and because Thuy hadn't ever referred to him as a living relation.

When Thuy's sister Nguyet set one of the final bowls down beside me, I tried to exhibit a little cultural savvy and reminded her not to have the food right away. Nguyet spoke English deliberately and with painstaking attention to grammar and enunciation. She was a teacher, like oldest sister, Nga. Nguyet had told me, when I met her, that her subject was math. Later, I found out it was actually English, and she'd just been hedging her bets.

"Correct," she said. "We wait for him to eat first."

Thuy's parents emerged from the back of the house dressed in black and gray *ao dai* dresses. Mr. Bang wore a mandarin's cap. In the courtyard, standing before a small table laden with areca leaves, betel nuts, flowers, and a clear bottle of ceremonial wine, Mr. Bang began to chant softly.

"He's welcoming his father," Thuy told me.

I looked at the old man, sitting alone at the tea table, smiling at a figment.

"Why doesn't he come out here?" I asked.

"Who?"

"Your grandfather?"

"He is here," she said. "Everywhere."

I looked at him again. But he didn't look that charismatic to me.

"He's right there," I said, gesturing inside at the old man and the family altar.

"My grandpa is dead," Thuy said, making no audible concession to her father's reverent muttering. She sat on the verandah's flat banister, turned partly away from her father's ceremonial observance, legs crossed at the knee, bouncing her foot like a girl. "He died on this day many years ago, and today he's visiting from the Permanent World."

I looked at the old man again. He looked ancient and perhaps even cadaverous, but I could see his chest heaving.

"He looks fine," I said, thoroughly confused.

Her parents' expression betrayed deep bereavement, but no one else looked aggrieved. Several conversations flared around us. For a pair of admiring nephews, Thuy's younger brother, Thang, was demonstrating his facility with a pair of noon-chucks, complete with vocal stabs and breathy effects of a Bruce Lee.

Mr. Bang burned paper images of gold and silver, then clothes and currency that would reconstitute itself as the real thing in the Permanent World. He was about to burn an icon of a horse when he examined it more closely and an expression of disgust soured his face. He beckoned a grandson, who reluctantly peeled away from Thang and who retrieved a paper car from inside the house.

"For when he has to go back to the Permanent World," Thuy explained.

The dinner was cold by the time we ate, sitting in groups on a half-dozen straw mats rolled out on the living-room floor. No one cared. The oldest member of each group filled everyone's rice bowl.

In our group, every diner was as apt to place a morsel from the communal bowl in someone else's bowl as his own.

I sat between Nguyet and Thuy, across from the old man whose name was Tru, not Tuu as I'd noted before.

"How old is your grandfather?" I asked Nguyet, still not sure who he was.

"Too old," she said, chuckling.

His voice, as he turned to Nguyet, croaked, a condition I immediately ascribed to years of barking commands over the sounds of exploding artillery.

"My grandfather wants to know, do you speak French?" Nguyet asked.

"I studied for five years in school," I said. "But not really."

"Vang," she told Tru. Yes.

"Bien, bien," he said.

His French was labored and, though steady, slow enough for me to grasp. I always had better luck communicating in French with people who spoke the language poorly than fluently.

Tru told me he was happy to meet me. Some people in his family had told him about me, and he had been looking forward to our rendezvous. "I can speak English a little," he said. He'd had a lot of American friends during the war.

I had a lot of questions for him, about the imperial court of Vietnam, the Dalat Military Institute, his relationship with the family of Ngo Dinh Diem, whose brother Can, I'd learned, had torn up his papers when Tru refused to convert to Catholicism.

I began with a reference to the photograph on the wall. *"Est-ce que vous avez gardé ce saber?"* I asked. Do you still have the saber?

He shook his head. *"My brother threw it into the lake in 1975. He was very afraid of the communists."*

"You weren't afraid?"

"Not really."

"Your medals. You kept them?"

A hurt, troubled look swept across his face, and I feared that my queries were resurrecting bad memories. Except for cyclo drivers, who hoped that telling you of troubles stemming from involvement with Americans before 1975 would engender sympathy, a big tip, and perhaps more, not many people liked to talk about the past. I'd asked Thuy about how her family fared in 1975, and all I got out of her was "okay."

The old man spoke to Nguyet in Vietnamese.

"You are confused," she said. "He is not that man."

"He is Ong Tru," I said.

"Yes, but that is his brother, Ong Tuu."

The old man hushed Nguyet. It was better not to say aloud the names of the dead.

"I see. And that man," I said, gesturing toward the photo, "is your grandfather. Not this man."

"No, he is my grandfather," Nguyet said, nodding solemnly at the photo. "And so is Bac," she said, moving her hand in Tru's direction.

The first time Thuy had introduced me to her nieces and nephews, she'd referred to them as her grandchildren. She addressed anyone slightly older than herself as *anh*, for older brother, or *chi*, for older sister, even when there was no blood relationship. She addressed those slightly younger as *em*, younger brother or sister. If your culture's language embraced strangers this way, then you might also confer the honorific of grandfather upon a grandfather's siblings.

I guessed that the man in the photo was not her real grandfather, and Nguyet confirmed my suspicion. The portrait had been misappropriated, like the oil painting of an early nineteenth-century sea captain that hung over the hearth of a man I knew on Martha's Vineyard, or people who buy highboys and old sea trunks and conveniently forget they are not heirlooms. Having the resplendent Tuu on the wall had been a hedge, for me, against the wattle and the thatch. His image had built a bridge for me. Yes, Thuy came from a Third World country; yes, the culture was halfway around the world from my own; yes, there was no phone in her house; but, her grandfather was a mandarin. It was one of the first details that I revealed about Thuy when I tried to paint her portrait, for no one so much as myself. I'd let that detail loose as if it were incidental, but I realized now, as the medals slipped from the chest of her grandfather, that Tuu had mattered.

Going home that night, I felt bad that Tuu had mattered. I understood my dependence on him as a blight in my own character. Thuy was beautiful and funny and discreet; she was smart, and yet for some reason I wanted Tuu as well. As I pedaled, I distanced myself from other, normal people with solid value systems and hierarchies of priorities that didn't merit factors like Tuu's. I'd thought that my own response to Thuy was purely visceral or at least emotional, but that too might have been a bit of naïveté.

Miller, during the days he preoccupied himself with the papers of his own girlfriends and his friends, once told me that it should be as easy to marry a woman of means as not to. Easy, I thought then, if you came from means. Later, of course, he tried to persuade himself that her papers had nothing to do with his love.

"So if her father just sold Westinghouse and didn't have an equity stake, same deal? Same love?"

"The same."

"Bullshit. What about papers? They used to mean a lot."

"They merely help filter the pool," he'd said. "So it can be all clear swimming."

CHAPTER EIGHT

The first time I noticed a man place the tip of his middle finger upon the tip of his forefinger, I reciprocated the gesture and waved back. We were bicycling, Thuy and I, to one of the many pagodas in Hue we'd begun visiting, if only for the sanctuary provided from people who gawked at us. I often felt like a public figure in Hue, and if through some osmosis of thought, the passing bicyclist had known I'd proposed to Thuy and was wishing me good luck, it wouldn't have surprised me. What did surprise me was the abrupt way Thuy stopped and hopped off her saddle.

"Why did you do so?" she asked, visibly shaken.

"Do what?"

"Your fingers?"

"Oh." I crossed my fingers again. "Good luck. A man—"

"Never do so," she said.

"Why?"

She looked away, and when she looked back her face winced in disgust. "I cannot say what that means, so terrible."

I thought about the gesture for a moment, and suddenly I understood it was actually an obscene reference to a woman's anatomy and moreover to a prejudice of my interest in Thuy. As soon as I got it, I whipped my bike around and sprinted back the way we'd come, trying to remember his face.

Thuy still hadn't told me who or what had been said to her in the Morin's courtyard. I'd narrowed my suspicions to the several guards who manned a small, windowed room that gave onto the hotel's tunnel entrance. One of them wore a billed military cap; another wore a tunic top with a row of brass buttons—garb so ill fitting and out of environment that I thought of those Sioux and Cheyenne warriors who'd worn the uniforms of Custer's massacred troopers like trophies. I didn't doubt one of them had muttered something to Thuy. I stopped at their window one morning and told them that my friend would sometimes visit me here. I was sure they understood, but their indifferent regard left me feeling that I'd have done better to keep quiet. I complained to Mr. Hue as well, but Mr. Hue didn't seem to feel much responsibility to customer service. Frustrated, I told Thuy I would change hotels. She advised against it. It would be the same elsewhere. Although people were delighted that I was dating a Vietnamese woman, most thought it was terrible that a Vietnamese woman was dating a foreigner.

After trying to track down the obscene bicyclist, I returned to Thuy. Her outrage had cooled. "Welcome to Vietnam," she said.

Boi hadn't ever heard of the "shrinking bird," but he understood the idea behind Truc's metaphor of the resentment that Vietnamese men felt toward foreigners who took a romantic interest in Vietnamese women.

"That was before, right?" I said to him, "during the war when boom-boom was the big deal." I looked around the café. "The only foreign men you see here are with foreign women anyway."

Boi started to say something but then stopped. "Not here. Not now." He looked around at his fellow cyclo drivers. Most of them were former soldiers in the Army of South Vietnam or the sons of prominent officers and officials in the government of South Vietnam, men shackled to the lower rungs of an employment ladder in a country whose present leadership could not bring itself to forgive and forget. It was a sympathetic crowd but a loose one, and Boi could never be sure who talked and who did not.

When I'd first met him, and he found out I was American, he gestured at the red-white-and-blue tarp he wrapped around the front of his cyclo to protect his passengers from rain. But that red-white-and-blue tarp material was ubiquitous in Vietnam, holding down cargo on the roof racks of old Desoto buses and as cover for sidewalk vendors. The colors didn't carry any political overtones in Vietnam.

"The Stars and Stripes," Boi had said, insisting on the relationship between his tarp and the U.S. flag.

Many Vietnamese men I met played the U.S.A. card, believing a premium would be paid for the sympathy. "I see that tarp everywhere," I'd said. "It doesn't mean anything."

"Most don't," he said. He held a finger to his lips, shushing me to conspiracy. "Mine does."

The sun was high that afternoon when I met Boi. I was wearing a wide-brim straw hat that I'd picked up at the Dong Ba market, but Boi wore nothing. He never protected himself that way, just as he never wore a poncho or took medicine. He lived alone with his sister in an old French house near the cathedral, and though he'd never said as much, I suspected Boi was Catholic. I didn't ask because questions that scratched at his history drew blood immediately. "Later, my friend," he'd replied once when I asked whether his parents were living. The things I learned about Boi came indirectly, from friends. His father had been a prominent diplomat in the government of South Vietnam. He'd lost siblings in the war. His reluctance to wear a hat or a raincoat, his asceticism, was a memorial of sorts, a smoldering immolation, an individual life-long protest against Hanoi's victory in 1975. His name, Boi, was a diminutive for "little boy," ordinarily a name he would have shucked sometime in adolescence for his given name, but that name, whatever it was, didn't matter any more, he told me once. "It died too," he said.

As we started down a straightaway along the An Cuu Canal, Boi lit a cigarette and, like a subway commuter, pulled a paperback periodical from his pocket. Absently, he hummed the melody of "Hotel California" and leafed through the pages.

"Very good poem," he said. "Good poem for you. It says about why the Vietnamee man love the Vietnamee woman. I will translate for you, near."

> *Because your eyes are blue,*
> *I have to love the sea.*
> *Because your skin is white,*
> *I have to love the clouds.*
> *Because your cheeks are pink,*
> *I have to love the sunshine . . .*

"No, not sunshine," he said, pausing his translation. He demonstrated what he meant by drawing his hand in simulation of a stream of light.

> *Because your smile is bright,*
> *I have to love the flowers.*

Because your hair is black,
I have to love the dark after the sun goes down.
Because . . .

"Ooh, la la," he broke off again, chuckling. "Why do you think the man have to love the mountains?" he asked.

I guessed.

He slapped my shoulder with his paperback. "But not like the American woman. So big you can ski down."

"What do you know about skiing?" I asked.

"Not much," he said, and then after a pause, more for himself than in answer to me, "Colorado."

Several kilometers outside Hue, Boi steered onto a rutted, reddish track that wound through a lush forest, far beyond the din of motorbike engines. We locked the bike outside a small house whose people Boi knew and followed a trail through the woods until we came to a looming twenty-foot-high wall curving off in either direction. The cement-plastered walls were deeply fissured. Fish-mouth gargoyles gaped around the wall's upper rim. Boi found a ruined stairway and led us to the ramparts of a deep coliseum, perhaps 100 feet across. "For when the elephant wants to fight the tiger," he told me. "In the king time."

The Tiger Arena, Ho Quyen, wasn't in any of the guidebook entries for Hue. It was remarkable that such a place had yet to be found out, fenced and picketed by preservationists. Vegetable patches consumed most of the level ground inside the arena. Banana plants fringed the perimeter, and all kinds of vegetation grew out of cracks in the wall. It seemed only a matter of time before the forest reclaimed it. I asked Boi whether many people, beyond the locals, knew about Ho Quyen.

"The French know," he said. "But the tourist, he doesn't know."

Five doorless pens at the base of the wall provided egress for the gory Southeast Asian spectacle, at which the elephants, symbols of royal might and prestige, always won. The ceilingless pens were filled with crumbled brick debris, but the cement was crisscrossed with what I figured were the swipe marks of tiger's claws. "Not right," Boi said. The tiger's handlers always declawed the tigers before battle, he said. They starved them as well, weakening the animals, and sewed their mouths shut. "Rulers around here, my friend, they do everything they have to to make sure they win."

At the king's reviewing stand, Boi kicked off his sandals and, using them as a seat, reclined in the sun. He seemed more sober out here, less the innocuous rock 'n' roller cracking jokes outside the Morin. He had to be careful, he'd told me once. In modern Vietnam, the sins of the fathers were always visited upon the sons. That, and he spoke English outside a hotel that catered to foreigners.

"You have to be careful too," he told me.

I nodded. Boi watched me closely for a moment, assessing the depth to which his caveat had sunk. I guess he decided it wasn't far enough.

"It wasn't an accident, you know," he said.

"What wasn't?"

He stood, walked around in a circle, as if to shake out the muscles. He rolled the fingers of each hand in a habitual little calisthenic, five times each, then sat down.

"The motorbikes."

I hadn't told Boi. I hadn't told anyone but Relin, and then not until Thailand. I asked him how he knew, but he only moved his hand between our faces. What mattered, he said, was that I continue to be careful.

· · ·

The day after I accidentally left my knapsack at Thuy's, I nudged the gate to her family's courtyard in the early morning. The squeak of the gate was usually enough to bring someone onto the porch, but the guys in the motorcycle shack next door were revving a reconstructed engine. They were always revving an engine, no matter the hour, and no one seemed to mind. I spied Thuy and Minh through a porch window. They were hunched over a table, poring over something as captivating as petri dishes.

Here was an opportunity.

Since I'd come back, they had both delighted in my clumsy efforts to manage the everyday life of Vietnam. They reveled in my ineptitude with the language, my ignorance of protocol in the pagoda, and especially my obvious aversion to some of the dishes they'd order at restaurants. This was Thuy's turf. And because I was trying to demonstrate how far I was willing to go, how broadminded, how much I was capable of spanning the cultural gap between us, I repeatedly left myself vulnerable. I hardly ever caught her unaware. When I did, I made the most of it.

I crept along the side of the house and stopped to crouch below the window facing them. They were speaking quietly to each other, the clandestine patter of their Vietnamese occasionally broken by Minh's awkward pronunciation of an English word. She would say the word out loud first, then spell it using Vietnamese pronunciations of English letters. Thuy would flip through the pages of their Vietnamese-English dictionary and provide a translation. Their work sounded to me like pornography, the meaty pages of an English-language romance that Minh had borrowed from a classmate.

"Tumescence," Minh said.

I heard Thuy hurry through the pages. *"Khong co,"* she said. Not in here.

"Roi, johnson," Minh said.

"Khong co."

"Dung roi, masturbation."

When Thuy found it, her chair scraped away from the table as she made more room for her laughter. In the midst of it, she managed a translation for Minh, who chimed in with her own, higher pitched laugh.

Then it hit me. *Tumescence. Johnson. Masturbation.* They were my words.

I popped up. They shrieked and pushed backward in their chairs. On the table was my journal. Wide open. Naked. A hostage. Baring my secrets as they translated my entries. It was why I had pedaled to their house at dawn, and yet I'd forgotten all about it when I saw an opportunity to send Thuy off-balance. I shoved my arm through the mullion but too late. Thuy snatched the book and stuffed it down her shirt.

I ran to the front of the house, remembering that a hurricane lamp had been burning on the table. Had they been up all night, translating?

I charged through the windstrips at the door, my face gone slack and heavy. It was no longer funny. I held out my hand. "The book, please?"

"Be Nho?" Thuy called out. Thuy propped her leg on a chair and hiked her pant leg up to reveal the lower portion of her calf.

Minh got a crazy, hungry look in her face and began scribbling furiously with an invisible pen in an invisible notebook. She looked up at the calf again wildly and bent to more scribbling.

In that notebook, which I'd started in the States, I had written a one-page elegy about the calf of a woman I'd seen jogging through Edgartown one day. "That was like painting a bowl of fruit," I said in defense. "And that other stuff, I tried to read a book by a writer named Philip Roth and couldn't get through it. I was writing why."

Thuy hiked her eyebrows and nodded vigorously. "Yes, I believe you."

I lunged for the book, and she jumped onto the bed platform. She had a finger wedged in the back of the 120-page National notebook I kept my journal in. I'd nearly filled it in a month. Everything went in there. I'd never put a governor on my journals, and it looked to me now like they'd read most of it.

"I'm sorry, Jim, but can you open your shirt?" she said.

"What?"

"Yes. I want to see"—she started laughing hysterically—"the monster that lives in . . . a cage . . . your chest."

Minh added her own belly laugh to her sister's.

"I want to know if he still agrees with me," Thuy went on, fighting for the words.

"Lurch," Minh blurted. "It lurches."

This was the monster that lurched out of a cave in my chest, the ogre in my spirit that transmogrified my attraction to women to disaffection after I latched onto a particular attribute that I would begin to obsess about.

"Are my fingers too short?" Thuy asked Minh, modeling her fingers.

"Yes."

"And how about my torsey?"

"Torso," Minh corrected her.

"Is it not right for the length of my legs? The proportion is wrong?"

"Yes. Yes."

"This is wrong, you know, Thuy." I sat down and with humility and righteousness put my hands in my lap.

"Then what about this?" She flipped through pages, and I realized with horror that she'd bookmarked it. " 'Marriage is the comfortable way to spend the winter.' What does *that* mean?"

"It's a line from a movie," I said plaintively, on the defense again. By rights, my privacy had been violated. But playing defense seemed to be the only recourse now. "A funny line from an old movie I saw just before I left. Shirley MacLaine."

"Why is it funny?" she asked, her upper teeth biting down on her lower lip in a mock threat.

"Why are you reading my journal?"

"You write *everything* in here," she said. "People talking, everything. We can't believe."

"Jim works for the . . ." Minh said and then covered her mouth and whispered, "CIA." She said this seriously. She was still admitting it as a possibility.

"Why are you reading it?"

"You left it in my house."

"That was an accident, and this," I lunged for the book again and she shoved it back up her shirt, "is private."

"Private," she said. "I don't agree. This helps me know your temper."

"It's the wrong way. Give it back."

"Never."

"Never?"

"Nho," Thuy said, calling to Minh for help.

"*Dung roi,*" I said, starting for the back of the house.

They'd never allowed me access there. It was where they slept, where they cooked, and where they kept the pigs they'd never admitted to keeping. That shamed them. That was private. They thought it very unsophisticated to admit they slept under the same roof as a pig. When I'd ask what all that oinking was back there, they would tell me it was a radio. It was pig music, *nhac heo,* playing on the radio as a lullaby for the chickens, which they didn't mind me knowing about.

By the time I turned my first corner into a room with a large wooden bed furnishing, Thuy and Minh had flung themselves upon me. I hadn't ever so much as shaken hands with Minh, she was that demure, and now here she was with her arms around my waist, trying to take me down. Thuy threw an arm around my neck and locked the clutch, grasping her wrist with her free hand. I dragged them with me.

"Okay, okay, okay, okay," Thuy was shouting. "Here it is, the book."

But the advantage was all mine. I turned another corner, and they scampered in front of me. They had their palms open and were dancing back and forth in front of me, singing nonsense and trying to block my view. But I saw it, a pair of them, dirty white and mottled black, two enormous hogs laid out on a concrete pen above the high watermark of the monsoon flood.

CHAPTER NINE

GRAEME WORKED AS A DIVER in Hong Kong and before that, according to Thanh, had been a member of Australia's Special Forces. "He used to jump out the plane when it's so high," he told me one evening, "and then fly, silently, very low, before he open parachute." In Hong Kong, Graeme's job required that he dive hundreds of feet, through hollow concrete forms as wide as a sewer pipe, to check the structural integrity of footings that would underpin the city's skyscrapers. "Down the bottom, it opens like a bell, and he . . ." Thanh got to his feet and like a blind pantomime, turned a circle, feeling up and down with his hands. Everything Thanh told me about the Aussie betrayed a similar Superman/Aquaman theme—enormous, powerful hands, "yellow" hair—until it began to seem that Graeme was more of a marvelous figment than a reality. Through the end of spring into midsummer, Thanh kept promising that Graeme was on the brink of a return, but he never materialized.

I didn't doubt that there had been an Aussie named Graeme who did live in Hong Kong, who had passed through Hue and had taken an interest in one of the daughters at 3 Le Loi. Southeast

Asian cities were littered with young women who had "boyfriends" of European heritage. In Thailand, especially, I'd seen photographs of these boyfriends, men standing on the shores of Lake Geneva and before sandstone Roman archways, men who for the most part had ricocheted through the region, dropping promises like coins in a jukebox. For all the sincerity of my first and second passes through Hue, and despite my pledge to return, I could easily have been one of them.

Eef was not one of them. Although born and raised in Holland, Eef was an archivist in Germany and spoke French, he said, better than he spoke English, which was almost note-perfect. He wore granny glasses and had the sort of coifed hair you don't wish on anyone, an uncontrollable sprout that looked like Hollywood's version of madness. His girlfriend, Mai, worked as a tour guide in the Palace of Supreme Harmony within the Imperial City. During his first pass through Hue, more than a year before, he had met her and chatted with her in French for an hour on the morning of the day he was catching a train to Hanoi. Back in Germany, he thought about her often, but he had neglected to ask her name. Scores of women worked in the Imperial City as tour guides, and there was no real way to contact her. No name, no address. When an acquaintance mentioned his plans for Vietnam, Eef drew the man a map of the gift shop at the palace, and the desk where he'd met Mai, but his courier never made it to Hue. Months later, with yet another courier, he dispatched another map and a letter for Mai. Weeks after he'd stopped hoping for a reply, he got one. She'd been thinking about him too.

He returned to Hue once for a two-week holiday and was back now for a five-week stint. Several weeks into this trip, he asked Mai to marry him. She accepted at once. But then, the following night, he let go of something heavy. He told her he was sterile.

Mai retracted her acceptance. She told him she needed time to think about things.

"She's already thirty-one," Eef told me the morning after Mai withdrew her acceptance. "In Vietnam, if you're not married by twenty-five, people start thinking of you as a spinster. We've never talked about kids, and I'm not sure what her dreams are. Maybe she doesn't want them. But of course I had to tell her about my condition."

I wanted to ask him how he knew he was sterile. How, if you were in your early thirties, if you've never been married, would you know that about yourself?

Several days later, and just a few days before his departure for Frankfurt, Mai asked him if he could love an adopted child as his own. "I told her I needed a night to think about that," Eef told me.

His candor no longer surprised me. "So what have you decided?"

"I don't know. I've never thought about children. Have you?"

I let out a fake gasp. "No. I mean, I still have to figure out about Thuy. That's why I'm here now."

I had guarded my own situation closely. I hadn't told him I'd proposed to Thuy, not once but twice now, a second time in the midst of a long embrace at 242 Café. The question sobered her. "I think I'm getting to know your temper," she'd said, and then nothing else.

I could have explained my situation to Eef, but I was afraid to reveal myself as a guy who, as one graduate-school friend noted, liked to close fast. Eef, by comparison, was a virtual tortoise.

Two days later, Eef told Mai he'd decided he could love an adopted child as his own, and they agreed to marry. The next day, Eef left for Germany. He would be back in a year's time when he got his next five-week break from the archives.

In the meantime, Graeme was on his way back to Vietnam. Thanh wasn't sure about the day. Any day is what he said.

I'd seen the pigs, confirmed their presence in her house. They had berths on a concrete loft. But Thuy, even after I knew this, would not admit to them. "We keep them for a neighbor. Temporary occupants," she said one day as we pedaled toward the mausoleum of Emperor Dong Khanh.

The gulf between our worlds was great. By denying the pigs, she denied the gulf. She'd let nothing from the First World astonish her, at least not outwardly. The North American cities we saw in the music videos they played at the Cercle before a movie, summery spreads in the Hamptons, the chic dress of urbane young people—she marveled at none of it. To do so would only widen a gulf that might or might not be bridged. She was still trying to figure that out.

Inside the main gate of the mausoleum, the guide led us across a spacious pavilion of cracked, clay tiles to Ngung Hy Temple. The building was wide and, like lots of Vietnamese architecture, made most distinctive by the dominance of its roof. Three pitches rose in terraces to a low wall, crested by dragons, that ran along the peak. More dragons, in bas-relief, spiraled up the lacquered pillars supporting the temple's lower pitch.

"Inside this Ngung Hy Temple," Thuy said, translating our guide's remarks, "French filmed the wedding scene of a new movie about Vietnam."

"People get married here?" I asked, looking around.

My proposal, the one I'd made at 242 Café, still hung between us, unanswered and undiscussed. I kept picturing it like a boomerang, out there spinning somewhere, though not necessarily on its way back, it seemed.

"No," she said, "just that movie."

Up several steps, we entered the temple through a set of accordion-style teak doors that fronted the length of the building. Inside, the vast hall was supported by colonnades of shiny, lacquer-red pillars. On one wall was a lithograph of a Napoleonic battle scene that the French had presented to Dong Khanh at his coronation in 1885. The gift had been a veiled threat, for earlier that year the French had deposed Dong Khanh's predecessor and cousin for subversive activity.

There seemed to be a subtext to everything the French gave Dong Khanh. The beautiful stained-glass windows carried the tricolors of the French flag. Opium pillows, for his pleasure and degeneration. Nearby, a tray of crystal perfume bottles for his concubines, no doubt. Thuy picked up a bottle of Japonais perfume. The delicate bottle pictured a Japanese girl in a kimono, kneeling, her eyes downcast, her bunned hair shot with a chopstick. The address at the bottom was 10, rue Strasbourg.

Thuy pulled out the glass stopper and sniffed the residue.

"You want to be a courtesan of Emperor Dong Khanh?" our tour guide joked.

"I'm already having trouble with dead people. I don't need any more," she said.

Dong Khanh had died of malaria at twenty-five. By then he had acquired nine courtesans, but his harem was paltry when compared with his predecessors Minh Mang and Tu Duc, who'd acquired so many courtesans that they were grouped in ranks. Minh Mang was especially randy. He would summon five concubines each night and could, if the stories were true, impregnate three of them before dawn. To ensure that the children sired were indeed his, his eunuchs would compile situation reports of the night's activities. With 56 concubines, Minh Mang had 142 children—78 sons and 64 daughters—before dying at the age of fifty. Tu Duc bested his father's courtesan count with 103, but to no avail. A bout of small-pox had rendered him impotent.

Taking multiple wives was not merely the privilege of Vietnam-ese royalty. Thuy's favorite brother-in-law was the son of a man with six wives. Her father's oldest brother, a seventy-year-old man from the village, kept a second wife in Danang.

"That doesn't bother his first wife?" I'd asked Thuy.

"It does."

Even after the advent of communism, and the eighties, and now the nineties, some Vietnamese men were still taking multiple wives. At Dzach Lau restaurant one evening, we had just sat down to dinner when a procession of motorbikes cut their engines in the courtyard out front. The other diners hushed uncharacteristically and watched as the wedding party moved among the tables. The bride looked to be in her early thirties, which was old for marrying by Vietnamese standards. She wore a blue dress and clutched a bouquet to her dress as she walked slowly, smiling shyly at the other diners who, as if by telepathy, knew exactly what was going on. The bride was followed by the groom's two young daughters and then by the little girls' mother, who was still married to the man and whose eyes were glued to the same patch of wall near the ceiling as the procession made its way toward the stairway upstairs.

By custom, a husband resorted to a second wife if his first wife failed to produce a son. After Dong Khanh's first wife, the queen, delivered two girls, he swapped her eminent position with the first courtesan to bear him a son. At the Ngung Hy throne, the woman whose painted likeness was propped on the seat to the emperor's left was his former first wife. To the more prestigious right, the mother of Dong Khanh's son, the future emperor Khai Dinh, is garbed in yellow, the color reserved for the king and his queen.

Outside, cicadas scratched through late-afternoon heat. Exiting the funereal city through a back gate, I took Thuy's hand and wondered whether to follow up now, here, crossing a rising field toward the tomb proper of Dong Khanh. I had no template for action and no idea how to tread water in limbo, not in America and definitely not in Vietnam. All I knew was that I hated limbo, and I hated treading water.

Neither seemed to bother Thuy. Not answering questions was one of her prerogatives. Several times, she'd related to me the questions that people had put to her about me. Who was I? How long did I plan to stay? Did she like me? She didn't answer them. "I only smiled," she'd tell me. And that seemed to suffice.

Twelve-foot stone walls plastered in drab gray concrete surrounded Dong Khanh's cenotaph. Fearing grave robbers, his remains, like the remains of his predecessors, were buried in an undisclosed location.

Inside the arched entryway, out of sight, I pulled Thuy close. We held each other until I heard the piping voices of schoolchildren. Opening one eye I found myself staring at one of those incongruities that occasionally surfaced in Hue, a man in a tricornered hat, standing in a flat boat, poling himself across a moat before a castle of European origin, the image contained in a fragment of porcelain with which Dong Khanh's son had decorated his father's tomb.

The voices shrieked close by, and Thuy snapped to and pushed herself from me. We descended several terraces before the cenotaph and sat on our sandals, looking out over the mausoleum. Pylons, denoting tombs of lesser royalty, rose out of the dense foliage in the near-distance, all but forgotten since the royals fell out of favor in the 1940s. The children stopped and for a long moment stared at us from the roadside, weighing a detour and further investigation. But they moved on.

Thuy unsnapped the long blade of my Swiss Army knife and started on one of the Chinese apples we'd bought from a vendor in Hue, but after a moment quit in disgust and looked at me accusingly. "You," she said, "are lazy."

She crossed the terrace to a small decorative stone dragon and, back to me—in fact, angling her posture to keep from view— scraped the blade expertly back and forth, sharpening it. Then she turned the skin off the pulp in a long, single peel. She bit the apple and gave it to me.

"One thing I remember from your journal . . ." she said, the words trailing off into her memory of what I'd written.

That she should be able to summon content from my private stash, as fodder for conversation, didn't seem fair. And it amazed me that she should propose talking about it with such equanimity. I couldn't imagine this happening in the States.

I said nothing, hoping my silence would deter her. But in the same way that she could litter with flair, without any drag on her conscience as she discarded some wrapper while bicycling down the road, she skipped along. "I want to ask about that," she said, meaning that passage in my journal.

"How long did you and Minh read my journal?"

"Long enough?"

"Long enough for what?"

"To learn some new things."

"Isn't it better if we not talk about what was in there?" I could feel an anger rising in me, but because I could recognize it, I could also deliver my words on an even keel, like a person who does not respond emotionally and rashly but with thought and consideration. "I mean, think about it: I haven't read your private thoughts."

"I don't write them down."

"If you had, I wouldn't, and I wouldn't ask about them either."

"You write too much, all those little notebooks, like dust. No wonder so many people are sure you work for the CIA."

"That's my illness." I took a notebook out of my back pocket and scribbled *That's my illness* into it.

"Troi oi!" she said. "A new one already."

"Do you know this model?" I asked, closing the cover, which pictured a shapely Vietnamese woman in a tight pink dress and pendant earrings, twirling a yellow umbrella. It seemed to me we were moving away from a place I didn't want to go.

Thuy yanked it back. "When did your parents divorce?"

I hadn't ever told her. That was the first level of shock that propelled me to my feet and pacing away from her. But the resonant part of the shock came from the depth to which she'd plumbed those pages. I hadn't ever directly addressed their divorce in that volume, yet she'd discerned it from some oblique allusion. I paced back.

"I meant to tell you."

"It's a big thing not to tell."

"It's a pretty big thing to figure it out the way you did."

She ignored that. "Especially after what you asked me two times."

"Oh, so you heard me. I wasn't sure you heard me."

"I had no answer for you."

"Had?"

She smacked her head the way she did whenever she made a grammatical error, but my heart was leaping at the prospect that it hadn't been a grammatical error, that a decision had been made, and all I had to do was look back to our embrace beside the cenotaph to find the answer I was looking for.

"Have no answer," she said.

"Nineteen eighty-three," I said. "In America, it's no big deal. It's not unusual at all."

She made a face. "Fifty percent, I know. Terrible."

Like most Vietnamese, she had a suspicion that Americans cared less about each other than Vietnamese. She equated nursing homes with prisons and couldn't understand how a parent could send a child off to a prep school. Where was filial piety?

"So you think Vietnamese customs are better?"

"Of course," she said.

"Maybe you're right. Divorce is terrible. Maybe it's just better to take a second wife."

She smiled, and I smiled with her.

"How common in America?"

"Divorce?"

"Some people say half."

"Yes, it's common."

"How about your grandparents?"

"Which?"

"So one did?"

This, I thought, didn't deserve revelation. I hadn't ever known my father's parents. I didn't feel that I had to be responsible for their precedent. "Yes," I admitted.

"And their parents?"

Oh God. It was as if she knew and had her laser on me. How many people in America could claim such a lineage of separation? The only male Sullivan of my line who had not split from his wife was the immigrant ancestor from the nineteenth century. My father blamed it on proteins. I blamed it on booze. But I sometimes believed what he did and that a part of my attraction to Thuy was for the antidote she'd bring to whatever was running in my blood.

"Maybe. I'm not sure. Separated. It was all in the bottle," I said vaguely.

She stood and walked back to the wall surrounding Dong Khanh's cenotaph. With her thumb, she rubbed a smooth porcelain fragment of foreign china. "I can never make divorce," she said softly. "Because *nghia*."

Nghia was the name of her aunt's oldest surviving son, a man I'd met briefly when he was up visiting from Saigon and who had asked me if I'd heard of John Paul Vann, an American he said he'd worked with during the war. He was Thuy's first cousin. He was old enough to be her father, and I couldn't understand the relevance until I remembered that Nghia had a sister named Hieu and another sister named Tinh, that her aunt had named her children after the cardinal virtues universally respected by the Vietnamese.

Nghia, Thuy told me then, had to do with a sacred obligation that people had to each other, depending on their relationship. She understood it as a kind of glue that held people together. It was what happened between couples after the curtain closed on a Shakespeare romance or a romantic comedy, the stuff you rarely saw after the mantle was turned down on the brilliant light of a love affair. *Tinh* was the Vietnamese word for this, for "passion," and I said the word aloud.

"Yes *tinh*, but *nghia*," Thuy said, turning around. Her tone was adamant. "Do you believe that when you fall in love, you will always love that person?"

"I hope so. Do you?"

"I'm not sure about that. But I'm sure about the *nghia*. Even if the *tinh* goes away, couples will always have *nghia*. I don't know if in another country, for example America, people think about *nghia*. Maybe not."

We didn't, or didn't acknowledge it. People preferred to believe the romance never died, that wedding anniversaries could truly reignite it. If your marriage was right, the passion never went away. If the passion was gone, so was your marriage. I remembered something a friend had told me about his own marriage. He was older, moving through his early forties, and he'd managed to scrape away a lot of what he called the hype. A romance has a beginning, a middle, and an end, he liked to say, but they rarely proceed in that order. Instead, there is the beginning and then the end, and then the long, long middle part that most people never make it through.

That middle part was the *nghia*, and I knew now that Thuy was trying to figure out whether I had the *nghia* in me. She seemed to believe that you had it or you did not, that it was in there like bone plates that reveal how much height you'll eventually have. I knew I was subject to the *tinh*, but I had always been bad at *nghia*. Maybe Thuy had suspected as much.

Graeme arrived at breakfast one morning, walking down Le Loi Street at the head of three cyclos laden with hard-shell suitcases and dented cardboard boxes on which the café's address was written in black marker. A swarm of kids surrounded him, and as he walked, he peeled dong notes off his wad and dispensed them judiciously, making sure the smallest kids on the fringe got a share.

The train station was just a few hundred yards from 3 Le Loi, but Graeme's walk looked like the confident final leg of a much longer journey, a man coming out of the jungle, certain of destination and reception. No one told me that was Graeme—I was having breakfast across the street—but there was no mistaking him, even if physically he didn't live up to Thanh's image of a Special Forces type. He was on the shorter side of average height but thick-limbed. The temperature was somewhere in the upper eighties Fahrenheit, but he was wearing a durable, long-sleeved rugby shirt, the sleeves pushed halfway up the forearm. Two of the 3 Le Loi daughters stood at the edge of the café, awaiting him, while one of the brothers beckoned the rest of the family.

His boxes were full of gifts. Clothes from Hong Kong for Kim Anh and her sisters. Bottles of various clear and amber liquors for the old man, including Johnny Walker Black. Within fifteen minutes of his arrival, Kim Anh's mother was wearing a bush hat garland with crocodile teeth. On the backs of two of her sons, she was tentatively cracking a short-handled bush whip. Kim Anh, through all of this, stood away from the fanfare, somewhat shyly and somewhat, it seemed to me, disinterested.

"So please," Mr. Tam said again, drawing me back from the reunion. "Say again." He nudged my untouched glass of beer.

I glanced down Le Loi Street again, beyond the café at number three to where Mr. Gioang had motored away too long ago, promising a prompt return from the Entry-Exit Police Station. He had my passport and visa, and in my impatience, it was difficult to unravel whether I was more bothered by what was keeping him or what was keeping me. Mr. Tam, and his older colleague and mentor, Mr. Phuong, had joined Gioang and I at the tail end of coffee, a meeting Gioang had requested as the prelude to his trip to the police station, where he had decided to formalize my registration as a sometime CENLET instructor. This was Gioang's idea, not the police's, as far as I knew. Gioang liked to keep all his t's crossed, and my unsanctioned trips to CENLET worried him.

"Isn't it easier to ask for forgiveness than permission?" I'd asked Gioang again that morning.

"Not in Vietnam," he said gravely.

"No, especially in Vietnam."

Despite the weight of Gioang's pronouncement, as if he were

imparting some profound truth about Vietnamese society, I was
sure he was wrong. During my bicycle trip, request for permission
was invariably bogged down in bureaucratic muck. Forging ahead
without permission—to take pictures of an old American combat
base, to bicycle through places not identified on our travel permits—yielded better results. But for weeks, Gioang was insistent
about the wisdom of his choice, and I wished now that I'd told
him it might have been better for me not to teach at CENLET.

At Gioang's departure, Tam ordered an opening round of Huda
beer and recited a poem Mr. Phuong had written during a recent
trip to Paris as a member of and translator for an official educa-
tional delegation. Mr. Phuong was in his mid-fifties and wore his
long, raffish hair like a bohemian. His mouth was perpetually wet,
almost sloshing, a consequence, I'd come to believe, of the near-
ness of beer.

Tam loved Phuong's new poem. Thought it was brilliant and
had helped me commit it to memory:

> *Don't look at the sun*
> *The moon will be jealous*
> *Don't look at the moon*
> *She never wants to be famous.*

> *Instead, look into your own heart*
> *Asking,*
> *Is it bleeding for neighbors.*

I couldn't quite make the connection in the poem between the
first and second stanzas nor the idea behind the moon's jealousy.
But Tam was convinced the poem was a marvel, to be published

in a Vietnamese literary journal. Now that I had it memorized, Tam wanted to know, would I make some overtures to some American periodicals.

When Gioang returned, he slumped in his chair and took a long draught of beer that Tam had promptly poured for him.

"Well?" I asked.

"Maybe you were right," he said.

To register as an irregular, part-time CENLET instructor, the police wanted my signature on a permit. Gioang said he hadn't known this would be required. If I had known, I'd have declined to continue at CENLET. The less contact with the police, the better as far as I was concerned. Now they had my passport and visa, and there was nothing to do but go get them.

The entry-exit police occupied a villa not far from the Morin, a tired old flat-roofed place with a cement courtyard that, any time I passed, seemed to be filled with bicycles and motorbikes. I didn't pass often. From what I had gathered, the entry-exit police had an arbitrary appreciation of the law, and the assumed threats posed by foreigners.

I couldn't distinguish the immigration officials from the traffic police from the soldiers. To my eye, they all wore olive-green uniforms and lofty military caps too big for their heads. Moreover, they all seemed to regard the world with the same dour, institutional frown or else the same chronically righteous expressions of half-bored cops everywhere.

Inside the station, a half-dozen table-desks faced the center of the room. On one side of each desk was an officer, or pair of officers; on the other was a local civilian. I took a seat beside the door and watched an animated civilian, pulling document after document from a satchel at his side, make his pitch to a disinterested official. While the policeman perused the field of papers before him and listened to the ongoing appeal, the petitioner nervously stitched his leg up and down. Ringed around the ankle of his socks were the letters USA, peeking in and out from beneath his cuff.

I pulled a paperback from my knapsack but couldn't absorb the sentences. The harsh northern accent of the cops, all of whom were known pejoratively to the natives of Hue as *bo doi*, or carpetbaggers, because they came from the north, marched through my head with the cadence of a goose step. These were the men who'd won the war, who had persevered through a $150 billion barrage of American might so that Vietnam could chart its own course. When I read through the history of my country's involvement in Vietnam, it was obvious that the United States had been wrong to wage the war and as obvious that the guys in the entry-exit police office had been in the right. Intellectually, I knew where my sympathies were supposed to lie. But I couldn't make my heart buy it. Secretly, I was pleased that Thuy's father had fought as a soldier in the army of South Vietnam.

On the hour, a wall clock jingled the ditty from "There's No Place Like Home." The man with the USA socks was still pleading his case, and an official from the far side of the room was calling my name.

Dich was beckoning from his desk, palm down, the hand gently flapping, as affable as an old friend. "Please," Dich said, gesturing to the now empty chair before his desk. "Sit down."

As I crossed the room, his goodwill slackened momentarily, like a flickering light. It was the briefest lapse, but in it, I glimpsed the resolve of a man who would lie down on runway tarmac, and I remembered that I'd passed a sidecar on the way in.

"I haven't seen you for a long time," he said, reaching to shake my hand. "When did you return my country?"

"Some months ago."

"Oh, long time." He glanced at his desk mate, a cold-faced official whose aggressive indifference hardly rippled under Dich's attention.

"Not so long," I said.

An official passed beside me, followed by the man with the USA socks and the satchel. From behind a partition, I could hear the sound of boxes and bottles being placed upon a table.

"What's your business in Hue now?" Dich asked.

"No business."

"Pleasure?" He jiggled the bait with earnest nodding.

"My visa tells my story."

"Right, your visa," Dich said, sliding open a drawer in his desk. In the brief span between Gioang's visit and mine, it was remarkable that my visa and passport could have found their way to Dich's desk.

Dich flipped through my pages again slowly, wetting this thumb at every page, his facial expression flexed in appraisal. When he was done, he passed the documents to his neighbor. The official lit a cigarette and propped an elbow on the desk.

"You want to teach English in Hue?" Dich asked.

"Occasionally. Did you talk to Gioang? Did he explain this to you?"

"No."

"I sometimes drop by CENLET. Not often. Just occasionally when they're looking for a native speaker to help out."

"And what do you want to teach these students?"

I laughed. The question supplied so much motive to my efforts. "Pronunciation. How's that?"

The other official went through the passport slowly, deliberately, as if every page might contain evidence of something he was trying to prosecute. His face was lean, and the muscle in it looked exercised and hard. *"What were you doing in Germany?"* he asked in Vietnamese, which Dich promptly translated.

"What could it possibly matter to him?" I asked.

The snap was out of my mouth before I could check it. And as quickly, I was wondering over my own stupidity. Where was my equanimity? I hadn't showed up in Asia yesterday. I knew obvious displays of anger worked against you, and yet here I was again, letting my blood have its way with my mouth.

"You went to West Germany?" Dich asked, knowing without looking.

"Yes."

"But not to East Germany?"

"That's correct."

"Something is wrong with East Germany?"

"There is no more East Germany."

"Yes," Dich said, "very unfortunate."

"Do you need my signature on something?" I asked.

"East Germany was poor but noble," Dich went on.

I knew little about East Germany, but pure was not the first attribute that came to mind, not before my mind tossed up half-formed thoughts about the Staasi secret police and the drug-enhanced performance of its athletes.

"Many people don't like countries that are poor. Or people who are poor," Dich said, dropping his gaze from his lofty purchase above the doorway entrance. "Like Miss Thuy, for example. Do you know why I don't like Miss Thuy?" He didn't wait for an answer I wasn't about to give him. "Because she doesn't like the poor man. She's only interested in the rich man."

In Vietnam, where the per capita income was about $300 a year and men like Dich were earning about $30 a month, I still had trouble reconciling my own identity to Dich's appreciation of me as a rich man. Of course I was rich, relative to the Vietnamese, but I'd always understood the term *rich* as a measure of one's place in society. I didn't move in those circles. My family's place in America was about where Thuy's family's was in Vietnam. I'd been tempted to argue this point with Dich. I'd considered distancing myself from his bias with a reference to my income tax returns and my dependence on brown rice and black beans as a staple. The point was not to drive a wedge between being miscast by this official but to defend Thuy, and the foundation of our relationship, against this prejudice. But I knew better than to engage him and risk another harangue in this office.

Over the next few days, I tried to persuade myself that Dich was actually referring to those other suitors, the dentist and pilot, as rich men, but that was just evasion on my part, evasion in the same way I'd tried to tell myself there'd been nothing deliberate about the way those motorbikes had veered into me that night. At Ho Quyen, Boi had stamped out the still live embers of my hope that the crash was an accident. And of course Dich had me in his crosshairs as he referred to the rich man. He couldn't have been any more explicit if he'd removed his shrunken bird and laid it for me to see on the table. I was rich, and he was poor, and that—he'd persuaded himself—is why he'd lost Thuy.

He'd quit stopping by Thuy's house. For a while after our encounter in the entry-exit office, I didn't see him. And then one day I did. He was sitting alone in a café outside the Cercle Sportif on the river, nursing a glass of lime juice. It was as uncharacteristic for a Vietnamese man to choose lime juice as it was for anyone in Vietnam to sit alone, unless waiting for someone. I stopped at a sidewalk kiosk under the pretext of browsing the ranks of paperbacks, first to confirm that this was indeed Dich and then to hope that he was waiting for someone and not simply watching the sampans pass by. But for as long as I flipped through English-language textbooks, no one met Dich. He was the guy in a Sinatra song, leaning against a brick wall with his collar upturned and a three-day beard. I couldn't quite bring myself to pity him, nor could I quite jettison the notion he'd stowed in my head about Thuy's love for the rich man.

At the Ong Tao restaurant that night, I told Thuy I'd seen Dich earlier at the Cercle. "He was drinking lime juice," I said.

"Nuoc chanh?" Thuy asked. Lime juice?

"That's what I was thinking."

I hadn't told her about Dich's appraisal of her in the entry-exit office that day. And I knew now, as I watched her order off the menu, that the insidious little remark was gnawing on me. To start, she ordered bowls of crab and asparagus soup, each dropped with an egg yolk. For an appetizer, she ordered *bo la lot,* luscious shreds of beef wrapped in a minty herb that was a specialty at Ong Tao. "In the summer, we like to eat *la lot* very and very much," she said. "We believe it's very refreshing."

Next came a whole sea fish fried in tomato sauce and then a fired-up tureen of simmering vinegar and water, seasoned with cut tomatoes, scallions, and pineapples. This was *bo nhung*, and there was a nice process to the preparation of the food. We dipped wide, thin strips of exquisitely cut beef flank into the vinegar for no more than a few seconds, then lay the strips on a triangle of moistened rice paper. Next we added greens like basil and cilantro, then rice noodles, and then rolled everything up in the rice paper. That dish cost about three dollars or what the average Vietnamese made for three days' labor.

"My mother says the scrambled eel spine here is very good," Thuy said.

"Let's get it."

We sat in an outdoor courtyard of cracked, terra-cotta tiles surrounded by high, mossy walls. Overhead, the lower limbs of the lychee tree were hung with tubes of blue and green fluorescent light. It was a slightly garish touch to an otherwise venerable old place inside the Imperial City. In the same house that the proprietor, Mr. Minh, prepared his food today, the emperor's cooks had prepared royal meals a hundred years earlier.

At the beginning of our meal, a waiter filled a small bucket with ice and, unbidden, laid in several bottles of Huda beer. It was a good restaurant for drinking. Near us, another waiter was rounding a banquet table of men with a shallow red bucket and tongs, plopping ice into the men's beer glasses while one of the diners followed, filling the glasses. A clutter of pint bottles of Saigon beer lay around the legs of their table and chairs like shucked peanut shells. Occasionally, the volume of their talk and the boister of their laughter was incongruously loud, as if emanating from a party in a much more crowded, noisy space where boosted voices would have been necessary. Eventually, one of those men drew a pint bottle from a nearly depleted wooden chest and, rising unsteadily, started toward my table and my still empty beer glass, his bottle raised in generosity and fellowship.

"*Troi oi*," Thuy said softly. Oh God.

I waved him off and feigned illness, grimacing and placing a palm over my stomach, but he would have none of it. He filled my glass and then, as if Thuy were not present, invited me to join his table. Several of his cronies beckoned me. It took several minutes of protesting before he gave up.

When the bill came, I glanced at it quickly, and then Thuy

scrutinized it for the errors that often showed up on a foreigner's bill. But Ong Tao was a better restaurant than that.

"It's okay," she said, handing it back to me.

The total was about 70,000 dong.

"Imagine," I said, pulling the dong notes from my wallet. "In college, you used to spend 10,000 dong for lunch and dinner for an entire month." She'd recently revealed this fact to me. She was still hiding the charcoal streaks on her fingers, but every now and then, she was opening a window on her life and her past. These details were coming at me, I realized, the way the revelation of her wattle and thatch home had come, in the name of full disclosure.

My own remark had no place to go for her. It was simply a matter of irony, and she smiled at it.

The neighboring table erupted at a shared joke, silencing us a moment, and turning the heads of all the other diners.

Thuy placed her elbow on the table and cupped her chin. "In college, we always did things together, boys and girls. We were very close. But then, that changes."

I looked around at the other tables, most of which were filled by men. Always, it seemed, the men came out together. The women stayed home.

"Even the smart, university students, eventually the men want to go to play with just each other," she said. "I never like that."

At the arched gate, a detachment of local, uniformed police parked their motorbikes, and Mr. Minh rushed from the kitchen to welcome them and make a table for them.

"It's expensive for police to come here, isn't it?" I asked.

Thuy turned and looked at them. "Never," she said. "They love to eat at this restaurant."

"Isn't it too much for them? They only make thirty dollars per month. How can they afford this?"

She stared at me incredulously. "More than that," she said, meaning how much they made per month. Thirty dollars per month was the base salary, but Vietnamese officials thrived on unofficial pay. No official was as poor as thirty dollars per month. Thuy's old dentist made far less per month than the average well-appointed policeman, like Dich.

"Dich," Thuy said as the officials took a seat near us. "He always wanted me to come here with him, but I never agreed."

CHAPTER TEN

AFTER BARGING THROUGH to the pigpens, I stopped using the toilet at a café near Thuy's home. And Thuy stopped pretending her home didn't have a toilet because her family, as she'd argued previously, did not engage in such nasty business. If there were pigs in the house, I was sure there had to be a toilet.

"Not true," she said.

"What do you mean, not true? Now that I know you sleep under the same roof as a pig, you can't tell me there's not a toilet back there."

She was telling the truth. There was no toilet; there was an outhouse with a shallow porcelain basin that had two inclined foot treadles flanking a hole to the sump. On a small shelf beside the basin were rolls of toilet paper and sometimes discarded assignment notebooks whose pages were to stand in when supplies ran low. Occasionally, there was nothing, in which case, I returned to the café.

One day, undone by a stomach ailment, getting to the café was out of the question. As discreetly as possible, I walked to the back of the house, reached through the window and grabbed a notebook

from the discard pile. On the cover was the colorful Japanese cartoon character Doremon. A half hour later, Minh bustled out of
the back room for an afternoon class and, while I sat reading at the
tea table, went straight to the discard pile. She thumbed through
the pile frantically, checking her watch all the while. "*Chi Thuy oi
Thuy,*" she finally sang out, and asked whether her sister had seen
the notebook with Doremon on the cover. I volunteered nothing.
Thuy said she had no idea. Minh made much of the search, checking under the bookcase, the wardrobe, her mother's niche. Finally,
she asked me. I held up my hands. I knew nothing. Eventually,
exhausted, she ran to the outhouse and shrieked. At the window,
she held the defamed notebook dangling from her hand. "Hours
and hours of work," she yelled. Thuy turned to me with her hand
over her mouth. "Did you?" she asked. I shook my head vigorously.
"You did," Minh shouted back. "How can I tell my teacher? My
dog didn't eat my homework, but my sister's boyfriend, he . . ."

Weeks after the incident, neither of them would admit they set
me up.

The mundane facts of their domestic situation gradually fell
away. The family cooked on a brazier, stoked with split wood.
Beneath the legs of their kitchen hutch, rice bowl footings filled
with water kept ants from climbing into the food. At night, men
with empty jugs rapped on the concession shop Thuy's mother ran
out the side of the house, not for cigarettes or bottled soda water,
but something that any member of the family might pour from a
three-gallon decanter of hard white plastic. One night, when none
of the family responded, I filled the cup of a crippled man who'd
dragged himself to the concession on a dolly and who then be-
seeched me to forego payment. After he left, I sampled the clear
rice liquor.

Later, Thuy tried to tell me that it was wine, that her mother came from a famous wine-making village outside of Hue. Had I heard of Bordeaux? Champagne? Did I know the great wine regions of France? California?

"That's not wine," I said. "That's grain alcohol. Maybe 50 proof."

"It's wine," she insisted, crossing her arms.

"Is that legal? Can your mother legally make that stuff?"

She kept silent.

"It's illegal." I laughed. "So not only is it not wine, it's moonshine. Your mother's a bootlegger!"

"Be Nho," Thuy called to her sister Minh, and then said something quickly in Vietnamese.

Minh grabbed my knapsack. In a moment, before I could rise from my seat, she'd absconded with my journal and was out the door. I chased her to the street, but by then she was ducking through the open doorway of a neighbor's house.

Thuy walked up beside me. "I'll give it back in a few days," she said, "after I learn a few more things."

In time, I learned that Mrs. Bang's village, several kilometers from the center of Hue, was indeed a renowned source of wine. She'd learned from her mother, who had learned from her mother. The recipe was good, and closely held. The flavor varied; sometimes it smacked of papaya, sometimes banana, sometimes pineapple. She added formaldehyde as a preservative. Whatever was peculiar about the wine was successful, because in 1975, when Mrs. Bang cranked up her operation, customers started coming in droves from as far away as Quang Binh and Vinh in provinces north of the DMZ. They would buy fifty liters at a time for weddings and other celebrations. While the country limped through 1975 and 1976, the Nguyens prospered. They moved out of a wattle and thatch-roofed hut and built the stuccoed brick house on Nguyen Trai Street. They made incremental improvements, tiling the roof in terra cotta, pouring concrete floors, adding a wing to the house, and then an addition out back. When it was time for Nga to go to college, there was money.

The neighbors weren't blind to this, and neither were the police who raided the house occasionally, sometimes with dramatic, bursting-through-the-doors commotions that the Nguyens countered with the pleading wails of seven girls. Vietnam had tremendous rice shortages directly following the war. Rice that went into distillation was rice that wouldn't feed a family, but Mrs. Bang could not afford to think of other families. They all knew hunger. It stalked them. Because she could, she bought the rice, and when the rice was spent, she fed the pigs. That part I figured out on my own.

"Smart economics," I said offhandedly to Thuy one day. "Wine and pigs."

"What pigs?" she asked.

On the day Thuy returned my journal—no keepaway this time, no references to content—we followed her mother out of Hue along Highway 1 and turned east on a causeway of rutted red earth. It was mid-afternoon, and the sea of rice paddies we moved through was relatively quiet. Egrets waded in the shallow paddy water, pecking for tiny field fish. Occasionally, we passed teams of farmers riding waterwheel pumps that transferred water between the paddies. After several kilometers, we neared a palm and bamboo–fringed island. "My village," Thuy said.

The road into An Thuan passed beneath a lashed bamboo gate, a ceremonial entrance, then twisted paveless and narrow as a cart path among thick stands of bamboo and hedgerows of elephant grass. We motored past tidy thatched homes set deeply in yards bordered with eucalyptus and casurinas. Stalks of sugarcane stood in small, cultivated front-yard patches. Fruit dangled everywhere in Edenesque proportions: loganberries, tamarinds, guavas, bananas, papayas, oranges, pomelos, and jackfruit.

Until 1967, Thuy's family had lived in this village. All the Nguyen kids, except the four youngest, had been born here in a place that was only recently wired for electricity. Vui's birth in 1966 had been particularly trying, Mrs. Bang explained. When the tell-tale contractions began, she left Nga in charge of the kids and started to make her way toward the home of a midwife. She didn't make it.

"It was near here," Mrs. Bang said today.

She stopped at the edge of a small rice field inside the village proper and glanced quickly in several directions as if to get her bearings by triangulation. Finally, she hopped off her motorbike and paced steps beyond the thick trunk of an old tamarind. When she stopped, she was standing where a bush had once grown and where, overtaken by the contractions, she had lain down and given birth to Vui, alone, in the middle of the day, in the middle of the war.

"But don't tell Vui you know this," Mrs. Bang told me through Thuy. *"She becomes shy when people know she was born in the bush."*

Through the afternoon, we stopped in a succession of homes that belonged to Thuy's aunts, uncles, and cousins. In some way, she was related to everyone in the village, which was why she considered it her village. Her father had been born there, as had his father and his father, one old woman explained to me, waving her hand in a gesture that took me back centuries, or whenever it was the Viets had migrated south and subsumed the Cham people who'd lived on this land before them.

As with the rest of the country, the war with America had divided the Vietnamese here, not because of any diametrical sense of allegiance but because on some nights the Viet Minh swept through, drafting young men to their rebellion against the French. Other days, the French would come through, demanding recruits. Like his oldest brother, Thuy's father found himself fighting for the Viet Minh (later, the Viet Cong) during the First Indochina War, but when he contracted malaria and returned to An Thuan for recuperation, the French recruited him.

The villagers found themselves caught in the crosshairs. One night in 1967, acting on a tip from an informer that there was some Republican activity at large in the village, the Viet Cong ambushed the Saigon soldiers, killing them. They went hooch to hooch, rooting out sympathizers. At that time, Mr. Bang was stationed at Mang Ca, the "Fish Gill" fortress in Hue, but one of his uniforms was hanging in the An Thuan house. When the V.C. knocked at the door, ten-year-old Nga deposited the uniform in a large mortar bowl they used to grind banana leaves for pigs. When Thuy's mother finally opened the door, the cadre asked why it had taken her so long. *"Her voice was so pitiful,"* Nga once told me, laughing, teasing her mother with the memory. *"She blamed Vui, the baby."* The excuse seemed to satisfy the soldiers.

After the French, the Americans started blowing through the village, soldiers mostly, men on field sweeps, looking for Viet Cong. One of Thuy's father's sisters told us about an American dentist who'd passed through An Thuan, perhaps in an effort to win the hearts and minds they were losing as American soldiers followed General Westmoreland's fatally flawed search-and-destroy strategy. This old woman's teeth were lacquered black, but the dentist had given her a clean bill of health.

"Good," she said today in English, the only English she had, remembering the diagnosis of the American who'd probed her teeth with his pick and mirror. The word came up out of her stomach, almost grunted. "Good."

The incongruity of hearing this seventy-year-old woman resurrect this little bit of remembered English made me wonder whether Thuy's mother also retained some. While Thuy's non-English-speaking sisters occasionally tried out a phrase or two in English, for fun, I'd never once heard Mrs. Bang utter a word. Not *hello*, *okay*, or *same same* or any of the usual suspects. I asked her if she had any English.

Mrs. Bang shook her head and looked shyly into her lap, a gesture Thuy had inherited exactly. The old aunt laughed at her sister-in-law, and said all people from An Thuan knew a little unforgettable English. She urged Mrs. Bang to speak it.

Mrs. Bang shook her head again, but she was relenting. I could see it in the dim smile that perked her lips and the moisture in her eyes.

"Please," I begged in Vietnamese. Mrs. Bang was the voice behind the wardrobe; she was the caution in Thuy's reserve, an indomitable survivor of war and privation. I'd known her as a woman who'd never sallied an English word for so long, it hardly seemed possible, but Thuy's aunt knew she knew, and as Mrs. Bang cleared her throat, we all knew that she did have some, a little, and she would share it.

She said it once, hoarsely and quietly, as she dislodged the weight of the one remembered phrase from her memory. There was a vacancy in her face, and she mumbled the phrase several times now, practicing it as if listening to the clacking echo of long-gone helicopters and picturing a skirmish line of GIs moving through An Thuan, looking for Viet Cong, knowing she would have to speak it, knowing they would ask her, was she one of them, did she know them. "No," she'd told them then, and she told me now. "No V.C."

At another relative's home, Thuy's grand-uncle Tru was playing cards with Mr. Mai, a man so short that our arrival, and my presence, generated a discussion of his height. Tru stumbled out of the discussion to insist several times, in barely intelligible English, that Mai was eighteen inches tall. I nodded vigorously, hoping to convey that I got the point. Mai was very short, but the conversation bore on, and I felt bad that my arrival had brought the spotlight down on Mai again.

He seemed unaffected by the discussion. For all the abject attention the Vietnamese gave to any unusual sight or incident, I guessed his skin, through his sixty or seventy years, must have grown pretty thick. He wore a brown beret, cocked at a jaunty angle, and a long, dirty shift that fell untailored, except for sleeves, from shoulders to feet.

Eventually, the hubbub over his height subdued, and Thuy announced the consensus that Mai was actually eight-tenths of a meter tall. He'd never married, and for years he'd earned his living as a bamboo-basket weaver, specializing in gourd-shaped fisherman's baskets and a conical-shaped basket with two open ends used to catch fish in shallow water. It was a subsistence living. Briefly, once in his short life, Mai had had a shot at some big money. This was during the French colonial era. During one of the festivals in Hue, Mai had been pulled around Hue in a small oxcart, covered by a glass dome. People showered him with piastres. The traffic was good, but the French put a stop to it.

While Tru told the story and Thuy translated, Mai busied himself with the cards, shuffling them with remarkable dexterity and, blindly, pulling the same card out of the deck, the joker, which he flashed at me with a defiant snap of the fingers, a magician's grunt, and a grotesque twitch of the face.

Before the oddities of Mai's life had exhausted everyone's interest, a neighbor and her young son stepped into the home. The boy, glimpsing Mai, flung himself against his mother's thigh. Mai reached out his stubby fingers and pinched his thumb and forefinger together, a gesture that elicited a shriek from the boy and laughter from everyone else.

"Small boys have to be careful around Mai," Thuy told me. "If they pass too closely, he'll press their penis."

The home belonged to Thuy's father's oldest brother, a man who'd just recently turned seventy and looked it. His face was blotched with black age spots. His sister tended to us from a horrible stoop that looked to me like a consequence of years in the rice field, bent over the crop. Their lives, obviously, had been filled with labor. The roof overhead was made from thatch; the floor was packed earth; and the walls were made from wattle. The place was as tidy as a museum exhibit, and I complimented Uncle on the house and asked about its age.

"Fifty years ago, my father built this house with his own hands," he said.

His father was Thuy's grandfather, the mandarin, a man whose home I'd imagined as a much grander affair, not the simple hooch we were now sitting in.

"Wait a minute," I said, turning to Thuy. "You told me your grandfather was a mandarin."

"He was," Thuy said.

I glanced around the hut.

"Maybe not the kind of mandarin you thought."

Tru explained that their were nine classes of mandarins, and that his brother had broken into the ranks at nine and ascended to eight. He occasionally worked in Hue's Imperial City, but mostly he worked here in An Thuan, as the village chief.

Her mother was a bootlegger, and her father's rank in the Army of South Vietnam was so low that the communists hadn't bothered sending him away to reeducation camp. Her grandfather was a village chief, and if not for her mother's decision to abandon the village a few years earlier, Thuy might have been born here. If I'd met her here, instead of Hue, if I hadn't raised a pedestal beneath her beauty and garlanded her past with military officers and the Imperial Court of Hue, if I'd known then that her university education was actually a community-college education, would I have persevered through my doubt in Boston? I wondered as we walked down a short path to a tributary of the Perfume River, escorted by a dozen child relatives.

But as we stripped the clothes we'd worn over bathing suits, and I saw her for the first time in a way I'd never seen her before, it occurred to me that her challenge was far greater than mine. At least I had a chance to see her in her environment. I could see what had built her, the people who'd informed who she was. All she had on me was my journal.

"You're not afraid of Ong Mai?" she asked, ducking underwater before I could answer.

"Not unless he presses my penis," I said.

She swam in circles around me. "Some months ago, I was sure you were going to go home."

"Some day I will."

"I meant, sooner."

"The weather is nice here."

She stopped treading water and threw her arms around my neck. Her hair was slicked back, and the river water was beaded on her face. She kissed me once, delicately, and pulled away to look in my eyes. "I'm glad you stayed."

"I'm sorry your grandfather was eighth rank."

Her hands slid down my neck, my back, through the water and below my waist. I closed my eyes and felt something brush the front of my shorts before she splashed away.

"What was that?" I asked.

She swam underwater for several yards, and when she surfaced, turned, treading water, and smiled at me. "I don't know? Ong Mai?"

That year, every day was another twenty-fifth anniversary for Gary Klaggs. One day, it was twenty-five years since Gary sat with his platoon on Foxtrot Ridge and watched the marines blow the ammo dump at Khe Sanh. Another day, it was twenty-five years since one of his buddies "liberated" thirty tins of pound cake from a pallet of rations with the flash suppressor of his M16. That was how he referred to them, as "anniversaries," and though some might be mundane—the shower he took on LZ Stud one day after two straight weeks in the bush, for example—they were all to be observed. Most of the anniversaries he talked about with me smacked of excruciating incidents: the death of his best friend, for instance, a teenager from Philadelphia who was killed while stationed on a three-man observation post. Gary had led the detachment that found them, and when he did, there was Kool-Aid splayed all over his friend's chest. As Gary related this to me one afternoon, he lapsed into a real-time remembrance of his communication with his company commander when he came upon the dead soldiers.

"Be advised, we have located Oscar Poppa (Observation Post)," Gary radioed back.

"Gary, what's the status?"

"Be advised we have three COORS [KIAs]."

"Gary, I copy. Three COORS. Return to POS [position]."

It was all so fantastic I sometimes wondered whether Gary could be telling the truth, just as I'd wondered whether my customer at the bar on Martha's Vineyard was really a combat veteran or just borrowing the trappings of one for the postraumatic anti-glory of it all. I didn't seriously doubt Gary, and I had no more reason to doubt him after he showed me a picture of himself as a marine in Vietnam. Although he was teenage skinny and lacked a moustache in this picture, it was unmistakably Gary, the same close-set eyes, heavy brow, and short, stiff sandy hair. Beyond them was the crest of a hill with a few mangled trees and ground that had been so pumped full of explosives it looked extraterrestrial. The date penciled in on the back of the picture was twenty-five years past to the day.

"When we got word that morning that a resupply chopper was coming in, I couldn't believe it," Gary said. "We hadn't had food in four days. We'd been drinking water out of fuckin' bamboo, we were so thirsty. But then we find out the chopper's a priority-one flight, which means they're coming in with ammunition, with mortar rounds, not food. I couldn't believe it. My company was India Company, and we were known as the Hungry I because we were always the last to be resupplied. Now here it was again. Ammo, not food. It broke me down. I saw a lot of shit, but nothing made me cry like I cried that day."

Gary had enlisted after high school in Cape Gireaudea, Missouri. The reason for his enlistment swarmed around the legacy of his father, a veteran of the D day landings who died when Gary was ten, and the precedence of an older brother who'd enlisted in 1965 and lost a leg to a Bouncing Betty several days after Gary had pitched a no-hitter for his high school baseball team. He described most of his time in Vietnam as time in the bush, engaged in long field operations like Purple Martin and Herkimer Mountain. He was a rifle leader and a squad leader and, after he reenlisted for six months so he could get out of the marines early, a platoon guide.

He'd left the marines, but the war hadn't really ever left him. He redounded to it in his khaki shirts and shorts, his short crew-cut hair, his drill-sergeant demeanor, and in an otherwise tranquil moment over coffee when he might suddenly explode into a rant about another goddamned "dink" who'd tried to cheat him out of a few thousand dong. There was no talking to Gary. He talked to you, jerking from one topic to the next with little regard for transitioning. He could leap from a memory of Staff Sergeant Sinkfield bashing in some gook bastard's head with a rifle butt to America's sudden infatuation with the waterbed in the mid-1970s without skipping a beat, as if there were relevance, as if nobody would have needed waterbeds if not for the trauma of Vietnam.

Beyond the observance of anniversaries and trips back up into the DMZ to revisit places he'd been going back to in memory for years to see them again for real, maybe to see if they were real, Gary had another agenda in Vietnam: to replace every month he was at war here with a month in peace. The New Age take on that might be atonement, but with Gary, the gesture felt more like a canceling out: there'd been matter, now there should be antimatter. "I got no satisfaction out of combat," he told me once. "There was absolutely nothing fulfilling about that experience."

He was finding fulfillment in his relationship with a poor Vietnamese family who lived in a shanty residence near the university's library. Gary liked to say he "sponsored" this family—sponsored, as if there was some sort of competition imminent and he was preparing them for it. Other times, he referred to them as the family he'd "adopted." The more I saw of him, the more I think he had that part backward.

He paid to have the family's house wired for electricity. He bought them a refrigerator. He financed the kids' schooling, so they wouldn't have to hustle lottery-ticket sales on the streets. He trooped all the kids to the dentist, and he harangued them about dental care.

"Every day, I ask Nha (the oldest daughter) whether she's brushed her teeth. I know she's tired of me asking, but I tell her, I will be very angry with you if I learn you're not brushing your teeth."

He'd never had children of his own. His life, since his discharge from the marines, looked like one long downward spiral through jobs as a ranch hand, a waterbed salesman, a construction consultant, and film-production troubleshooter. He'd never married. Relationships never worked out.

Lately, I'd started shying away from Gary, partly because I'd begun to feel trampled by the march of all his ghosts and partly too because he led a high-profile life in Hue. One night after the cafés closed, he marched down Le Loi Street, chanting old Marine Corps ditties. One day in a café, a Vietnamese man I didn't know began to ask me questions about him. Occasionally, if I'd ducked him for too long, Gary would rap on my door. There was no use trying to ignore the knock. He had a sixth sense that told him you were in the room.

"Mis-ter Sull-eee-vaan," he called in one afternoon, moments after I thought he'd given up.

"Ah, Gary," I called out. "Napping." I opened the door, squinting for good effect.

He stepped around me and into the room, carrying a fine leather garment bag that looked empty. "Trying to get an audience with you is like trying to see the pope. I'd have a better fuckin' chance of meeting John Kerry than slowing you down."

I pressed a hand to my forehead and gestured at an empty ice bucket beside my bed. Every couple of weeks now, I was subject to mysterious sweeps of fever. Their harbinger was dizziness. A few hours before any fever came on, I would begin reeling under a light-headedness that was so abrupt and so powerful, it was as if something had clobbered me and here was its resonating consequence. From the onset of dizziness, I usually had enough time to get to the Morin and load up on ice. Whether that worked or not to break the fever, I couldn't tell. But it was a balm, and it kept me out of the local hospital, which looked more like a halfway house to death.

"Fever," I said to Gary.

"The F-U-O," Gary said, theatrically, as if this were revelation. "The fever of unknown origin. I know it well."

He sat down and promptly started talking about his goddaughter's bank account. He had checked it earlier that day and found that Nha had withdrawn the money to buy a television set for her family.

"A real fuckin' nice one too," he said.

Somehow, the television sparked a memory of a mine sweep during the war that cost the U.S. Marines thirty-seven dead one foggy morning. Then he wanted to know whether I knew that most of the marines at Khe Sanh had died under mortar attacks. I hadn't.

Gary wasn't going to ask Nha to return the TV, but he did have a talk with her about the absolute need to make judicious financial decisions when there was so little money. He'd had to have the same talk with his "old lady" in Saigon after a recent holiday they'd had in the resort town of Vung Tau.

He hadn't ever talked about a girlfriend. "She's come over to visit?" I asked.

He looked at me strangely for a minute. "No, I went down to visit."

"She's Vietnamese?"

"A hairstylist in Saigon. A real dragon lady."

I wondered whether Gary knew about Thuy. Because our dialogues were more like his monologues, I'd spoken little about my reasons for being in Hue.

In Vung Tau, she'd insisted they stay in the best hotel and that part of each day be devoted to shopping.

"How's her English?" I asked.

"She doesn't speak one tenth of one tenth of one syllable of English," he said.

How he had that talk with her, I couldn't say, because Gary was talking now about a woman he'd dated in the States. She was an actress, he said, whose previous boyfriend had been Dave Brubeck.

"Do you know Dave Brubeck?"

" 'Jeepers Creepers.' "

"Well, the Dave Brubeck Orchestra has played around the globe, in every country that's worth its salt. Anyway, I'd thought about marrying this woman, but she had an annoying habit of crying on cue. And there was only one way to stop it. I'd pull out the old American Express, and the crying would stop like shutting off the lights. The 1970s fucked things up for women," he went on. "Women's lib and all its politics simply won't let them be. It's the beauty of Asia. They do not traffic that bullshit here. Guys like us, we've figured that out, but we're few and far between when you reckon the male population of the United States of America."

I stood up. "I better get more ice," I said, pressing a palm to my forehead. And then so as not to look too much like a sissy: "Fuckin' fever."

My gesture did little to uproot Gary. He crossed his legs and lit a cheap Dalat-brand cigarette. "That Vung Tau trip cost me," he said. "Nha and that television. I'm broke."

I was standing in the doorway, looking for one of the hotel staffers and more ice.

"I've got to leave the country," he said.

"I'm sorry." I was and I wasn't. Gary was like a bellwether for me. If they'd put up with him, they'd put up with me. But now they were tying me to him, and he was tying himself to me.

"I need a stake so I can get out of the country," he said. "I've got nothing. But I'm going out. I'm going to teach English in Taiwan, and then I'll be back, flush." He picked up the garment bag. "I bought this for $700. Any luggage vendor worth his paycheck would pay $200 for this tomorrow. I'll leave it with you as collateral."

How much do you need?"

"A couple of hundred."

I gave him eighty dollars and let him keep the garment bag. Later, at that same café, that same man asked me whether I knew what Gary carried around in that garment bag.

One afternoon, I found a monk in brown vestments sitting at the Nguyen's tea table. He was gaunt, and a few days of black stubble showed on his bald, shaven head. He stood upon my arrival and immediately assumed the role of the host. He rinsed a tiny cup for me, poured some tea, then offered me some of the jellied fruits the Nguyens had set out for him. No one else was in the room, but I could hear Minh washing dishes at the spigot outside the back window. She was softly singing an old American song, "Saa-aaaa-aaaa-aaaad movies, always make me cry. Oh, oh, oh, saaaaaad movies always make me cry."

Minh's life revolved around the acquisition of English. She listened to slowly enunciated Special English broadcasts by the Voice of America and BBC in the morning and evening. She listened repeatedly to old American songs, jotting the lyrics and singing them during chores. When she was really stumped with a home-work assignment and needed immediate help, she would pedal across the river and waylay a friendly looking English-speaking traveler walking or bicycling along Le Loi Street.

Meanwhile, I had been studying Vietnamese with a tutor and thought I was making great strides, and with my cultural savvy in general.

"Tu thay," I addressed the monk, *"chua nao thay o lai?"* Reverend teacher, what pagoda do you come from?

He smiled brightly at me and squinted with incomprehension. I repeated my question, once again addressing him with the honorific I'd heard Thuy use during our visits to the area's pagodas.

Outside, the water stopped gushing. "Jim," Minh called, "don't speak to the monkey."

I looked at him, wondering did he have any English, but his beneficent smile was unwavering. He hadn't understood her, let alone picked up on the mistake. Nor did he seem to understand my question. So I asked again.

"Jim," Minh said, her face in the window now. "Please don't speak to the monkey."

"Monk, not monkey," I said, annoyed by her intrusion.

"Ahh," she smacked her forehead. "So stupid. Yes, the monk. Don't talk to him."

"I'm practicing my Vietnamese." But then it occurred to me that he hadn't spoken a word since I showed up and that he was perhaps engaged in some rite of ascetic silence that I was now violating.

"Okay to practice, but you must not call him what you called him."

"Tu thay is polite," I said.

"No. *Thay tu* is polite. *Tu thay* means 'hate foreigners.' "

The monk left a short time later, and because no one was around I started browsing through the Nguyen's bookshelves. There were Vietnamese translations of *The Grapes of Wrath*, *The Moon and Sixpence*, *One Hundred Years of Solitude*, and *The Sound and the Fury*. I'd once asked Thuy whether she'd read any of them, and she replied that she'd read them all.

"This one too, *The Sound and the Fury*?"

"Of course."

"For what?"

"For fun."

I doubted her, and my face showed it. "No one reads *The Sound and the Fury* for fun."

"The story is very strong."

"Okay, tell me about Caddy," I said.

"Caddy?" She frowned, and a spasm of confusion troubled her face. "Oh yes, Caddy. She smells like trees."

I could have sharpened my Vietnamese by digging into a translation, but there was an English-language book in the case, a history of St. Petersburg, brought back from Russia by a brother-in-law who'd studied there five years. I was making my way through it during my long in-house waiting spells.

Minh finally finished her washing and came inside to work on her French. "Do you know why the monk was here?" she asked after awhile.

"Bananas?"

"Not polite."

"I'm sorry."

"You want to know?"

"No."

She went back to her French, and I returned to the construction of the Winter Palace. After several minutes, she looked up again. "Do you want to know where my sister is? Or don't you want to know? I'm confused. *Do you or don't you*—what is the difference?"

"No difference. Positive and negative."

"Okay, don't you?"

"Yes."

"That means you don't want?"

"Correct."

"Why?"

"I'm happy just sitting here with you."

She stared dumbly at me for a moment, then frowned. "We are learning about irony my class. I can guess more about you when I learn more about this."

"Your sister's whereabouts don't concern me in the least," I said.

"Not even if I told you she went out with Sister Vui?"

"Not even then."

"Across the river."

I didn't answer her.

"Ahh, now he is curious."

"Not curious," I said.

"Curious, I know."

"Not curious, concerned. There are a lot of dangerous foreigners across the river."

"Hmmm, must be irony again. Okay. They went to visit the home of a woman, she works at *So Tu Phap*."

"What's *So Tu Phap*?"

"Hue Justice Department."

Again, I said nothing.

"Oh, you're such a bad card player. I want to play cards with you on the Tet New Year. I can earn a lot of money from you."

I looked into the book, and she let me spend a minute there.

"Pretend," she said. "Reading the same sentence over and over. I said something, and now your mind is like a wheel. Hue Justice Department. Why do you think my sister went there?"

"I give up."

Minh looked from side to side, as if to see what other sport could be made of this. But there was nothing. "They are going to ask what documents you need to marry my sister."

I merely nodded. I felt heroic all of a sudden, but anxious, needing to go somewhere and do something physical and fast. I was trying to look stoic as I walked to the door. "I'll stop by again later," I said.

Minh skipped after me. "Jim, the light is bad, but I saw."

"Saw what?" I asked, unlocking the rear wheel of my bike.

"Your face. It's become the color of . . ." Her tongue flickered to the corner of her mouth, and she started trying to pronounce a difficult word. She garbled *crustacean* several times, then resorted to a simpler word: "*Lobster*. Your face look like a lobster."

CHAPTER ELEVEN

THE STORYBOOK RITES OF MARRIAGE PROPOSALS—the bended knee, the proffered diamond, the popped question—had never appealed to me. I couldn't picture myself as a character in such a scene. It was too scripted, too much the stuff of Harlequin romance, and so mendacious, to be raged against. The other side of a proposal, however, was a different story. I was a sucker for the magical moment of acceptance. I expected magic, however stale the traditional imagery associated with it: the eyes glistening and over-run with emotion; a desperate, falling-together embrace as we re-alized, with the power of epiphany, that our long, lonesome journey was over. There was moonlight in my notion, and the twining flights of ecstatic birds. If none of that would come to pass, at least I always thought I'd be present when a would-be fiancée said yes. It surprised me to learn about Thuy's acceptance secondhand, from her younger sister, but then again, that was no more surprising than finding myself at twenty-eight, living in an old French colonial hotel halfway around the world from the architecture of all the expectations I'd built through my teens and twenties. You walk through life thinking you know where you're going, and then a leg is stuck out, you trip, and when you get back up, you're heading somewhere else.

As soon as Thuy agreed, I crunched another set of numbers in a notebook one morning, calculating fixed costs and variable costs, and found that my fellowship money was draining at a faster rate than I'd hoped. Every three months, I had to leave Vietnam to renew my visa. Whenever I came back, the Morin jacked my room charges. I could afford a wedding, a modest one, but only if I indulged nothing.

Since calling home cost more than a night in the Morin, I considered that an indulgence, but revealing my engagement in a letter that wouldn't reach Quincy for two weeks would itself be considered, I knew, a breach of fealty not easily forgotten. I had to call home, and not only with the news but a request. The birth certificate and passport might suffice for marriage elsewhere, but not Hue.

On Thuy's first attempt to get a list of documents necessary for a marriage like ours, she'd been turned away from *So Thu Phap,* the Justice Department, by a clerk named Hang, who had told her she didn't have time to dispense such information at work. So Thuy visited her at home, where Hang preferred to conduct certain aspects of her business.

The first time Thuy visited Hang, she showed up empty-handed. Coincidentally, Hang was busy and didn't have time for Thuy anyway. The next time, Thuy went with her older sister, Nga, who recommended that they stop to buy some cakes and sweets for their visit. Not coincidentally, this time Hang was able to produce a mimeographed sheet that listed the necessary documents.

"An affidavit from the Quincy police?" my mother said slowly, writing the words as she repeated them.

"I'll spell it all out in a fax," I said anxiously. It had taken her a minute to find a pen, and I could feel another night in Hue slipping away during the wait.

"So we should start to make plans? To come over," she said.

"I don't know how long this process is going to take."

In the slight pause that followed, I knew she'd read in between the lines.

"You don't want us there," she said flatly.

She was right. I didn't. The prospect of mixing these two worlds, Quincy and Hue, was more than I wanted to imagine. They felt as mutually exclusive to me as friends from boyhood and friends from college. You didn't mix them. You loved them both, separate but equal.

Then again, I wouldn't have wanted a wedding in the States. Insofar as she knew me, she'd always known that, and I hoped it would occur to her that this kind of ceremony, as much as I yearned for its consequence, was not the kind of special moment for me that Western culture celebrated so sentimentally. I couldn't tell her this now, not unless I wanted to risk several more nights in Hue by way of explanation. So I lied.

"Wrong. I'll let you know how things develop. We can plan from there."

Among the regulars at 3 Le Loi was a Vietnamese man about my age who wore a Member's Only knockoff. His hair was parted in the middle and worn stylishly long, and his eyeteeth were just prominent enough to be noticeable. He was vaguely familiar, but most of the regulars at 3 Le Loi were. One morning, a man I knew at the café, who was also a regular, told me the Member's Only fellow had asked him what kind of coffee I drank everyday.

"I don't want to say anything," the regular said. "You have to understand me. I'm only drinking coffee here myself. Not looking around at everything. Look at this. Look at that." He was paging through a copy of *Paris Match*.

"If I have to say anything," he went on, "I want to ask why does he ask me something like that. He's having coffee here every day too. He should know what kind of coffee you drink."

"So what did you tell him?"

"I tell the truth." The man slapped the table with the magazine and let out dry raspy laughter. "Coffee like the woman."

I took my robusta on a thin bed of condensed milk, the only alternative to the plain old homogenized milk I took with coffee at home. Most men in Vietnam drank their coffee black. Women wanted milk.

"Maybe he's a spy," I said. "Maybe he's going to open his own café, and he needs to know what kind of coffee foreigners like."

"About the first part, you are right," the regular said. He was an older man, a sometime photographer who'd shouldered a camera for one of the American networks during the war, he'd told me. I couldn't quite understand why he was crawling out on a limb for me this way, unless he continued to feel some responsibility to revelation.

"Spy? Spying on who?"

"You." He looked around and then turned another page of his magazine and spoke softly into a spread of colored photographs. "Some days ago, he wants to know what does Mr. Jim write in his notebooks all the time?"

"He did?"

"You have to understand me. I don't want to say anything. But he knows I speak English, and he knows my comprehension is good. He asks about your notebooks, but I tell him I never pay attention. The foreigner is always writing in a notebook." He had begun to look distressed.

"That's their job. To watch out for foreigners." I gestured around the café and finally lit upon Graeme, whom I'd finally met and liked, now sitting at the back of the café in yet another seemingly interminable discussion with one of Kim Anh's brothers. "I bet they know everything about Graeme."

"Not Graeme," the regular said, rising. "You."

The first of my documents to arrive from the States was from the secretary of state's office in Massachusetts, an affidavit attesting that no record of marriage for James D. Sullivan had been filed in that office. A handwritten note accompanying the affidavit said the secretary of state's office was the best alternative.

"I phoned Kennedy's office, then Kerry's," my father wrote, "to ask what was SOP when it came to a single statement, and they referred me to the secretary of state. It looks like the best we can muster, kid. Next stop: Quincy police. I'll forward documents as they come in."

For months now, I'd held this vague idea that my father was hoping his parable about the encyclopedia saleswoman from England might finally sink in. He hadn't mentioned Thuy in his letters. I hadn't mentioned her in mine to him. Instead, I'd nurtured the conceit of a young man on the go. Here I am in Thailand; here I am in Hanoi, Hoi An, Ha Long Bay, like someone engaged in field study, plumbing the source of a great natural phenomenon. I was out there, having adventures; eventually I might just come home.

He wasn't fooled. I'd kept my mother up to date on how things stood with Thuy, and she was keeping him up to date. When she brought home the fax of Hang's list, he assumed responsibility. It might have been what enabled his turnaround. As soon as he could ally himself with me, against them, he'd made a decision about which side he was on. Since Thuy was on my side, he was on her side.

In his next letter, he referenced a conversation with a cousin who'd told him of a mutual cousin who'd married a woman from Korea: Their child, she'd told him, was a real beauty. Then he mentioned another story that resonated from my boyhood, about the fiber of kids born to people who spring from different parts of the world: The combination makes for a much stronger child. I couldn't remember the particulars of why he'd told me this when I was a boy, though I did remember that China was the example he used. "Maybe," he wrote today, "it helps balance everything out."

As soon as we had my single statement, I was all for going to Hang's house to get approval. I wanted to visit, paper by paper, to count the victories and celebrate the milestones. Thuy argued against plaguing Hang with our case. I insisted. "Just this once," I said. "Let's make sure we're on the right track."

Hang wasn't home. A neighbor was, and as we left, the woman wanted to know whether we wanted to leave anything for Hang.

"Anything like what?" I asked Thuy outside.

"Anything to make friends."

"Like money? Like something under the table? A bribe. To get her to do her job?"

At Boi's suggestion, I'd recently met with a fellow in the province's department of foreign affairs, a high-level official who'd told me about the fast track and the slow track. The man drove a late-model Honda scooter, and one of his teeth was gold. He was part of Hue's privileged ruling class. The first time we'd scheduled to meet, he'd had too much to drink at lunch; he was too drunk to speak with a foreigner, according to one of his assistants. When we did meet, he led me to believe that a few hundred dollars placed here and there would expedite the process.

"Should we make friends with her?" I asked Thuy.

"How about your idea?"

"I asked you."

"My brother-in-law's young sister, she works as a bookkeeper for the taxation department in Hue. After I lost my chance to work as a bookkeeper at 2 Le Loi, because I didn't have $500 to buy that job, I asked that girl for some help. I thought, maybe because we shared a nephew, she might try to help me. But she wanted the money too. Always the money, the money, the money. I'm so tired of it."

I couldn't tell whether she was making an argument for acquiescence or fortitude.

"When I look at Hang's cold face, I never want to make friends."

"So we won't," I said.

At breakfast, Graeme was sitting alone, hunched forward in concentration over a mess of papers. His forehead was pressed against one palm while the pinched forefinger and thumb of his other hand tapped semaphore on the tabletop, oblivious to everything but the papers.

"Not very good feeling here this morning," one of the 3 Le Loi waiters said, glancing at Graeme. The waiter's features soured dramatically, and he sucked a quick hit of air through his teeth, the memory not only bitter but chilling. He set down a glass of freshly squeezed orange juice that I didn't have to ask for anymore.

"Not this morning," I said, pressing my palm against my stomach.

I'd developed a low-level upset stomach I couldn't shake. When a doctor friend of Thuy's sister Oanh was visiting the house the day before, he interviewed me at great length about my eating habits. When I told him I had a glass of juice at breakfast every morning, he clapped his hands. Here was the source of my problem. No more orange juice, he'd told me.

Meanwhile, Graeme had turned his attention to the contents of a plastic attaché that he'd bought locally, hence the collage of smiling kittens on the cover. I'd seen that attaché on a number of occasions and dreaded it, the way it bulged against its seams, filled with bent, creased tabs of manila envelopes and loose-leaf papers that came in a variety of colors. If all that paperwork was required of someone from Australia, a country that had diplomatic relations with Vietnam and an embassy in Hanoi, who knew what that meant for someone whose country was still waging a cold, economic war against Hanoi.

"Ah mate," Graeme said, looking over. "Mind if I join you?"

I pushed out a seat.

"Terrible morning," he said, sitting down, "not to mention last night, or yesterday afternoon when all this started."

I made a wish that whatever ailed him had nothing to do with his attaché, that the contents of his attaché was merely a means of diversion. "The rain is terrible," I said even though the rain hadn't started until that morning.

He removed a single paper and spun it to face me. It was an affidavit, notarized by provincial officials in the Northern Territory of Australia, which certified that Graeme Stewart was single. "What color's that piece of paper look like to you, mate?"

"Light yellow?"

"No, it's the wrong color. Wrong, according to the People's Committee of Thua Thien Province. Because last year, another bloke from Australia married a woman from Hue and his paper— they had this, they showed it to me—was light orange."

I laughed, but I didn't doubt for a moment that color was an issue. At the same time, my own anxious masons added a dozen more rows of brick to my dread. "You change the color of the paper, all set," I said.

"I don't know what they want from me now," he said, nodding up Le Loi Street toward the People's Committee. "But I've got to fix another problem first. Ol' Ma and Ba here, when they found out from Kim Anh that the People's Committee said no to my single paper, they reckoned I had a wife back in Oz. There was all kinds of shouting here this morning. I have no idea where any of it went."

His fingers thrummed the tabletop, keeping time with another torrent of rain. I'd never noticed how thick Graeme's fingers were. Looking at them, at the way they trembled moments later as he slipped his papers back in the folder neatly marked DOCUMENTS, I felt sad for him. Though he'd served six years in Australia's Special Forces, a guy who'd leapt from planes at 20,000 feet, his lack of guile and his naïve faith in goodness and the benefit of the doubt defined him more sharply. He told me once that he'd come to Vietnam "looking." He made no pretense of the fact that he wanted a wife and with her to build a family and have children. He was going to do right by Kim Anh, and her family, and the People's Committee, and yet they'd checked him. I couldn't understand how this kind of trouble could have come to him. If it were happening to me, I'd just figure I deserved it.

I looked at Kim Anh's father, an older man whose main function around the café involved the ignition of cigarettes while his wife and daughters ran the works. His brow was still furrowed from an argument that set him against his wife, who was also nursing a wounded expression as she made her way through several chickens with a cleaver. I doubted that Graeme had an ally in either.

"There's a bright side, though, mate," Graeme said. "It could be worse, yeah. Last time I came through Saigon, I ran into this bloke who'd got himself a fiancée in the city. They were pushing things a little on the romance side. You know, hitting the hotel for an afternoon here and there, until the cops grabbed them. They busted into their room one afternoon and later made him sign a paper, declaring that his girl, who was actually his fiancée, was a prostitute."

"And he signed it?"

"He did. They put the jacks on him. I won't say that I blame him, but I'll tell you, mate, his girl did. When I met him, he'd been trying for nearly a month to just get her to speak to him again."

The night before our first trip to the Justice Department, we bicycled to the Cercle Sportif—the only house in Hue that played foreign films—for a movie. The movies were videos actually, played on the kind of concave wide-screen television that resolved a beam of red, green, and blue light into washed-out images on screen. The same woman's voice, in a harsh, clipped northern accent, dubbed all the speaking parts, though I could often hear the undertow of English below.

It didn't matter that the quality of the presentation was poor or that the interpreter's voice, when I failed to strain for understanding, could shut me out of the movie; I simply liked being there. The Cercle Sportif was the old French leisure club in Hue, and redolent with the ghosts of the old colons. Outside, there was a drained and fissured swimming pool as well as the rusted pipe superstructure of an old diving platform. On the other side of the building was a netless tennis court. The building itself was a two-story nautical moderne design. Coping ran around the roofline, and horizontal grooves detailed the facades. Two wings extended off either side of the main function hall, where the cinema was set up, and a large oval tongue of a patio stuck out over the Perfume River. It was easy to picture the profligate French at play here, sipping aperitifs late in the afternoon, or celebrating on Bastille Day or Noel, waltzing the dark hardwood floors. The interior space had European dimensions, and in some vague way I felt slightly more entitled to be there than in native Vietnamese buildings.

Outside, a new motorbike corral attendant chalked my seat and made to help pull the Honda up onto its center stand, only then noticing my non-Vietnamese features. His eyes switched quickly to Thuy, then back as I passed a 2,000-dong note into his hand. *"Cam on,"* I said. Thanks.

"Khong phai," he said. Not right. *"You pay four thousand dong."*

I turned around. *"I didn't come to Hue yesterday,"* I said. *"I know how much to pay."*

"No," he said in English, twisting a loose upturned palm beside his ear. "No, no."

"You understand me," I said, patting his shoulder. *"I know you do."*

On a board that hung from the banyan tree out front, the film was billed as new and titled *Tinh Yeu va Thu Han. Love and Hate.* We knew better. All films, even the ones starring Marilyn Monroe and Brigitte Bardot, were labeled new. We'd already seen *Love and Hate* several times, and each time it had been a different film. The previous week's version was actually a movie called *Lower Level,* a B-grade thriller featuring a couple in garish mid-1970s garb, stalked by killers through a skyscraper. This week, it was Kevin Costner and Whitney Houston in *The Bodyguard.*

Costner Thuy remembered from another outing at the Cercle when we saw *Robin Hood,* the first movie we'd seen together. She responded viscerally and spontaneously to the scenes, clapping at Robin Hood's triumphs and squirming out loud under the dramatic tension. Her reaction thrilled me, the purity of her response, so unaffected and unselfconscious, she'd devoted herself completely to the on-screen action. It was partly why I never cared what the movie was; I could always watch her.

"Are you worried about the Justice Department tomorrow?" Thuy asked.

We sat in back, choice seats as far as I was concerned but second rate for this crowd, which packed in from front to back. A preview set of Hong Kong rock videos played on screen.

I shrugged and shook my head. "Not really."

Thuy shrugged and mimicked me, " 'Not really.' Like the cowboy, that film last week, he doesn't care about anything."

"Why worry?" A slight edge sharpened my voice, and she felt it.

"Ah, so not really the cowboy?"

"No, not a cowboy."

"How about the bodyguard?"

"No."

"Some man, he attacks us, what do you do?"

"Run away."

"I see, not the cowboy. *Coward.*"

The rock videos ceased abruptly, mid–guitar riff, and the peeling metal was replaced with the sound of moviegoers cracking watermelon seeds between their teeth. As the movie began, Thuy produced her own plastic bag of seeds.

Her question ricocheted around my mind during the opening credits, from Graeme to Eef. I thought of Relin, the elaborate schemes he'd concocted in Bangkok and Saigon to obtain travel permits and visa extensions, the guides he'd insisted we hire through desolate portions of our route. I preferred to plow ahead and meet obstacles head-on, and Thuy seemed to be telling me they were coming.

An inaudible stream of English flowed beneath the dubbing, and Thuy took it upon herself to translate critical moments and reversals, leaning forward, one finger held aloft as she vaguely pointed toward the action and whispered. The reflected light of the screen upon her face. The even, monotoned keel of her voice. This responsibility she felt, to keep me in the loop. I'd begun to notice that she was, in many ways, a vigilant guardian of my welfare. At a wedding the previous week, when the guests segregated, the men to drink beer and make loud jokes, the women to swap talk, she reached for me repeatedly across the crowd of guests, lifting up off her seat to hold me for a moment with her eyes. Could I bear this? Was it too much? Lately, I'd been telling her that the lines that distinguished her as Vietnamese were blurring in my eyes.

When the movie was over, we waited for the Cercle to empty and then left. The streets were deserted except for a few night vendors and the sweepers. It was only as the motorbike bounced over curbing onto Le Loi Street that we realized all the air had been drained from our back tire.

The Justice Department building was on Ngo Quyen Street, not far from the Morin. It was another French place, with a broad stairway lined with potted plants rising to the first floor. Our business was on the ground floor, in a small cell-like room bereft of plants, decoration, and excess furnishings and administered by a woman who did not look up when we entered. This was Hang. Her face was riddled with acne scars, and the bridges of her teeth bulged against the lips she fastened over them. She gestured toward a pair of wooden seats set facing her desk, not near enough to enable conversation but across the room against the wall.

After several minutes, she looked up at us for the first time. *"I won't do business with you if he comes to my office in short pants,"* she said. Her accent was northern.

We all looked at my legs. *"But he's wearing trousers,"* Thuy said. *"I'm just telling you,"* Hang said.

Ten minutes later, Hang was still studying the papers on her desk. "Maybe she is busy. Maybe we should come back later."

"No problem," Thuy said. "Just sit."

Ten more minutes passed, and I was fidgeting. "Not that," Thuy said. "Just sitting."

Finally, Hang scraped her finger tips across the desk, like a gambler calling for another hit, and Thuy presented my documents in a neat folder that she'd purchased at a stationery store.

Hang shuffled through them quickly and with no more than cursory regard. She seemed to know what she was looking for. *"Where's his health certificate?"*

"Yes, we're making arrangements for that. Is everything else in order?"

She pushed the dossier back across the desk. *"I'll tell you when I see his health certificate."*

CHAPTER TWELVE

Mɪɴʜ ʟᴏᴏᴋᴇᴅ ᴛᴇʀʀɪʙʟᴇ. Her slacks were wrinkled, and her hair, beneath the wretched straw hat her father used in the garden, was uncombed and not braided. Down the corridor of the Hue hospital, she shuffled behind us, head bowed and silent. She was eighteen years old but capable, frequently, of lapsing into adolescent postures, usually of innocent giddy delight but sometimes, as now, steadfast funks. Minutes earlier, when I'd greeted the two sisters with bananas on the hospital's steps, she merely tightened her lips at my hello.

"She's angry with me?" I asked Thuy, wondering whether I'd offended her. I'd been less willing to play the willing part of an English tutor lately. It could be exhausting, like spadework, and Minh was like a terrier going at the language. Sometimes her tireless efforts to pronounce a single word correctly wore me out. I hadn't been curt with her, I knew, but certainly less enthused than I'd been through the first few months.

"She's mad at me," Thuy said.

Though several steps behind us, and though Thuy had made a pretense of whispering, Minh's antenna picked up her sister's remark. "You know, Jim, every and every day I listen to VOA Special English and BBC, but this morning my sister insisted I come to the hospital. And so I am angry."

While Thuy waited in line to talk to a nurse at reception, I sat with Minh on the floor across from check-in. Dozens of patients and the families of patients sprawled on the hard benches and floors around us, some groaning. One boy's leg was bent at an obscene angle; his mother could do little but swab his silent tears and look anxiously at the admitting nurse when she stood to call someone. Another old woman held a bloody compress to her head and rocked slowly back and forth. Nobody's pain fazed anybody else. Competition for medical attention took precedence, and commiseration would only weaken your case.

When it became clear that we'd have to wait awhile, I asked Minh about her studies, a question that I used to ask often and that always opened the door to a tutorial. From her satchel, she produced a transcript of a recent VOA Special English news report about a dolphin rescued after several wayward days up a New Jersey river. We read the report aloud, and her pronunciation was remarkably competent. I told her so.

"But I still don't understand," she complained, slapping the pages against her lap.

I took the pages and started down with my forefinger, summarizing in even plainer English what had happened.

"No, I understand what happened. But I don't understand is why. Why so many people and why so much money to save the life one dolphin?"

VOA had reported it cost more than $1 million to save the dolphin; the whole community had been emotionally snared by the fate of the animal and experienced a collective sigh of relief when it swam free off the Jersey shore. In Vietnam, for Minh, for her classmates, there was some debate over whether the news was a hoax, or a joke. It didn't seem possible that they could live in a world that would spend so much money to save a dolphin and so little money to help old women with head wounds.

From reception we walked through corridors past wards where lucky kids and adults were recuperating from long-dormant ordnance, a mine that had exploded under the errant footfall of a boy out walking his water buffalo. There were two wounded gunpowder prospectors for whom the risk of exploding a dud dropped from the belly of a B-52 was offset by the dire straits of trying to make it in an embargoed economy. As my glance swept past one room, the nurse asked if I wanted to meet any of the patients. I did not.

I'd met some of these casualties on a hospital tour during my bicycle trip. An eight-year-old boy who'd lost his right hand, one of his testicles, part of his jaw, and both of his eyes, whose still-moist remains curdled black and fibrous in his sockets. The boy's vigilant father sat beside him, cooing songs and waving the cardboard of a cookie package over his face to keep the flies from his eyes. All the patients, I remembered, were attended by family members. The head of one man in a chest cast rested on a vinyl gym bag.

"We want to forget the last war," an orthopedic surgeon named Pham Dang Nhat told me then, "but it doesn't want to forget us."

Listening to the shortwave these days, I occasionally heard Americans lobbying against a lifting of the U.S. trade embargo, men like Senator Bob Smith of New Hampshire and the families of soldiers still missing from the war. It hardly made sense: Twenty years after a war we'd started was over, and a critical mass of Americans were still blaming the victim. In 1945, we'd embraced the axis powers immediately upon defeat and ushered Japan and Germany back into the mainstream of world affairs. Vietnam had yet to achieve anonymity among a random lineup of nations. The name of the country wasn't an ordinary word. It had power, resonance. It still vibrated when you said the word aloud, as though an exclamation point were permanently attached to it.

At an office deep within the hospital, our escort nurse retrieved mimeographed pages for twelve different tests for Thuy and thirteen tests for me. The thirteenth test was for AIDS, or SIDA.

"Why do I have to have a test for SIDA, and you don't?" I asked.

Thuy was shelling out dong notes to the nurse, who was mumbling along, counting the money as it fell into her palm. "Because I don't have it," she said.

I let the implications of that pass, then asked the nurse why I had to have the SIDA test and Thuy didn't. The nurse was recounting the money and answered me without breaking stride in her count. *"Because she's Vietnamese. So she doesn't have."*

Over the next several days, we roamed the hospital campus, from the bland, white multistoried main facility built during the American era to the antiseptically uninspiring but charming villas built during the French era. A nurse drew blood. A technician took X-rays. One doctor didn't bother to check my blood pressure and pulse; instead, he jotted healthy figures into my chart and brushed me off. He wore a circular reflector on his forehead and a surgeon's cap outside the operating room, more like someone imitating a doctor. I didn't argue, but the gesture shocked me. I hadn't suspected that the institutional malaise that deadened so much of the Vietnamese workforce had also spread among the ranks of doctors.

The ratio between my height (5'8½") to weight (158 pounds) warranted an "A" rating on the bottom line of one examination. Most foreigners, according to this nurse, came in at "C" and "D," usually because they were too heavy for their height. *"Too fat because*

too old," she said. Thuy also received a "C" rating, but for the opposite reason. At 95 pounds, she was too light for her height (5'2"),
according to the Vietnamese nurse. Her proportions were characteristic for most women in Hue, but the Vietnamese always believed
they should be heavier.

The same nurse told Thuy I was the youngest foreigner to be
examined for marriage, a fact that heartened Thuy. While people
in Hue might question the financial subtext of a match between a
younger Vietnamese woman and an older foreigner, our five-year
split was like wind on that chatter.

Thuy's sister Nga accompanied us on the morning of our last
trip to the hospital, to pick up the results of my HIV test. I'd never
been tested for HIV before. It hadn't ever been necessary, and I
hadn't ever worried about it. But after the nurse filled one vial
destined for the microscope of a lab tech looking for HIV, I felt
as if my fate had been sucked out of me. Where there had been
nothing but blue skies, clouds started massing, high, thin, and wispy
at first, but as the day approached, they descended and thickened.
A bolt of lightning seemed more possible every day.

I began to dwell on the six weeks in 1989 I'd lived with my
father's brother, Paul, who'd died from AIDS in the fall of 1991.
He was the uncle who'd spent two years at Cam Ranh in the late
1960s, who'd commissioned my portrait from a Vietnamese painter
and the only one of my father's five brothers whom I'd gotten to
know well. After I showed up at Paul's place in Santa Cruz in
1989, we tuned up my car, each of us combing the engine with our
hands to replace spark plugs, filters, and hoses. At one point, his
hands emerged from the engine with a scrape of blood across the
knuckles. Later, I noticed nicks in my own hands. I thought nothing of it. At twenty-four, I hadn't admitted the fact of my own
mortality or that anything truly bad would ever happen to me. In

Hue, those nicks on my hands, and the bathroom I'd used at Paul's house, his coffee mugs and forks, turned ominous. Cowards die many times before their deaths, and I'd been stabbing myself now for days with phantasms of Paul's forks.

At the back of the hospital compound, Nga left Thuy and me at a bench outside one of the old labs and went inside to get the results. I'd tried to tell them the lab probably wouldn't release the results to anyone other than the person whose blood they'd tested, patient confidentiality and such, but that notion mystified them. Of course Nga could get them.

"What would you do if I had SIDA?" Thuy asked as we sat and waited.

"You're Vietnamese. You can't have it," I said.

"But if I did?"

This was a test of a different sort. The way she'd turned toward me and looked for the hint of an answer in my face told me I couldn't get out of this without giving her one. It would have been easy to say the noble, selfless thing, but as soon as she had begun to look for an answer from me, I began to wonder myself.

"I'd want to know where it came from," I said.

"That matters?"

"It might."

"So you mean we've agreed to be married, but there may be something—you don't know now—but if you found out, it might change everything."

"Right."

"You might run away."

"Let's say you had SIDA. I'd want to know where it came from. If you were an intravenous drug user, I'd want to know why you decided not to tell me about that."

"You don't just accept my past?"

"Well."

"Like I accept your past. For example, I don't ask about other women you've been with."

"That's not the same as doing things that might bring on SIDA."

"Sex can cause SIDA." She lifted the statement like a question, meaning she wanted to keep beating the path. I didn't. I'd never believed it was wise to rout that deeply through each other's past except, perhaps, in a situation, like the revelation of SIDA, that warranted it.

I looked toward the villa. Through the open doorway, I could see an HIV poster on the wall. "Okay, what if I had SIDA? What if I have SIDA? What if Nga comes out the door and tells us I've got SIDA?"

"Go away," Thuy said.

"You'd go away."

"We'd have to go away, for example, to some small island."

She delivered her response so flatly that it seemed to carry the weight of deliberation and resolution. No doubt, she had considered the possibility of my having SIDA. It had to be lurking somewhere in her thoughts. After all, the doctors were testing only me. And little kids all over Vietnam now were shouting SIDA at foreigners, as if we all carried it. I didn't say anything about her reference to the island. The idea seemed as shimmery and fantastic as a mirage, and for a moment, I stared at the conjured image of such a place. From the corner of my eye, I saw Nga exit the doorway. She stopped at the top of the stairway and looked at me directly. Nga's eye contact with me had always been glancing; now, she'd settled a steady, sober gaze on me.

"*What?*" Thuy asked.

"*SIDA. He has it,*" Nga said. She'd set her arms akimbo. My papers, the results, were furled at her hip.

Thuy's arms encircled me at the lower rib cage. Her hands clasped, and I felt the vice of her embrace and the confirmation of her declaration to escape to the island.

I couldn't look at her. But I was raging against the verdict. The lab was a sham. Tests for HIV could only be conducted in Saigon or Hanoi. The results were fixed. Dich had a hand in this. If these results were legitimate, they would have come directly to me. Why had Nga gone in there in the first place? Why had I let her?

A moment later, the lab technician stepped onto the porch, smiling cheerfully. He waved at us and, eyes on me, said something to Nga. I looked at the woman's purple plastic sandals, and in that instant, knew that Nga was joking. A grave joke, indeed, but death, for people in Vietnam, was far closer to home than it was for those in America and hardly the stuff of taboo. It could be joked about.

"Yes," I said, rising in relief that was not yet complete. Nga still retained a sternly indignant expression. "I admit it. I am SIDA."

She buckled then, laughing. Her hand went to her mouth, covering the dead, broken eyetooth she didn't have the money to repair.

Thuy marched on her oldest sister, scolding her in transit, and reached for the papers, which confirmed that I was HIV negative.

The following day, the skin along the side of my right forefinger erupted into a hideous field of tiny, translucent bubbles, filled with yellowish gray pus. They hadn't only ruptured the skin from just below my nail to the bottom knuckle, but seemed to rupture from each other, layers upon layers. My finger looked like an amusement from a joke shop.

"No problem," Thuy said. "Your finger wants a suntan. That's all."

"There's no sun."

"It'll go away."

We braked our bikes in Hang's courtyard, and Thuy took the dossiers from my basket. She looked my clothes up and down, then nodded. "Keep that finger in your pocket," she said.

Inside, we waited in chairs on the far wall, like suspects, while Hang paged through a copy of the national army newspaper, or so it looked to me. At the top of the hour, her wall clock chimed the ditty from "Frere Jacques," and moments later a boisterously happy woman whisked into the office with a bag full of clothes. She removed one outfit after another: a little boy's sailor outfit with a cap and trailing red ribbon, a small *ao dai* with a mandarin's cap, and a set of pajamas featuring a steamer-trunk sticker motif: one sticker was for Galveston, another for Texas, a third for Lubbock. All the clothes looked like just the right size for the little boy pictured in a photograph on Hang's desk.

"Have we gotten anything for Hang's son?" I asked Thuy.

"No."

"Should we?"

"Do you want?"

I looked at the woman's grim, acne-scarred face, her evidently expensive makeup, and found cause to blame her for the old woman's bloody head at the hospital. "Not particularly," I said.

When Hang finally got to my papers, all duly notarized, translated, and bound per protocol, she stopped immediately at my health certificate. *"What's this?"* she asked.

I felt my finger throb in my pocket. She was going to ask to see it. She was going to want to know why I was sitting there like that.

"Health certificate," Thuy said.

"This is a Vietnamese health certificate. He is American."

"Right."

"These are not his doctors. I need a certificate from his doctor." She closed my dossier and passed both folders back to us.

"It doesn't say on the list of documents required that I need to have an exam from a doctor from my country," I said loudly to Thuy. I began to say as much in Vietnamese to Hang but stuttered for the right words. "Please, tell her this." I went back to the documents and opened the folder so lovingly assembled the previous evening and pointed at the health certificate.

"No, Jim," Thuy said.

My finger was out now. "Ask her."

"This is not the way."

I turned to Hang myself. Her eyes had drooped to half-mast, and I believed I saw a smug smile on her lips. *"Why?"* I asked her. *"Other foreigners had exams at Hue's hospital."* I turned to Thuy. "Can she understand me?"

"This is not good."

Hang looked around me at Thuy and asked her what country I came from.

"You know what country I come from. You've seen my papers," I said, though I have no idea whether my inflection rendered my remarks comprehensible.

"America," Thuy said, gathering our things from Hang's desk and taking me by the elbow. At the doorway, Thuy turned, smiled, and made a slight bow toward Hang.

"Right," Hang said. *"I know that country."*

CHAPTER THIRTEEN

IT TURNED OUT THAT MY HEALTH certificate was the least of my paper problems. That fix was fairly easy. Since my mother worked in billing for my doctor, she simply retrieved the records of my most recent physical exam and sent them. Two weeks later, they arrived as much of my mail did these days, in a plastic pouch and accompanied by a note from Vietnamese authorities stating that my mail had been damaged in transit. Mr. Gioang translated the results of my physical exam and, moreover, agreed to act as an intermediary for future visits to Hang's office.

"That's better than taking a chance with Jim in that office again," Thuy told her family.

"I was reasonable," I said.

Thuy hopped to and stalked across the room to the dinner table, mimicking my act in Hang's office, leaned over a niece, then deepened her voice and harangued the girl, pointing her finger like an angry Russian official.

"It was nothing like that," I said.

"That's because you couldn't see yourself."

Later, after visiting Hang's office with my new health certificate,

Gioang believed it would pass muster. Hang didn't tell him it was okay; she didn't object to it. But there was another issue.

"You need a document from your parents, a paper on which they grant their permission for you to marry Thuy."

"My parents are dead." In my indignation over this latest complication, which was mentioned nowhere on the list of requisite documents, it was my first impulse.

"You'll have to get death certificates." Gioang said this with such alacrity I wondered whether Hang might have anticipated this feint and explained the necessary recourse.

"They're not dead, for God's sake. But I'm twenty-eight. Why do I need their permission?"

"Why is the sea blue?"

My parents granted their permission, notarized it. We translated it. Gioang ran it by Hang, and she wanted to know where the document was that provided a history of my relationship with Thuy.

"I want to ask her where that requirement is on the list she gave us," I said.

Thuy put down her glass of iced sugarcane juice and spoke to Gioang. "I told Jim I wanted him to stay in Vietnam for one year so I could know his temper. I am getting to know."

"Forget about one year. How about two years?" I said.

"You have to write everything," Gioang said.

"For example?" Thuy asked.

"All," Gioang said.

We wrote a page. Gioang translated it and recommended that Thuy and I visit Hang's together again, calmly. This time, Hang sailed quickly through all my papers and then looked up at Thuy. *"Where's the stamp from his embassy?"*

Thuy opened her mouth but didn't say anything. I knew the

word for embassy to be *Toi dai su,* and as soon as I heard the martial cadence of the word spit from Hang's lips, I fell into a hole I couldn't rise from. No danger of losing my cool over this. *"America doesn't have an embassy in Vietnam, as you know,"* Thuy said.

"I need an embassy stamp," Hang said, closing my dossier.

"It doesn't say so," Thuy said, her voice spiking. She stood up and opened her arms in a benediction. *"On your paper, it doesn't say."*

"Some embassy."

"Any embassy?"

"A U.S. embassy."

At the consulate of the U.S. embassy in Bangkok, I took a number and waited my turn before a high counter whose clerks were, to all appearances, American. None of them were reading army newspapers. Posters of New York City and Wyoming hung from the walls. The room was air conditioned, and the chairs were drab but redolent of waiting rooms all over America: one-piece stainless-steel arms and legs and neutral, cloth upholstery on a large square seat and a rectangular support for the back. The chair was more comfortable than anything I'd sat on in Vietnam. The room felt like a sanctuary, and my confidence buoyed as the clerks efficiently handled one petitioner after another.

When my turn came, I was grateful for the opportunity to talk to an American in this fashion. I hardly knew where to begin. I was tempted to tell her the whole story from the start. My gratitude was gushing. I wanted to thank her for being there.

"I don't really know what I'm looking for," I said, chuckling.

Her eyes slid away from me to a wall clock and then deliberately back to me. "How may I help you?" she said again, as officiously as before as though I hadn't noticed the first time.

"I've been in Vietnam," I said. "I'm engaged to a woman there,

and I'm having a world of trouble with the authorities in the province . . ."

"How may I help you?" she asked again, as if she hadn't asked
twice already. She was sitting on a high stool and had leaned forward, forearms braced against the edge. On her desk, I could see
a copy of *People* magazine.

"I need stamps," I said, "stamps from my embassy. I can't move
my marriage application without them." I slid my dossier across the
counter to her.

She glanced through my papers, and I explained their contents,
annotating as she casually leafed through them, laughing over the
parental permission slip, desperate to pull her in league with me.
But she was immune to my appeal.

"It's ridiculous, I know, but they're stamp crazy in Vietnam. This
one official requires that I have a U.S. embassy stamp my documents."

"We can't do this," she said. She pushed the documents through
the crescent opening in the Plexiglas shield. She didn't say she was
sorry. She didn't offer an alternative or any guidance. It stunned me.
I'd walked into the embassy, encouraged, warmed by its mundane familiarity, believing that here there would be commiseration and that
if not, then at least pretensions of concern. I was sure the embassy
staff had been groomed for this overseas assignment. They didn't
work here; they'd been *posted* here. But this woman might as well
have worked at the Registry of Motor Vehicles or at McDonald's. In
her lazy, dispirited tone was a desire to be somewhere else.

"I've got to have something," I said. I looked at the poster of
New York and then away quickly. "Is there someone you can talk
to?"

"No."

"Why not?"

"We can't be putting embassy stamps on anything anybody asks us to."

"Why not? I'm not asking you to attest to anything or authenticate anything. I'm stuck over there, and I need a stamp to get me through."

"I'm sorry."

"What's your name?"

She tightened her mouth at my question. "I'm not allowed to give out that information."

"You're kidding."

She didn't deign an answer. She hiked her eyebrows on me and pursed her lips, a tough girl sizing up an opponent on a city sidewalk.

"Let me speak with your supervisor."

She pushed back from her stool and went to a man heading toward a door into the rear of the consulate. She explained her version to him. His glance swept the counter, locating me but not making eye contact. One of the neighboring clerks caught my eye, and the corners of his mouth stretched in a brief sympathetic smile. Moments later, my clerk returned to say her supervisor could not speak with me now and that he agreed with her decision.

I stared at her through the Plexiglas while anger spewed inside, threatening expulsion. I might have reached her through the crescent in the Plexiglas or called her a fucking bastard or worse. I had a history of leaping from high to low ground and thus losing the good ground to fight another day. But a pilot of hope still burned in my gut, ignited by the neighboring clerk. I couldn't ditch yet.

That day I phoned Beatty, a college friend who'd showed up in Bangkok to lawyer at an international law firm the year before and who now declared he'd never leave. He was Canadian, personable, and connected, I hoped, to someone at the U.S. consulate, or he knew someone who was. He proposed a rendezvous that night in Patpong, where he would be entertaining a client from the States.

Outside the Freddy III guest house, I hailed a cab. "Patpong," I told the driver.

"Evening comes, where else?" the driver said. "Patpong, Patpong," he chimed. "Sing a song about Patpong."

He left me outside McDonald's on Silom Road. Across the street was Patpong, Bangkok's red-light district, a pedestrian mall of go-go bars, transvestite follies, and erotic floor-show venues. Neon bar shingles blazed ruby red, lime green, and deep purple come-ons for go-go bars like King's Castle, Lipstick, Peppermints, the Safari. Fan-blown plastic-strip curtains draped the entranceways, shredding vistas of bikini-clad girls dancing on stages, their hands blithely attached to gleaming, brass-plated poles.

"Have a look, sir." A young Thai male handed me a small menu card, detailing his club's acts: live boy-girl sex show, girl-girl sex show, pussy smoke cigarette show, pussy hide razor blades, pussy Picasso, Ping-Pong ball race, girl-dog sex show.

"This is a joke," I said. "Girl-dog."

"Today, dog is sick."

It turned out the dog was always sick. They went far on Patpong, but not quite that far.

I walked from one end of the strip to the other, checking either side of the horseshoe-shaped bars at King's Castle, the Limelight, and the Goldfinger before I found Beatty at the Safari, standing outside a semicircular booth with one arm thrown over the shoulder of his client. A Thai woman in a bikini top sat on a stool before them, as close as a woman about to read a palm. Her hair was iron-straight, and long. The shape of her eyes reminded me of a girl I knew from Denver in college.

From my first pass through Bangkok more than a year before, I recognized two other guys in the booth; Brett, a communications specialist from Australia, and Tim, another lawyer at Beatty's law firm and a Vietnam vet who'd had his first exposure to Patpong twenty years earlier. They were regulars in the district. It didn't matter that HIV was rampant among the bar girls, that the songs they danced to on stage, whether disco or AC/DC, were really just movements of a dirge. These guys wore condoms as armor. "I get tested every three months," Brett had told me. "That way I know whether to keep making investments or start spending all my money."

Bravado, maybe, but a fact too. They got tested. They passed. And they began to think of themselves as invincible, as mosquitoes in the rain, dodging death sentences.

The longer you stayed in Bangkok, the more likely you were to "break" as the expats called the end of your resistance to the city's harlots. Under the temptation of its siren song, chaste passage from one side of the night to the other required an Odyssean harness and a vigilant maintenance of knots that loosened with every beer, every hour, and every other dance string of Thai women whom many deemed the most beautiful women in the world.

Among Beatty's set, the extremes of indulgence—not your vehicle, not the cut of your suit, not your handicap—were the arbiter of your relative worth. How many different girls you "went with" on a given night. Whether you had the courage to hang in there with a *katooey*, a lady-boy transvestite who'd had the operation. During my previous stay, one of Beatty's colleagues had gone with a girl who was deaf and dumb, and who raised the bar to a new level. After spending a night with her, he declared, "You're not a man until you make a mute girl moan."

I'd stayed away from Patpong until then, but the query chased you down in Bangkok. "Not yet," I said one night at a Japanese steak house.

"But you've been here more than a month," Brett said.

"Yeah, well, you know, it's like Russian roulette down here . . ."

Light laughter rippled around the table, and I realized that raising the specter of AIDS with these guys only made me look like a hypochondriac.

As I slid into one end of the booth, Beatty glanced around. "Sully. Good. We just got here too." He gestured at one of the waitresses, ordering me a beer. "Francis here just got into town, and we're giving him the royal tour of Silk City, eh."

Bangkok was ineluctable for Beatty. In college, he'd belonged to a voyeuristic fraternity whose brothers kept photo albums of their sexual conquests and who would huddle on a ledge outside each other's bedroom windows, snapping photos with high-speed film. He was barrel-chested and as handsome as an underwear model in the Sunday newspaper. In school he had a reputation for being lusty but never lewd. Women seemed to forgive his addiction with the same pity that people in liberal circles extend to alcoholics.

Francis, on the other hand, looked out of his element. His beaming, genial gaze leapt from Beatty to the girl at his shoulder, who was twirling the hair at the nape of his neck, to a fresh string of stiletto-heeled go-go girls who were stepping on stage to Right Said Fred's "I'm Too Sexy."

As one of the dancers caught Francis's eye, she winked, and he rocked back and forth over his stool in time with the music. "I'm surprised at how tall these girls are," said Francis. "I'd always thought Oriental woman were, you know, petite."

"They are," Beatty said, nodding confidently like an on-air reporter responding to a pat question from the anchor. "On stage, they're about five-eight or so." It was the slimness of the hips, he explained, that made for a disproportionate appreciation of the height. "You'll see when they come down off stage and stand beside you for the chat, they seem a bit shorter, let's say five-four, five-five. The moment of truth comes when you get them home, and they step out of their heels. They're rarely taller than five foot." He swilled off his beer and shook off that last observation. "But that doesn't matter."

When the waitress delivered my Kloster, she gathered the empty beer bottles, then darted a hand into my lap, where she squeezed my crotch. "What's wrong? You don't have good time? Maybe you meet my friend Noi."

"I'm engaged," I said.

"No problem," one of the girls said. "You know *mai pen rai*? In Thailand, mean 'everything okay.' "

I smiled warmly and shook my head.

"Tim not engaged," one of the other expats volunteered.

"Tim old," the waitress said.

"I'll remember that," Tim said.

"I remember *you* last time," she said, fixing him with an accusatory glance that made everyone look at Tim.

Nervously, he raised his palms and shook his open hands. She turned back to me. "You no eat same food everyday. No good for you."

"I'm sorry," I said.

Carrying a platter that held a shot of tequila, the cut halves of a tiny lime, and a wooden shaker of salt carved in the shape of a stupendous penis, another waitress stepped between Francis and the girl in the bikini top. The girl removed her bikini top.

Beatty lifted the cut lime from the tray and handed it to Francis. "First, lather her left tit with the lime."

"Jesus H. Christ," Francis said, the laughter bubbling out of his generous midsection. "I got two kids at home . . ." He glanced at his wristwatch. "Probably getting up right now to watch *Teenage Mutant Ninja Turtles*."

That fact didn't keep him from screwing the lime around the woman's nipple.

"Now, juice the other one," Beatty said.

Francis twisted a fresh lime over her other nipple, then cupped her breast from below, lifting gently. "Is this infidelity?" he was saying. "I don't know from infidelity. I love my wife. I've always been faithful. Even after this I think I'll still consider myself faithful."

"We'll see how you do tonight," Beatty said, grinning. He picked up the salt shaker. "Now go on in and season your mouth for the tequila.

Tentatively, like a man tiptoeing through shallow cold water, he moved his face in on her breast. His tongue flicked at her nipple, quick and snakelike, before his mouth mashed around her aureole. A minute later, Beatty said, "grab some air."

The man surfaced and downed his tequila while Beatty sprinkled salt over the woman's nipple. Francis looked at the nipple with the dull, veteran gaze of a junkie, then honed in with the single-mindedness of a heat-seeking missile.

"Oxygen," Beatty said after another minute, tapping the man's shoulder.

The man looked up, licking his lips with exaggeration.

"Now look around," Beatty said.

"Where?"

"Around the bar."

There were two foreign women, known in Thailand as *farang*, sitting alone in a darkened corner booth, scowling at the man with unapologetic contempt.

"The last leg of the Tequila Titty," Beatty said, "is the glance around the room to see how many disgusted *farang* women will remember what you've done for the rest of their lives."

The music changed, the medley ongoing—"Groove Is in the Heart": "It's getting . . . it's getting . . . it's getting kind of hectic." The foreign women stared after Francis and Beatty as they went to the bar, where Beatty was introducing him to a girl who'd just come down off the stage. They—the two foreign women—were speaking rapidly to each other without looking at each other, and if one of them had pulled a notebook from her lap and begun scribbling, an engaged sociologist at field studies, it wouldn't have surprised me.

This was how Western men behaved in the East. Far from the tether of the priest and the emancipated woman, here they could indulge every fantasy with a willing, pliant, submissive girl. You wouldn't have to talk to her. In fact, you probably could not, and that was part of the attraction. Do away with the complicating clutter of speech, and the eroticism is only enhanced. How much of what the *farang* saw in Francis, I wondered, did the embassy clerk see in me? Perhaps, as I made my pitch over the counter, a whole set of givens had fallen into place for her. Here was another megalomaniac. Here was just another guy looking for an Asian cup of tea. Boom-boom. You go boom-boom?

Beatty slid into the booth beside me and clapped my back. "Sully," he said, deadpanning. "How's Thuy?"

I hurried down the rest of my beer. "Fine," I said. "I got to talk to you later about something. Billable stuff." The revelation of her name here, with all these guys and all their girlfriends, spooked me.

"Billable? What the fuck. No billables between us." He turned to the other expats. "Sully's engaged to a Vietnamese girl."

"Vietnamese?" Brett asked. "How are they? I have to go there next month."

"Good," I said, trying to nod off the subject. "A lot like the Irish."

"He's having a wedding," Beatty said. "What? Next month. In a couple of months."

"I did that," one of the other expats broke in.

"That's right," Tim said. "I forgot you were married."

"We went up to her village, up near Mae Hong Son. It was great. There were firecrackers and paper lanterns, the whole bit. A real to-do." He gripped the shoulder of the bar girl beside him, number seventeen according to a tag on her bikini-top strap, and pulled her close. "You made a good move, mate. I keep telling these poofters they ought to take the plunge, but do they listen?"

Beatty didn't know anyone at the U.S. consulate. So the next day, I pulled my number and bided my time, watching the line move and gauging the likelihood that I'd end up with the same clerk. If I did, if she beckoned me, I'd step aside, feigning scrutiny at a sudden problem with my documents. I didn't have to. I got another consulate official, a real one, the vice consul.

I explained my situation. I told him about my bike trip, about my article, which had been published recently in *Bicycling*, Thuy, the intransigent Vietnamese clerk, the need for stamps. My request troubled his face with worry or confusion. He thumbed through the documents, mumbling the numbers. I could see that my request did fly in the face of their policy, but I also sensed that his mind was churning on a solution. He was the picture of the kind of diplomat I expected. Yesterday's clerk had been the picture of a brick.

And then the brick was at the vice consul's side. "I dealt with this case yesterday. I went to Bill about it, and Bill says no."

She was a nightmare. I'd thought Hang was trouble, and she was. But I'd also thought that Hang's kind of terror was peculiar to Third World communist bureaucracy. It was not.

The vice consul nodded at her and continued his worrisome perusal through my papers. Just then, the clerk who'd sympathized with me the day before, stepped up to the vice consul's other side. The brick crossed her arms. The new clerk suggested something, and the vice consul's face relaxed.

"What if we listed all of your documents on a separate affidavit and stamped that? Do you think that would help?"

CHAPTER FOURTEEN

MY EMBASSY STAMP PASSED Hang's inspection. In a gesture that I'd come to believe was nearly impossible, she closed our dossiers and placed them in the top drawer of her desk. From there, they would go to the People's Committee, then to Hanoi, then back to Hue, where we could check for them at the entry-exit police bureau. It would take some weeks.

It was a perverse irony that our papers would route back into Hue through the entry-exit police bureau where Dich worked, but that circumstance couldn't dampen the élan with which we fled the Justice Department. Nobody would be as tough on our documents as Hang, a good cop official at the People's Committee had told us. If our papers worked for her, they'd work for them. Our documents' journey to Hanoi was merely a formality.

Evenings now, in each other's arms in the sweetheart cafés upon the ramparts of the Citadel, at 242, and Blue River, we yielded to forces that were larger and more compelling than any hold custom had upon us. We whisked each other toward thresholds that would hold for a time and then crumble under the weight of desire. Then we would honor a new threshold, until it too succumbed.

Thuy's mother and sisters maintained a vigilant watch over her romance. One morning, after Mrs. Bang noticed a garland of mosquito bites around Thuy's ankles, she scolded her daughter for letting the moonlight—her euphemism—make her mindless. "Remember the mosquitoes," her mother had told her. Her sister Nguyet cautioned her against kissing on the lips because "you may never want to stop."

After several weeks, we decided it was time to stop at the entry-exit police bureau to check on the progress of our papers. The job fell to me. I'd thought that Thuy might have a better chance of success, but she nixed it.

"You're the one they'll want to see."

Dich never had a day off. When he finished with one of the local petitioners, he waved me ahead of several others in line, ensuring still more contact. I told him I'd come to check on our papers, and he told me we'd have to check with officials from the foreign ministry. "And you are lucky. We have a man from that office here today."

He nodded slightly at the young fellow in a gray Member's Only knockoff. It was Vinh, my sometime shadow.

"Hi, Jim," Vinh said, taking a seat beside Dich.

"This is Mr. Vinh," Dich said.

"I recognize Mr. Vinh," I said, and they both laughed.

Vinh received my passport and made a run through, then handed it back. "So what do you hear from Andrew Sherry?"

Sherry was the Agence France Presse correspondent in Hanoi, and a friend of a friend of mine from school. I had stayed with Andy and his family at the AFP villa several times in Hanoi, and he had come down to visit in Hue a few months earlier. It floored me that they knew Andy.

"Fine," I said.

"Did you learn anything . . ." he shook his head, frowning as if broaching some mystery, ". . . from the monks at Linh Mu Pagoda?"

One of the trips Andy and I had taken was to Linh Mu Pagoda, a Hue landmark. I shook my head. "Nope."

"They can make a lot of trouble, those monks," he said.

Earlier that year, during the weeks I was at home in the States, the Buddhists in Hue had staged a street demonstration. The monks were complaining about infringement of their religious prerogatives, something about the nationalization of Buddhist properties or the selection of a government-ordained leader. No one was sure about the details. But the reaction had been tumultuous; some were saying more tumultuous than any in Vietnam since the end of the war. I'd heard that a crowd sympathetic to the Buddhists' complaint had turned over a police car on Le Loi Street and that a man had immolated himself beside a shrine at the back of Linh Mu.

"I don't know much about that," I said.

"What did you tell Philip Shenon about it when he visited you in your room at the Morin?"

Shenon was the *New York Times* corespondent in Bangkok, and he'd come to my room for leads about the Buddhist action. "The same. I don't know much about what happened then."

"And George Esper? You are friends with him."

Esper was yet another newspaperman, a legendary longtime AP corespondent in Vietnam before 1975 who had recently returned to Hanoi as the AP set up shop in the country again. He was a friend of my mother's friend, and when I was last in Hanoi, we had dinner at a bistro downtown.

I ran ahead of Esper to wonder what else could possibly be coming at me. To know what they knew about meeting Shenon in my room and Esper in Hanoi meant they knew a lot, meant they were keeping tabs. It was ludicrous to be watching me this closely. If I were one of their priorities, then their priorities were all wrong.

"You are friends with Mr. Esper?" Vinh asked.

"No."

"But you had dinner together?"

"First time I met him."

"Do you have your books with you?" he asked.

"My books?"

"The book you write in."

"My journal?"

"Diary?"

"Yes."

"You do have it."

"No," I lied.

"May I look in your backpack?"

"Of course not."

Dich and Vinh laughed together. "A very private man," Dich said, slapping Vinh on the shoulder.

Vinh stood up and shook my hand. "Jim, please let me know if you know about some people, they want to make trouble around here. Gary, for example. Or Marian. Let me know."

"Nobody wants to make trouble, Vinh," I said.

Leaving, he patted me on the shoulder.

"You have some questions for Mr. Vinh?" Dich asked.

"Maybe later."

"But you came here with a question."

"I know."

"I have a question for you."

I smiled and nodded at him.

"Do you love Miss Thuy?"

A slew of wise-guy answers crowded my head, but I managed to reject them. Play the game. "Yes," I said.

"Do you kiss Miss Thuy?"

Now there was no room to maneuver. I looked at him, the small dark eyes and his small head, his hands placed palm down on his desk. A man who would not put up with a bird that had shrunk, a man who had all the rules in his pocket. "That's none of your business."

It was as if he hadn't heard me, because he had another question.

"At the Blue River Café? On Friday night, for example?"

Thuy heard a rumor. Although our papers had been dispatched to Hanoi, they'd stalled there for lack of one very critical document: a bank statement that showed that I had at least $12,000 deposited in a savings account. I pretended not to hear. I was looking for flat stones that I could skim over the surface of a small pond at Tu Hieu Pagoda.

"The problem with Vietnam, the really big problem," I told Thuy, "is that you don't run into many stones for skipping. When I was the boy, there was this small cove in a park near my house that was full of flat rocks, perfect for skipping out into Dorchester Bay."

Thuy jabbed the shallow depression in her temple with her middle finger, fighting a headache, and I gave her a bottle of menthol balm I'd begun to carry. The paper chase had taken its toll on her. She'd begun to have headaches she couldn't shake, and she believed she'd developed sinusitis.

"Bad?" I asked.

She nodded.

She sat on a rock, and I stood in front of her. With my middle fingers, I twirled small circular massages into her temples. She closed her eyes and let herself go with the rhythm. Bracing the sides of her head with my fingers, I ran hard lines of pressure from the temple, over the brow, and down the bridge of her nose.

"A nose so flat," I said.

"And such yellow skin," she murmured.

"Sloped eyes."

"A slope," she said softly. "No, a gook. A dink. Is it right?"

I worked my thumbprints into her hair, harder and harder. The monks had long ago ceased their afternoon chants, which we'd come out for, the way you go to see a sunset, and the dusky bugs were now scattered through the gloaming.

"I had a dream last night that you and I made a small baby," she whispered. I stopped massaging her head, but my fingers stayed on. "He was a boy."

"We're in a pagoda," I said.

She waited some time and then said, "Don't talk to the monkeys."

The rumor vanished with her headache, but of course it didn't go away. It circled back that evening, and I faced it in my room at the Morin. I counted my stash, something I'd been reluctant to do for weeks, then parsed my savings in another jotted budget. We weren't going to make it, couldn't. The money wouldn't last. We'd talked hesitatingly about plans for a wedding, and though we'd talked about a modest affair, the money wouldn't stand for it. I wrote a letter to my grandfather's brother, Tom Gallagher, an eighty-year-old bachelor who still lived in the house he'd grown up in and who was reputed, correctly it turned out, to have millions secreted away in dresser drawers: equities, bonds, titles to obscure but valuable land. I loathed the thought of asking for a loan. I had a history of making judicious financial decisions. I never carried debt on my credit cards. I lived within budgets that knew when an impulsive Snickers bar made an appearance. But there was no way around this. I wrote the letter. I spelled out my request as $10,000 and mailed it to him, care of my mother.

Ten thousand was not twelve thousand, but the rumored financial prerequisite had not reared its head and probably wouldn't. To be sure, and to check on the lethargic pace of the bureaucrats in Hanoi, I needed to talk to Vinh, though not in public. One evening when, coincidentally, we had our dinner at a fried-noodle shop near the bus station, I sent a Huda beer over to his table. When the waitress pointed me out, I toasted him, and he toasted me back. He picked his teeth while I dallied over my dinner, and when I ordered another beer, he checked his watch and stood to leave.

"Your taste in beer, it's very good," he said, stopping at my table on the way out.

After he'd turned out the garage bay entrance, I watched him unlock the fork of his motorbike and steer into Tran Phu Street traffic. I left payment on my table, went outside, and pedaled into the street, about a hundred yards behind him.

It was just after dark, and several times I was sure that I'd lost him. Each time, I just caught sight of the gray Member's Only knockoff, turning the same corners I turned on my trips to Thuy's house. On Nguyen Trai Street, I waited inside the tunnel of a Citadel gate while he braked and puttered into a small courtyard. Then, I slowly pedaled by. I'd been by the house dozens of times, oblivious, and grateful now to see that Vinh's family also kept a pay phone booth in their living room.

The following evening, Vinh must have seen me before I saw him because he slipped out of the living room as I entered. An older couple, his parents, welcomed me and ushered me into the phone booth, where I placed a call to Thuy's sister Dieu, who'd recently had a phone installed.

"My friends have a new phone," I told Vinh's parents when I came out. *"They like to talk on the phone."*

The older couple didn't respond to my Vietnamese. The old man remarked to his wife that I spoke Vietnamese, and then they looked at me again, beaming friendliness. I glanced around them at the television where Bugs Bunny was outwitting Elmer Fudd. I laughed at Bugs, and the old couple turned slightly toward the television. Then they did what they were obliged to do.

I watched the rest of that episode, then a sing-along Walt Disney tune from the 1940s. I sang along with the bouncing ball, delighting a young woman who'd just toted a baby into the room and sprawled on a webbed chaise longue. Then we watched Felix the Cat, and I sang that theme song.

Vinh didn't come out of the back room. His wife let me hold the baby, whom I got to giggle by impersonating a pig. Vinh's mother giggled too. Then I left.

The following night, I showed up for the phone too late. An accordion grate was dragged across the entrance. But the next night, I caught the phone booth open, and Vinh before he managed to slip out of the room.

"Vinh?" I asked, halting his flight.

"Ah, Jim," he said, turning. He looked at his parents and his wife.

"You live here? I sometimes stop to use the phone."

He nodded perfunctorily, then beckoned me to a room off the main street. We sat in elaborately carved wooden chairs, inlaid with pastoral scenes in mother of pearl. On his ancestor altar were photographs of men in the North Vietnamese army. His family too had come down from the North.

Vinh poured tea and offered me a carousel of sweet snacks. I kept this visit short. I complimented his English and told him that he spoke English better than many in Hue, and it was difficult to find good conversation in Hue. Then I excused myself. I placed another phone call to Dieu's house and left.

A week later, I stopped by again, not for the phone but to query Vinh on the rumor of the $12,000 bank statement.

"I don't think you have to worry about that."

"It's just a rumor?"

He shook it off. We were sitting in the back room of his house again. Though he was dressed casually in shorts and a T-shirt, the way Vietnamese men will at home, his manner was skittish. When people entered the house for the phone, he'd stand to glance outside at the customer.

"Do you have any sense of where our papers are in Hanoi? Would it be possible to find out?"

"Maybe I can?"

I put a white envelope down on the table.

"What's that?" he asked, straightening in his chair. He looked from side to side.

"In case there is a fee? I am asking you to make some phone calls. To ask about my papers. I don't pay taxes in Hue. I don't expect people to work for free."

He shook his head. "No, no. Please take it. I don't want. This is my job."

"There must be some fee to this process."

"Some day, you come back to Vietnam, if you bring me a picture book about police in America, that's enough."

I stopped by several more times, once for the phone and once, timing my arrival, to watch some more cartoons. To ensure an invitation, I very quickly noticed the cartoon and laughed as Wiley E. Coyote went through a box of ACME explosives. Vinh had also stood for my arrival, and he preempted his parents' invitation for me to sit.

"Jim, please," he said. "Come with me." He combed his hand through his hair, and we sat again to tea. He didn't know how to begin. I'd insinuated myself into his family, not intimately but far enough. He acknowledged that. "My parents like you. I like you."

He combed his fingers through his hair again, then scratched his neck hurriedly. "You see, it's my job. You know. I am police. I follow the foreigner. But you, you come to my house. It's not good my job."

"I see," I said, nodding soberly and with resignation. "I . . . I'm worried about my papers. You work for the foreign ministry. I am looking for information. I don't know . . ."

"Your papers are fine."

"What?"

"I know. I found out. They are coming back."

"True?"

He pressed a dopey look on me, as if to say he'd know if anybody knows. "They'll be in Hue. There are some formalities, but simple. Easy for you."

"Everything is fine."

He stood and shook my hands. "Congratulations."

That Hanoi had put its imprimatur on our application for marriage was a victory of sorts, and worthy of celebration. Thuy agreed; she said she did. But through lunch at Ong Tao inside the Imperial City, she met my euphoria with chilly sobriety.

Vinh's revelation had cut the restraints I'd placed on my faraway talk. Over lunch, I tried to describe in great detail the sound that loons make on lakes in Maine at night: at first, the prehistoric, mournful notes from a lonesome bird searching for another of his kind and then, upon discovery, the hysterical cackling that intimates an exchange of hilarious episodes from their shared pasts.

She didn't nudge me with questions, eliciting more detail. All of it came at her unbidden, from the well of my own anticipation; the loons, the balsam fragrance of a grove I loved to camp in, the trickle of a creek I'd tried to record once so I could hear it when I wasn't there. My enthusiasms were rampant. She rarely talked about what would happen to us.

After lunch, we pedaled to a place near her aunt's house, a cemetery that she'd visited as a girl and that she'd remembered recently. A place I'd like, she said. An abandoned Catholic cemetery. We parked near the chained, gated entrance and paid a kid to watch the bikes. Trash, like worthless flotsam, lay banked along the cement-plastered stone wall. Several kids hopped over the wall after us, fledgling tour guides, gnawing on long sticks of raw sugarcane. A long school building with broken terra-cotta roof tiles abutted one side of the cemetery. Clamoring children's voices issued from windows that looked like gun slits.

The cemetery was French, the tombs above ground but nearly subsumed by vegetation: once cultivated grasses gone wild and coarse from neglect, suffocating ivies and ground covers; the broad, lush leaves of ferns that had rooted inside the cracked-open tops of several crypts. Stone crosses persevered above the tangled growth and pillars, shorn deliberately at forty-five-degree angles. At the back of the graveyard, a series of mausoleums with oval entrances had lost their doors.

Our tour guides, gauging my cursory interest in one tomb over another, hugged great clumps of vegetation away from the inscriptions, revealing the names of Hue's former colons: one Victor Joseph Urdy, who'd served the colonial administration as surveyor of public works and had died January 18, 1918.

The resident superior of Annam had been buried here in 1941; an inspector with the resident superior's military bureau in 1908; a president of the chamber of commerce and agriculture died young at age thirty-two in 1916. They were dead, and their resting place too had achieved a kind of death.

"I'm so scared this place," Thuy said.

"Ghosts," I said.

"Not the ghost," she said and moved on to stare inside the mausoleum of Jeanne Derobert, who'd died at the age of twenty-nine in 1925. On the tiled floor of her tomb was a dead rat. I wondered what that rat might mean for Jeanne's descendants, if she had any.

"These people, they died so far from home, in some place nobody thinks about them," Thuy said.

"I never think about dying," I said.

"Sometimes I do."

A clump of human feces lay atop the tomb of M. F. Graffeuil, the resident superior, though I didn't think that kind of bitterness still lingered in Hue, not for the French.

"When I'm too old, I will say good-bye to you," Thuy said. "We'll come back to Hue together, two old people, and maybe we'll have a small holiday here and visit all our old places. Then, unless you want to stay in Hue, we'll go to the train station, and we'll say good-bye, like we said good-bye last time you went back to America. I will stay here and die and be buried, and you can go back to America."

Before I'd left Vietnam the first time, she'd told me she dreamed that I'd stay in Vietnam forever. We'd talked about that, about the

impracticality of that from both a financial and a political stand-
point: I couldn't work in the country, nor would the Vietnamese
make allowance for any other circumstance. Moreover, I didn't
want to stay in Vietnam forever. But the same was true for her,
and I hadn't ever thought about that before. She didn't want to
stay in America forever. While Vinh's revelation stimulated my anticipation, Thuy had heard the resounding toll of a bell that would
ring over her departure.

We peeked in each of the forgotten mausoleums. The last belonged to Marie Cosserat (1885–1951), whose husband, presumably, was Henri J. Cosserat (1870–1937). Marie wasn't like most of
the other colons buried behind Phu Cam. Beneath her name was
this: *Nee* DANG THI SIM.

"What does that mean?" Thuy asked. *"Nee."*

I didn't have the heart to tell her.

We'd decided to wait on approval from Hanoi before setting a date
for our engagement party, but after we had it, after confirmation
had come from Vinh, the date hung out there, as illusory as ever.
Several times I'd revved the engines of our process by recounting
my trips to Vinh's. I concluded the same way every time, mentioning that we now had the approval we were looking for. But Thuy
held onto the brakes.

"Should we be talking about something?" I asked one night.

She looked at me as if she hadn't understood, but I detected a
kind of percolation in her face, the pupils focusing on some invisible
kernel between us, her lips tightening on a silent resolve I knew
was weakening. The courtyard flooded suddenly with motorbike
headlight, and when the engine quit, a voice sang out *Thuy oi Thuy.*

Moments later, a pair of young women crashed through the
doorway together, loosely embraced. The trailing wind strips were

still sliding off their shoulders when they caught sight of us and froze. The girlish merriment vanished. One of the women bowed her head sullenly while the other drank me in.

"*Giao vien tieng anh cua Xuan Minh,*" Thuy said hurriedly to her friends.

"I can't believe you're still saying that," I said.

"I don't want the gossip."

"But they know I'm not Minh's tutor. How long have I been here? They know."

The curious friend was having none of Thuy's deflection. I felt her scouring glance lifting details off of me—blue-green eyes, lightly freckled—stuff to communicate around later. She only got so far before Thuy rose and ushered them back onto the verandah.

Minh reclaimed a Streamline English book from the shelf and asked me to please finish the last dialogue skit we'd been working on together, about a detective's interrogation of a man whose alibis were never consistent.

Outside, an inconstant yellow bulb lit a huddle in full swing on the verandah. Thuy led the conference, talking in a rapid whisper that sometimes flared. Her forefinger jabbed the air like a righteous speechmaker's. The curious friend occasionally glanced toward the doorway.

"Too curious," Minh said. I glanced back at her, about to agree that the one friend was too curious, when I realized she was referring to me.

"My sister is a troublemaker," Minh said.

I snatched one more glimpse out the window as the trio walked, arm in arm, toward the motorbike. When they were gone, Thuy returned, poured out some tea, and asked what I thought of her friend's cheekbones.

"The one with acne?"

"The other," Thuy said.

"I didn't notice."

"They're high," Thuy said, "and tomorrow someone is going to tell her boyfriend they are too high."

"Who will?"

"The fortune-teller," Thuy said. "Her boyfriend wants her to visit some woman, he calls her a friend. In fact, not a friend. In fact, she's the fortune-teller. My mother, she has visited that fortune-teller, and that fortune-teller will tell him his girlfriend's cheek-bones, they are too high."

Minh was already laughing and gesturing at Thuy. "Like my sister's."

"Many people believe high cheekbones on the woman means that that woman will rule her husband. My friend knows this." Thuy looked out the window, anger narrowing her eyes. "I told her already. I told her she must refuse. She should say good-bye to him because he asks her to visit that fortune-teller."

Minh was still laughing. "A trouble center."

"Do many boyfriends ask girlfriends to visit fortune-tellers?" I asked. The vigor of her speech and Minh's remark about Thuy's cheekbones led me to wonder whether she'd been put to the same test in the past.

"Some do," Thuy said. "The ones not worth."

"Well, I'll cancel the appointment I set up for you," I said, but it landed flatly. I swerved the subject back to our pending date. "That's what all this has been about, right?"

She shook her head.

"You should talk about it," I said. "Better to let it out."

She shook her head urgently, like a child. "Waiting."

One evening, Thuy emerged from the back of her house, face wet with tears, an uncharacteristic defiance in her voice. "If I was married before, does it matter to you?" she asked. Hands on her hips, she wanted an answer.

I put down the history of St. Petersburg. Its pungent, moldy pages overwhelmed the room. A preternatural silence filled my ears, and for a split second I felt a weird, disorienting fear of heights, as if someone had just opened a plane's door on me. The door shut quickly, but not before I heard the discomfiting echo of Thuy's remark at the hospital, about how things from the past could haunt the present and change everything.

"What are you telling me?" Of course she'd been married before, I thought suddenly.

She glanced sideways at the altar, then started unraveling the braid in her hair. "It matters to my mother."

Mrs. Bang appeared in the doorway beyond, speaking softly, almost in consolation. I couldn't catch her first flurry of words, but as Thuy bowed her head and teased her hair out into its fullness, she said, *"It's too late, Keep your hair braided."*

"Ma!" Thuy said. She crossed her arms and walked straight out the door into the courtyard, as if along a plank. I rose to follow her, but Mrs. Bang waved me back into my seat, nodding, then spoke to me at great length, in Vietnamese. She always presumed greater fluency than I had. When it occurred to her now that she'd lost me, she sat back in her seat and laughed. "No V.C.," she said. "No V.C."

Thuy was gone, plunged out of the front yard into the deep darkness of another power outage. I knew there would always be things I wouldn't know about her. Part of it was a consequence of her own discretion; she didn't feel a responsibility to kick back open the doors behind her thresholds. Part of it too was the reference points of her youth. She couldn't reference episodes of the Brady Bunch. Johnny Appleseed wasn't buried in her memory. She could

not resurrect ancient melodies skreeled by tin whistles. Her store-
house was built from different bricks. I didn't know them. And I
wouldn't.

At CENLET, I didn't need a lesson plan. I only had to show up
and start talking about anything: cemeteries, ghosts that inhabited
the bowers of trees, divorce rates, the height of a girl's cheekbones
and what that meant. The students listened attentively and followed
me down any road, content simply to practice comprehension and
speaking.

The classes, though free-form, were exhausting, and I welcomed
the break that came midway through our two-hour sessions. One
evening, a fellow teacher was complaining about a French delegation that had recently toured the neighboring Quoc Hoc High
School. The delegates were prepared to recommend funding ren-
ovations to the storied old lycée but only if the school's administrators swapped French for English as the school's principal foreign
language. He asked what I thought of that, and I fell out of my
chair. Three teachers leapt to their feet, and I scrambled to my
own, laughing, shocked to mindfulness by the cool floor tiles.

"You're sick," one of the teachers remarked, gripping my wrist.

"Another fever," I said, rising.

The fever was coming on in familiar fashion—the lighthead-
edness and the giddiness that always came with that—but faster.
I'd tried to ignore it. I'd thought my unsteadiness before the blackboard was lethargy, or boredom, but something else was brewing.
That morning, I'd had to scrape chunks of crust out of my eye
sockets before I could open them.

"Maybe I can't finish my class," I said.

"Yes, yes. Perhaps it's better if you go to the hospital."

"I will."

"I'll go with you."

"That's okay." I laughed. "I'll be fine."

Too dizzy to ride, I walked my bike down Le Loi Street. I couldn't quite manage a straight line. As I passed a sidewalk café, two men rose joyfully from their seats and begged me to join them for some Huda. I frowned them off and quickened my pace, but the brief spurt exhausted me. I stopped and pressed a hand to my forehead but quickly removed it, alarmed by the heat. *Part of that is exertion*, I thought.

At the Morin, I ordered a bucket of ice from the hotel staff, then went to my room and dialed up the ceiling fan's speed. From an oblong Tupperware box of first-aid supplies, I tore open a disposable thermometer and sat by the window. In the street below, a boy was beating two sticks rhythmically as he walked down the road, heralding a soup cart that followed, pushed by an older woman, presumably his mother. My thermometer read 101° Fahrenheit.

When my ice came, I tuned my shortwave to faint ballroom music and applied a series of ice packs to my forehead and cheeks, my arms and chest. I'd broken fevers with ice before; I could do it again. This time, my thermometer registered 103°. But they'd been stowed away in that Tupperware for months. I checked the ripped-open package for an expiration date. Surely, they had been degraded by the humidity, because I hadn't stored them in a cool, dry place. The expiration date was fine, and now my adrenaline began to run, as if in step with the march of my temperature.

I beckoned the hotel staff for another bucket of ice, a large one this time, and went back to the Tupperware and looked at the arsenal of supplies my mother laid in. Her handiwork was still in evidence: all the single-use packages of antibiotic cream bound by elastics here, the gauze squares there, packages of 500-milligram pills for respiratory infections, acetaminophen—"for fever," I remembered her telling me, then took four.

After another series of ice packs, I tore open another thermometer. I waited a few beats. "Okay, let's go," I said softly, then placed it in. The soup boy came back with his mother, and I opened my eyes on my Tupperware and the malaria pills I'd stopped taking after I'd arrived. I'd taken them faithfully during my bike trip, but the side effects were a nuisance, and I quit taking them months ago. Thuy wasn't taking them. Why should I?

While my fever heated the thermometer, I examined the flights of mosquitoes in my room. Malaria was carried by the long-legged variety, and all of them in my room seemed to be hung with dangling legs. Fearful that my traipsing after mosquitoes might have distorted the reading, I discarded my thermometer, then ripped open a new one. I was hearing merry-go-round music out of my shortwave now, the pipes of a band organ, bells, cymbals, and snare drums, all sounding faintly martial but off-kilter too. The cymbals weren't crashing when I expected them to, and the snare drum seemed to be keeping time to another melody. I couldn't read the thermometer in the dim light shed from the far wall and so, pathetically, I crawled back to the chair by the window and looked at how many of the tiny red dots I'd heated. I kept my fingers over the upper reach of the scale and moved my thumb up over the ladder of dots, one at a time, past 101, 102, 103, 104, and 105, every one of them burning like embers, no cool blue dots in sight, no hope.

I was on my knees by the chair, and when I looked over at the door I'd left open, it was filled with hotel people. The next thing I knew I was in bed, surrounded by them and urgent whisperings. I felt captured and bound, the big bass drum of the merry-go-round pounding from the corner of the room and my tinny little shortwave. They looked at me with curdled expressions, the sides of their mouths tugged down, the brows furrowed as if in the presence of something too horrible for words.

"Mr. Jim, much better you go to the hospital," the night manager said.

Of course he was right. But in my delirium, I believed a trip to the hospital would be a fateful move. If I went, I would show the hand of fear to whatever bugs had crawled inside me and, I rationalized, empower them. Going to the hospital would elevate the disease from simple fever to something serious. I was sure I'd never make it out. Or they'd evacuate me or deport me. I couldn't do this now. The green lights were coming on for us, at Hang's office, in Hanoi. I'd dispatched my letter. Reinforcement money was on the way. I had a horrible sudden vision of the colonial cemetery.

"No, I'm tired. I have to sleep," I said. I mustered the energy to prop myself on my elbows and laughed, if only to give them reassurance that they wouldn't find a corpse in room 34 the following morning. "I'll be fine, please."

When the hotel staff left, I collapsed off my elbows into sleep, forgetting entirely about the mosquito net. The mosquitoes devoured me. I felt them all night but believed they were characters in a dream, a dream made understandable by my neglect of the malaria pills.

In the morning, I groaned at a series of knocks on my door, and twice someone came in to look at me. The third time someone came in, it was Thuy.

"Troi oi!" she said.

My head was pressed uncomfortably against the footboard, and I'd curled up sideways against it, as if to escape the mosquitoes. I hadn't been able to. My face was a mess of tiny welts, as were my feet and arms, like chicken pox. The shortwave had peeled away to static sometime in the night.

She shut off the radio and turned down the fan. I felt her hand lift my head, then cradle it and adjust the angle. At my feet, she pulled out my legs, and then, by degrees, stretched me out.

"We have to go to the hospital," she said.

"Not now."

She left the room for some time. When she returned, I heard the water running in the bathroom, and then felt the cool application of a towel mopping up my sweat. She laid on ice packs.

"I talked to a doctor," she said softly. "I told him about you, and he said it's okay for you to rest now. But when you are done resting, you have to go to the hospital."

I slept deeply but emerged several times, as far as a doze, while Thuy took care of the sweat.

"Did you get married before?" I asked her once.

She laughed lightly. "Never."

"I'm thinking about that cemetery."

"Why? No."

"I have to sleep."

"Sleep."

She left again, but when she returned I couldn't eat the stew she'd brought back.

She wiped me down again. "Okay, let's go."

She drove to the hospital and led me to the same waiting room we'd become acquainted with during our physical examinations. We took seats on a long, crowded wooden bench, and I looked longingly at the people who had spots on the floor.

"I'm so tired," I said.

"Wait," Thuy said.

She went outside. In a few minutes, she returned with a straw mat, trimmed around the edge with a thin strip of red cloth. She found space for me on the floor, then rolled out the mat, all the while scrutinized by the other sick and their attendant family members. Several people asked her if I had SIDA. She wouldn't answer them.

"I haven't been taking malaria pills," I told her as I made my way to the mat. "Tell them."

"There's no malaria here," she said.

"All the mosquitoes in my room last night had long legs."

"Shhhh."

I laid down and inhaled the fresh straw of the mat and slept. When she roused me later, I felt capable of standing. Thuy placed a hand under my shoulder, and I asked her to let me try. I wanted one small victory, and I managed it. But on my feet, I felt a tremendous fear of heights and incapable of steps.

"Wow," I said.

"Wow," Thuy said. Because I'd frequently punctuated my speech with this, she had begun to do the same, partly in emulation and partly for the fun of adopting a new exclamation. "Don't worry about anything. I think, sometimes, you worry too much. You think too hard. Everything is okay."

I shuffled down the corridor alongside her, following a nurse who stopped occasionally and looked back at us with impatience. I looked at the floor tiles. At the base of the walls, there were stubbed-out cigarettes. Once, on that long walk, I heard someone shriek, a horrible end-of-the-world cry that no one tried to contain, or soothe.

"Don't worry," Thuy said. "Don't think about that cemetery. Don't think too much."

I nodded. I had no idea what had gripped me. I knew that I

was bad off, not in pain, but slammed by my something serious. Its consequences didn't plague me, not the way possible consequences will when you're in fine health and fear the ramifications of blood in your stool or lesions on your chest. The plague consumed fear of itself.

In a large cafeteria-style room, we approached two seated doctors who watched us come across the room. I sat, and Thuy described my symptoms to one doctor while the other looked back and forth between us, trying to fathom, no doubt, the nature of our relationship. As she wrapped up, the one doctor peered into my ears with a small flashlight that might have belonged to an auto mechanic. Then he sat back down and consulted with his colleague.

Thuy was sitting beside me, one hand in mine, the other resting on her thigh. Her free hand snapped rigidly and bounced upward several inches before she caught the gesture. "Forgot," she said. "I didn't bring anything."

"What?"

"You should give them something," she advised me quietly.

"I will."

"It's better you do so now."

Then I remembered a story Thuy had told of her sister Vui's most recent pregnancy. While in labor, roaming around the delivery room as she went through dilation, she'd taken refuge in one chair and propped her feet on another. But Vui had made a mistake. Her baby was coming early, and her husband had not yet visited the home of her doctor, ostensibly to consult with him about the baby's arrival and, more to the point, to supplement the doctor's salary. Because Vui had not taken care of the doctor, the doctors had not taken care of the nurses. While Vui was in the throes of labor, one nurse yanked the chair from beneath her feet.

One of my doctors lit a cigarette.

"Do they want to know my symptoms?" I asked Thuy.

Thuy asked them in Vietnamese. They listened and then looked away.

"They're waiting for something, I think. I didn't bring money. I forgot, you know. I made the soup. I hurried back to the hotel and I forgot to bring money."

I took the wad of Vietnamese dong notes from my pocket and not so subtly peeled off the equivalent of five dollars—the equivalent of a week's pay for the average Vietnamese.

"We don't have an envelope," Thuy said, looking around the room.

"We have to hide it? They're sitting there, waiting for it, and now we have to pretend."

She took the money from me and nodded at one of the doctors. A third doctor came into the room. He consulted with his colleagues and then diagnosed my illness as amoebic dysentery. He prescribed ampicillin and Tylenol.

On the way back to the hotel, Thuy drove past the Medecins Sans Frontieres station. The doctor's van was gone—as it had been when she visited earlier—but she stopped now and asked the housekeeper where they were. The Ashau Valley, on an inoculation tour. She asked when they'd be back. A week, she was told.

That week I laid in my hotel bed, drenching my sheets with sweat. I dreamed persistently of my boyhood, small vivid vignettes of the schoolyard cove where Kid Costa and I played stickball and dwelled on scenes from *The Lord of the Rings*. The drainage pipe we climbed to roam the school building's roof, as Gandalf and Aragorn, never Bilbo or Frodo, the slate-tile pitches of the Old Wing and the mastic/pebble surface of the New Wing. I remembered the fender of the car I was sitting on when Rachel Squires's older brother told us that Nixon had resigned. Things I hadn't remembered in years, made buoyant by illness. I walked my paper route, house by house, seeing the Astro Turf covering Lucky Luccini's porch and the peephole in Mrs. Johnson's door that darkened whenever I called collecting. I sat on curbstones, bored, waiting for time to pass, poking through the refuge in the gutters; popsicle sticks, bottle caps, and crumbles of street tar. I came out of a doze one afternoon, craving SpaghettiOs, and went back to sleep heating them in a Revereware pot whose copper bottom my mother could never quite scour back to the kind of gleam that would let her hang it for display. I had a few hours of lucidity every day, and now I had begun to fret, wondering whether I hadn't tapped the reservoir of remembrance that flowed before your eyes at the end.

I rarely left the hotel and couldn't eat more than a spoonful of the porridge Thuy brought each day. I drank water and wished for more direction about dysentery. I had taken the doctors at their word, grateful that it was not malaria. Diarrhea was consistent with dysentery, but it seemed to me that diarrhea was probably consistent with any tropical disease. There had been an outbreak of cholera in Hue that year. Yellow fever lurked in these shadows.

After a week, I awoke one morning with my eyes caught in a web of yellowed capillaries and my skin the color of draft beer. That was also the day that the doctors had returned from the Ashau.

After a description of my symptoms and a checkup, Dr. Damien said, "I am afraid. I am sure." Two sentences, like that.

He looked at me the way the Vietnamese had, and it suddenly occurred to me that I was about to hear one of those dreaded revelations in a doctor's office.

"So it's not dysentery?" I said.

"No."

"Malaria?"

"No." His one-word answers frustrated me. Suddenly, I felt a surge of venom for him, for his cagey bedside manner, and all of the French too, as if his hesitancy was indicative of the whole ethnic group.

"Cancer then?" I asked, only half in jest.

"No, it's viral hepatitis. It's clear. You have jaundice. Anorexia. Fatigue. Nausea. The question is, is it A, B, or C. I think A. But we'll have to check your blood to be sure."

Dr. Damien drew my blood. In a week, he said, we'd know for sure. In the meantime, I had to remain calm. It was the only real treatment for hepatitis, wherever it was in the alphabet.

"You mean, get a lot of sleep and stay away from noise."

"Yes, but keep your body calm. Your body is fighting a terrible battle, and what you can do to help is keep the playing field level."

On day seventeen, my appetite quietly called for more than the couple of spoonfuls that had been satisfying it. I ate a whole bowl. That sufficed for the day, but I could feel the lower rung of a ladder in my grip and knew I was going to be able to climb out.

In the meantime, the anorexia had taken its toll. My head looked gawky on my slimmer neck, and my wrists were loose inside my fingers when I encircled them, which was often. In my face, the definition of my bone structure was horribly evident, as if the tide had gone out and here's what the bottom of the bay floor looks like. I found new hollows beneath my razor.

I had to return to the hospital for a second round of blood work, and when I weighed in, I found that my weight had fallen into the one-thirties. Absurdly, during each trip to the blood lab, I'd hoped that the technician would be able to read the letter of my hepatitis from a simple glance at my blood. In America, they could never tell you such things, the techs who conducted X-rays and sono-grams, for example, but this was Vietnam.

"How does it look?" I asked anyway.

"*Do qua!*" Very red.

In the end, the hepatitis was A. "Garden variety," said Damien.

Nguyet lived with her mother-in-law and her husband's sister's family in an old French house on Chi Lang Street. From the wide vestibule, her sister-in-law rented paperbacks out of glass cases. I found Nguyet out back, in an open-air courtyard bordered by the high ochre walls of neighboring four-story apartments.

"Yes, there's a problem. But not the way you think," Nguyet said. She uncapped a bottle of soda water for us to share. "Thuy was married, not in any way that matters to you, but to my mother."

"How can it not matter?"

"There are no papers on this marriage. It's a marriage that happened in the other world."

In another world, the Permanent World, Thuy had been kidnapped by two rogues in the marketplace. If not for the intercession of an old prince, who took pity on Thuy's plight, she would have been hauled through bondage as a harlot. Instead, the prince rescued her. She, in gratitude, offered him her hand, despite their difference in age.

"How different?"

"Old. He's old. Ninety-one."

"Not ninety or ninety-two?"

"No, he's ninety-one."

And not so old that he couldn't have children. They had two together, a boy and a girl. For Thuy to abandon them was heresy.

This story had been divined out of an old book of Chinese characters, from a fortune-teller, but its provenance made it no less real to Thuy's mother, for whom those rogues were as perilous and compelling as the mandates of purgatory. For her, it was a real place to be reckoned with. How many times had I seen her and Thuy's father conduct ceremonies for the departed souls of ancestors and for their son, Uy, who'd died in a truck accident, and their miscarried children. Who was I to dismiss their faith as the stuff of superstition? Their oblations were not all smoke; they held substance. They mattered. They mattered to me.

Mrs. Bang had only recently begun to visit this new fortune-teller. She had given up on a previous intermediary when some of his divinings turned out to be false. I should have thought the other fortune-teller's failures might have put the lie to the whole costly enterprise of divining.

"No, my mother, she thinks it's because that fortune-teller is not good," Nguyet said.

Nguyet was a schoolteacher. Her husband, Dung, had a doctorate in physics and taught at the university in Hanoi. As we sat drinking soda water, her two young sons were reading children's science periodicals and, through their mother, asked questions about the glaciers that had covered my part of the world: Did I know the coastline near my home was still rising back up now that the glaciers had gone? I had not.

Nguyet allowed that Thuy had a problem, though there was a solution. Thuy could nullify her other family through a series of rites and oblations offered at sites around Hue. The separation would consume an entire day. It would cost more than $100, but Thuy was loathe to submit.

"You know, my young sister, she keeps her own idea very much. Maybe too much," Nguyet said. She held my eyes a moment, then tilted her head without breaking the gaze. "That's true."

True, but not intractably so. After the days cleared and the worst of my hepatitis had ebbed, Thuy relented. She would follow the fortune-teller's path through Hue, to various temples and other intersections between this world and the other. I wanted to join her, to witness her release from this covenant, but her mother objected. My presence would be too brazen, too spiteful. It was something they would have to do alone and with contrition.

On the appointed day, Thuy, her mother, and father burned effigies of three girls at a temple on the Perfume River. One girl for the prince, who was losing a wife, and a girl each for the two rogues, who might otherwise seize the opportunity to capture her again.

Her children too needed ministering. She burned sham gold and fruits for her son and daughter at the temple, and then again in a sampan they had rented and taken into the swiftest current of the Perfume River. There, she burned yet another effigy of herself, that this image might nurture her otherworld offspring. When she let the burning effigy from the stern of the sampan, the current took it. Remarkably, Thuy said, the paper effigy remained upright for several minutes.

"It didn't fall flat in the current?" I asked.

"No," she said, amazed. "I saw it. I watched. It's true."

I gained weight gradually, every pound a milestone on the way to recovery. Still, I had to persuade the tailor who was cutting the suit for my engagement to make allowances for fifteen more pounds on my frame. He asked Thuy a question, seemingly good-natured except for the one word that rang out, *SIDA*.

"I had hepatitis," I told him, patting my lower stomach after converting his centimeter measurement of my neck into fifteen skinny inches. *"In a month, I'll be fatter."*

Thuy interjected fluently, explaining that I wasn't always this thin. The tailor heard her out. He smiled obligingly but made no revisions. He was a tailor, and in more ways than one he had the true measure of people. He knew their dreams and desires. He knew that people inevitably missed the mark, that you should bank on their frustration, not their achievements. The suit was tight.

I had shoes made for nine dollars and Thuy was fitted for a new *ao dai* made of shimmery pink silk. We shopped for jewelry, composites of gold and silver, a ring of imitation ruby, pendant earrings, and a jade Buddha. I stopped making budgets. With the advent of the ceremonies, it would be freefall until my uncle's parachute blossomed overhead.

I'd never questioned Tom's beneficence. An aunt and uncle who'd fallen on hard times had asked Tom for three times what I was asking, and he gave it without reservation. Still, it had been weeks since I'd made my request, and the sound of his silence was starting to ring in my ears. I was checking at the post office twice a day, and more frequently now my mail was coming in plastic pouches, mangled, pages missing.

The rains went on, wilting the paperbacks in my room and rooting fungus on my shoe leather and nylon windbreaker. It weighed on me like melancholy, relentlessly, day after day, as steady as a march and subtly insidious. The rain swelled the Perfume River as well as its tributary canals and the moat that ran around the Citadel, every day more tumescent and perilous. In several shallow places, water lapped the edges of my route to Thuy's house and where the road dipped, raced across in a thin, threatening sheet of flood.

Thuy's family was vigilant, bracing for a surge in the rain and the insidious creep of water, up from the pond out back, in from the street out front, welling up the several inches of slab, and generally throughout the house. The seasonal floods happened more often than not, and no frenzy of sandbagging, no pumps, could staunch them.

Inside the house, the water never rose more than a couple of feet, and each year's level scarred the wall in a way that paint could never hide. In Tay Loc, all over Hue, families stayed home through the worst of it; abandoned homes invited looters. In the past, Thuy had fished successfully from the rafters of her home, dangling her hook over the living-room floor. As the waters receded, no matter the time, the family descended from the rafters and worked a fleet of mops over the floors, sweeping out the heavy accumulations of silt with the last couple inches of water.

That year, the sun hammered through the cemented layer of monsoon cloud cover in the nick of time, several times, and the flood held off. The fortune-teller set a date for our engagement party. Several days before, Thuy made an appointment with a video photographer recommended by a married friend.

The obtrusive presence of a shouldered camera and the requests to stand over here and stand over there bothered me. I didn't want the video. Thuy knew this.

"But what about your mother?" she asked. At the very least, she said, I owed my mother a video since she wouldn't be present for the event itself.

Our photographer was a tall man with a legitimate mustache. He wore Levi's that looked genuine and a rancher's long-sleeve shirt with silver tabs on the pocket flaps. A mesh photographer's vest was hung over a chair back, and one of his eyes squinted when he inhaled his cigarette.

In an entertainment console, he pointed out the small, orange Sony bubble decals at the bottom corner of his television screen and on each of his components. *"They're all genuine,"* he said. He let us chew on that fact a moment, squinting at us and exhaling two streams of cigarette smoke out either nostril. *"Some photographers will tell you they're working Sony, but some lie."*

He slid an example of his work into one of several decks and sat back on a vinyl sofa still shrink-wrapped in plastic. A pan-flute rendition of the music from *Love Story* provided the opening soundtrack as the component parts of the Chinese character for togetherness assembled on screen. The symbol danced back on screen toward a glorious cartoon sunset while a passenger jet accelerated down a runway in the foreground. Lifting off, an inset bubble opened in the middle of the fuselage. The image stilled and in the bubble was a shot of the bride and groom, wearing traditional wedding garb. The bubble-shot in the fuselage, and the bubble-shot in the ballon of a wineglass, which followed, were fixtures of the nuptial record. It was classic kitsch, but to the Vietnamese, it was simply classic.

The Vietnamese cherished trite poems about the sun and the moon, and if the moon could have been a huge disco ball, spraying purple and rose swatches of light, so much the better. They hung framed portraits of giggling kittens in their finest restaurants. In Saigon, they'd rung the staid Roman clock face of Saigon's Hotel de Ville with red blinking lights.

Now, on-screen, the video flashed an unbelievable, sampled image. "Did you see that?" I asked Thuy.

"I did."

The photographer told us to wait, then slid to the front of his seat in anticipation. He was, Thuy had said, the best video photographer in Hue. He was an expert splicer. He had stock footage no one else had. And then there it was again, foreshadowed previously in a fraction of a second, whetting our eyes, but played to fulfillment here: Minnie and Mickey Mouse, standing before

Disneyland's Enchanted Castle, waving and waving in welcome, then grasping hands and running toward the castle.

Most of the on-screen action was set to Vietnamese and English pop tunes, more English than usual on this video because the groom, in this case, was American. We heard "Kiss Me, Honey, Honey, Kiss Me," "Say You Will," "Fernando's Hideaway," and a cheerful rap song called "Oriental Boy": "I've seen the East, I've seen the West/Now I know which I like best."

As an eight-foot string of firecrackers writhed in explosion, the speed of the video throttled back to slow motion, indulging our enjoyment.

The American groom was the photographer's brother-in-law. I'd heard about this man, a sheriff from California who had met a girl working as a postal clerk in the Huong Giang Hotel. During the close-up of the couple's kowtow at the family altar, their age difference was obvious. He looked like her father.

"How old is he?" Thuy asked.

"Thirty-two. And my sister is twenty-six."

Later, the groom read a prepared statement. He looked shell-shocked, like a prisoner of war, reading propaganda. He wore a mandarin's cap and the ornate blue soutane of an *ao dai.*

"How remarkable," the sheriff recited, "to find myself here in Hue, in my forty-second year and to find the love of my life in a twenty-one-year-old girl who sold me stamps one morning."

CHAPTER FIFTEEN

O N THE MORNING of our engagement ceremony, a detachment of police from the local bureau followed our baker and her tiered cake into the courtyard and asked Thuy's mother, who'd been standing on the porch, whether she had a permit to hold such a celebration.

I was sitting in the side room, watching two sisters and a hired beautician preen over Thuy, setting the hair, applying makeup, each other's hands darting in and out to execute the next brush stroke with such finesse that I had to wonder whether this was practiced, if not choreographed. While the beautician went about her business impassively, Oanh and Vui looked slightly anguished. Through it all, Thuy kept her eyes closed and the muscles in her face completely at ease, at odds with all my expectations of how brides (although in this case she was merely becoming a fiancée) were supposed to behave. I had chalked up my own calmness that morning to my unfamiliarity with the props of this ceremony; the bulbous Chinese lanterns, the wheels of firecrackers, the bowls of traditional areca and betel offerings. They weren't the totems for me they were to Thuy, but she, sitting here through makeup, had entered her own trancelike state. If I could hardly believe this was happening to me, then maybe every time she opened her eyes and looked at the prop of her soon-to-be fiancé, perhaps she could hardly believe it was happening to her.

As the harsh, northern voices sounded in the courtyard out front, her eyes snapped open and fastened on me. Her three attendants quit their ministrations, literally freezing for a moment as the resonance of those words in the courtyard played through them. I couldn't understand the particulars of the policemen's lengthy address, but its substance was clear. A moment later, Vui's two-year-old daughter entered the sideroom with a gob of cake frosting on her fingers and threw it onto my pants leg.

"They want to know why my mother didn't apply for a permit to hold this party," Thuy whispered to me.

I nodded.

"My mother is telling them this is not a wedding, only an engagement. No one ever applies for a permit to have an engagement."

Thuy listened to a slightly indignant voice outside, then translated: "He is saying something about a permit because you are the foreigner." She lowered her face into her palms, ruining much of the beautician's work, but no one now seemed to think that mattered much.

The calmness I'd been feeling all morning wavered. I could feel it as a mutable thing inside me now, charged by the alarums and excursions taking place in the courtyard. Two more motorbikes came into the courtyard, the odds stacking against us, and Thuy's face was now rocking in her palms. My calmness, after my momentary seizure of nerves, went back to the same level, though it was dread calm now. These were the whistles I hadn't ever really convinced myself we wouldn't hear at some point. True, I'd been run into by motorbikes. There'd been the shifty hoops of paperwork to navigate and uncomfortable moments with Dich, but none had been of much consequence. Until now.

Thuy's uncle, the man who was to officiate the ceremony, parted the wind strips and stared at me for a moment. Like Thuy's father, this man was also in his sixties, but he was not a blood relative. This was Mr. Bang's best friend. An enormous goiter stood out on his neck, and he wore a clip-on tie under a collar that would not stay down. He held his hand up, gesturing for me to stay put, then went out into the courtyard.

This Mr. Mai had been a Viet Cong hero. He'd spent much of the war on the Ho Chi Minh Trail, a fact that no one in Thuy's family held against him, just as it didn't seem to matter much to Mr. Mai that Thuy's father had spent much of the war aiming artillery shells at his comrades.

Outside, Mr. Mai greeted the policemen in turn. I could hear the friendly pitch to his voice and the shuffling movements of this older man wending a way among the motorbikes to greet each of these officials in turn. He told the police he was an old man. Since he'd been a young man—since long before any of them were born—he'd been fighting, first the Japanese, then the French, then the Americans. His friends had been incinerated on the Ho Chi Minh Trail. He didn't have much longer to live, he told them, but he hoped that he'd live long enough to see peace at last between the United States and Vietnam. One manifestation would be the lifting of that trade embargo. Another manifestation would be the union he was going to officiate that morning.

Pretending to obliviousness, Mr. Mai thanked them for coming to extend their well wishes this morning and then invited them to a beer. These policemen knew him, or of him, and his unimpeachable history, and they probably hadn't expected to encounter him at this house. After their beer, Mr. Mai ushered them out the door and as promptly ordered that two bicycles be brought to the door of Mrs. Bang's concession. Thuy's brother loaded a crate of beer on the back rack of each bike, and two brothers-in-law pedaled away into the morning.

During the ceremony, Mr. Mai was long winded, and he continued the theme he'd started when the police were in the house. He spoke of the long-troubled relationship between the United States and Vietnam. The war. The cold peace. The embargo. But he believed change was coming. Any day now, we would wake up to learn that the United States had lifted the trade embargo against Vietnam.

Thuy whispered a translation of his speech to me, but after a while, she quit. At round tables set up all over her living room, her relatives and friends did little to mask their waning interest in his speech. Guests began talking to each other. Mr. Mai was not discouraged.

"Now what's he saying?"

"He's back to the war. American soldiers and Vietnamese soldiers did not want to fight each other."

A short time later, I asked her again, but she couldn't say. Her attention had butterflied out the window to the peanut gallery of little kids who'd come to gawk through her fence. Mr. Mai went on, making his separate peace, and at the end of it, Thuy and I were engaged.

We had rain after the ceremony, a good hard rain that augured well, watering the seeds sown that day. In the morning, it was still raining, so hard that the hissing off the tarmac outside the Morin's coffee café made conversation, for long spells, impossible.

"We call this *mua nho nha*," Boi said, looking up from a biography of Chopin. "It say about the rain so heavy you miss home because you cannot go back there."

I liked that and repeated the phrase. There was a shared sentiment buried in those three words, whether your rain was Southeast Asian or Northeast American. Growing up, we'd thrilled to heavy rain, contagiously enthused by my father, for whom powerful rain was recalibrating, a reminder to celebrate the snug comforts of a home. He always wanted to be home for the big rains.

"You miss your home?" Boi asked.

"No."

If he'd asked this question after my rearrival in Hue, I could have confessed to dislocation and even panic. Drastic reactions had sold themselves to me in my weakness. I was not cut out for this. I couldn't hack the lonesomeness so far from my reference points. In fact, it was wrong to have divorced myself from that. That kind of selling. I could have been a buyer, but I hadn't.

And now Hue felt like home. In the predawn, there was the clang of the Morin's train-track rail, rousing me momentarily like the percolation of my father's coffee when I was a boy. At night, there were the rhythms of the street sweepers, coming closer and moving on, like the slow-motion Doppler lullabies of buses on their night routes. I knew where to get my hair cut. I didn't have to haggle with certain waiters; they simply charged what they charged the locals. I knew that it was better to go over the Hai Van Pass for routine monthly visa checks with the police in Danang. I could have checked with cops in Hue, but that meant checking in with Dich. I preferred the day-long round-trip to Danang, sometimes by bus, though better by train.

The train's route through the Hai Van headlands negotiated terrain as spectacular as California's Big Sur. Waterfalls burst from the vertiginous flanks. In the secluded bays below were strands of beach that had never known a sunbather's towel, and might never. Later, *National Geographic* would rank this stretch of country as one of its "places of a lifetime," in league with Paris and the Pyramids of Egypt. And I was commuting over this route, from the relative inaccessibility of Hue to the slightly less inaccessible metropolis of Danang.

My monthly visits took no more than ten minutes. I sat down with a cop. He checked my passport, checked my visa, and stamped me for another month. Every third month, I went to Bangkok for a renewal. In Danang however, this time, the ten minutes stretched to an hour, and then a cop told me to go to lunch and come back afterward. After lunch, he said I would need to process my extension in Hue. They were no longer offering this service to people who were staying in Hue.

In Hue, an entry-exit police official told me I had to leave the country. The official had a mole near the back of his jawbone and a long, uncut hair grew from it.

"Actually," I said, leaning over the desk to point out the dates on my visa. "I've got two more months on this visa."

He didn't look at my visa again. He folded it blindly and pushed it across his desk. "Tomorrow, your visa no good."

"It's good," I said, unfolding it again and checking once more. "Look."

"No good." He folded it blindly, roughly, insisting it stay that way.

I listened to the pendulum of a wall clock, a sound I hadn't remembered hearing there before, a sound that, in a spasm of paranoia, I believed they had imported to make this moment all the more dire. I looked at the other officials, their languid postures and droopy lidded contemplation of the empty spaces of the room.

"May I speak with Mr. Dich?"

"He not here."

"He's always here."

"Not today."

"Okay, your captain? May I speak with him?"

"He not here too."

I could see one of his captain's shoulders through a doorway. "He's right there."

"Not right. I'm sorry. Much better you prepare to leave my country. Tomorrow your visa, it's no good."

I couldn't stand up. The last time I'd been standing, everything had been all right. Outside, the manic voice of a radio cartoon was playing from the handcart of an ice cream vendor. Thuy was in her computer class at the Hai Ba Trung High School, familiarizing herself with MS-DOS and the role she expected this to play in her future. I could hear something unbudgeable in the official's voice, some decision that he'd likely had no control over. I played the emotional card anyway.

"I'm getting married to a woman from Hue. *A Vietnamese girl,*" I added in his language, trying to elicit sympathy I knew would not come. "We've just had our engagement party."

"I know," he said. He looked at his wristwatch. "It's not my decision."

The cop's directive had lowered a scrim between me and all my haunts as I ricocheted through Hue that afternoon, to the Hai Ba Trung School, the EC office, Vinh's, Gioang's. It was an altered place, stark as a house that's lost its furnace and whose comforts recede gradually as the temperature inside drops. As I pedaled frantically around the city it seemed that everyone knew, the guy fixing flats on the corner, the women at their pyramids of fruit, and unless my frantic reboundings through the city straightened out into a line that led from the Morin to the train station or Phu Bai Airport, I would be subject to a great commotion of cop cars and sirens.

Marian Cadogan at the EC suggested I go directly to Hanoi and appeal the decision at the foreign ministry. Vinh doubted that would work. He mentioned Andrew Sherry again, and Phillip Shenon of the *New York Times*, and George Esper of the Associated Press, and my trip to Linh Mu Pagoda after the Buddhist protests. "Some people wonder, what do you do here," Vinh said.

I didn't believe him. My troubles started the day Dich walked into Thuy's house and asked to see my visa and passport, long before I had met Shenon or got my mother's note about Esper. My bad luck had less to do with them and more to do with the consequences of falling in love with a girl who was being courted by an official who worked in the city's immigration office. That was plain.

While I waited for Thuy's class to let out, I decided that I had to go to Hanoi, not only to make my appeal at the foreign ministry but to see people at Vung Tau Intourco, who'd processed my visa. To do this, I knew, was going to cost more than I had, more than I could muster and more, I thought, than I could bear.

Several days earlier, I'd finally got a reply to my letter to Uncle Tom. The reply came in a plastic pouch, not from Tom but my mother, writing in a big round hand on sheets of five-by-eight stationery. I got only page one of a longer letter, but what she did write was more than I wanted to read anyway. She felt uncomfortable about going to Tom for money. She explained to me then her feelings about not leaning on other people for help. She was a private person. She started back into her financial troubles after she and my father divorced. The letter trailed off on a line about her pride. I crumpled it, a thing I never did to letters, and tossed it in my trash.

As my financial challenges compounded my greater political challenges, I tried to think of a way to put some positive spin on this for Thuy. She was engaged to be married too, and now the whole proposition was rife with poison. The little pep-rally cheerleader in my head kept trying to rouse me from my torpor, but I knew that when it came time to tell her what had happened, I wasn't going to be able to put a positive spin on anything.

Her class let out as the nightly Voice of Hanoi Radio propaganda began spewing from the city's speakers. Rather than pedal back to her house for dinner, I suggested that we stop at a café. I had something I wanted to tell her. She didn't press me for what, as I would have done. At the Cercle, we ordered lime juice outside and wandered up into the empty theater. We took our usual seats.

"Okay, I've waited long enough," she said. "How bad is this?"

My plan was to cast my problem as a routine bureaucratic hassle, but my failure to say anything as we cycled down Le Loi, ordered juice, and walked into the Cercle got in the way.

"My visa's run out."

She looked at her fingers, motioning two of them. "You have two more months, I know."

"No. They told me today. No more time."

"Oh no." She looked around the room, and I could see that she was scrambling for something to anchor herself to as this current swept through the Cercle. Her family could play no political cards; even the Viet Cong hero who had officiated at our engagement had played out all he had when he turned the police away. When she turned back to me, tears had welled in her eyes, and I could feel a plumb rising in my own throat.

"What do we do?" she asked.

"I don't know." The full weight of my desperation came out in my tone. "I'm going to Hanoi tomorrow. If I can't fix things there, I'm going to Bangkok."

She shook her head, then placed her hands, one palm upon the other, against my shoulder. She pressed her forehead there, and started to sob quietly.

"I can fix this, Thuy," I said.

She shook her head. "They can do what they want."

"I'm sure I can fix this."

"Jimmy," she said, rising from my shoulder. She stopped sobbing and stared at me through glistening eyes. She kept silent for a moment, as if to let me guess her mind so she wouldn't have to speak it out loud. "I have been afraid of this for so long. You don't know."

Over the next couple of days, whenever things could get worse, they did. In the morning at the Morin, a knock on my door from a hotel desk clerk was followed by the revelation that my visa—he didn't know if I knew this—had expired. Did I need help with my bags? Was I planning to leave Hue by train or by plane?

From my room, where my clothes still hung in the wardrobe and my toiletries perched on the plastic shelf beneath the mirror, I'd spent the night weighing various fantastic alternatives to capitulation. I could see the steeple of a Catholic church from my window and had briefly considered the possibility of seeking sanctuary, in the nave, the sacristy, or the rectory, I wasn't sure where. Was this still done? Was it possible, and was I a candidate, estranged as I was from the church? I decided I was not. And that I was a fool to let my thoughts stray toward the melodramatic.

But later, lying awake in bed after midnight, other reckless possibilities occurred to me: barricades, hunger strikes, evasion, and, with Thuy, escape. I conjured the cadence of the theme music from *The Great Escape* in my mind and the existential defiance of Steve McQueen's baseball, rebounding off the cooler wall in that last resonant scene of the movie. But this never worked. You couldn't forge mettle with the notes of an inspirational soundtrack running through your head. You either had it or you didn't, and because I didn't think I had it, I persuaded myself that less inflammatory action was the better course. That was the right decision, even if I arrived at it through the back door, certain in my gut that I lacked the courage to make a bold stand against the entry-exit station's order for me to leave.

I had yet to exhaust all my reasonable chances for a reprieve, and an inadvertent reprieve was more likely than deportation. Despite the facade of communism, Vietnam was still a bunch of fiefdoms. The rules they made in Hanoi didn't necessarily apply in Hue or anywhere else. The old adage about all politics being local was especially applicable in Vietnam. From Vinh, I knew that most Vietnamese bureaucracies lacked computers and thus databases. The country was still running on stamps. Everybody honored them. If I could get one in Hanoi, where they likely had no idea what Hue had decided, I'd be free of this.

In the clear light of the North, as I cycloed into Hanoi from the train station, I paid particular attention to the billboards hailing economic developments for water-treatment facilities and industrial parks. These projects had marshaled millions of foreign dollars and sobered me. I reined in the dumb options I'd let scroll out of my overactive imagination. A system that was developing this kind of faith in foreign investors would not suffer the petty politics that was trying to bounce me out of the country.

At Vung Tau Intourco the following morning, an agent in a tweed jacket who, the previous day, had assured me that my visa was fine, told me there was a problem; he could not say why. Bottom line: "Your visa, it's no good."

"Okay, let's make a new application. Start over. A tourist visa. I go to Bangkok. Pick it up there."

The clerk grimaced, and I could see there was something in this situation that even he didn't understand. "Can not," he said.

I took two fifty-dollar bills out of my pocket. "Maybe it costs more money," I said.

The clerk glanced at the money. "Not about money," he said.

"Maybe it's about more money," I said, opening my wallet again.

"Not about money or more money." He went slowly through photos of our engagement party. "Maybe your case is special."

The city, which had until then felt like an antidote to Hue's sinister parochialism, turned on me. The government didn't function by computers, but somehow the change they'd made to the roster of undesirables in Hue had also been made to this roster in Hanoi. And for what? For being friends with Sherry or for talking to Shenon? For staying so long in Hue and keeping a journal I wouldn't show them? Or because I loved a girl one of their own had loved too.

At the Sophia Hotel, the desk clerk wouldn't let me register another night, not with an expired visa. The hotel at 22 Hai Tien said no for the same reason. So did the Trang An, where Relin and I had stayed during our triumphant arrival by bicycle. None of the hotels would let me stay, and now I had a new worst-case scenario to fathom.

At the foreign ministry, a clerk told me to return the following day and nudged me toward the door, and out of his hair, with brusque, compliant nodding and a repetitive stream of *vangs*. Yes, ten o'clock would be a good time. Yes, I could speak to a ministry official. Yes, it was possible to fix my visa here. He also said he could recommend a hotel, but when I asked for specifics, he simply said *vang, vang, vang* and pointed toward the door.

Going to Sherry's villa seemed like an invitation to more trouble, but I wasn't certain how much worse it could get. For starters, Sherry wasn't home, according to a saleswoman who sold apples on the corner outside the Agence France Presse office. Was his family? No. Had they taken the car? No. Which meant they'd flown somewhere.

After lunch, Phillipe Agret, the bureau chief, returned. Though Sherry was in Saigon, reporting, Phillippe was sure Andrew wouldn't mind if I stayed in the villa.

Overnight, I repeatedly played back the story Marian had told me about a friend who'd been teaching in Vietnam when she first arrived. After his departure, and because he'd fallen in love with the place, he'd tried repeatedly to come back, submitting applications from embassies in Laos, Cambodia, Thailand, even the Vietnamese mission to the U.N. in New York. He was denied everywhere. If they want to keep you out, she told me, they can. I countered her story with Gary. Gary always found a way back in, and if he could, why couldn't I?

I went to sleep on that little bit of solace and in the morning buoyed up out of sleep into sunshine. True, Marian's story was baleful, but she had also told me that she was very impressed by the caliber of people at the foreign ministry in Hanoi.

The ministry building was on Chu Van An Street, not far from the Ho Chi Minh mausoleum, in a neighborhood of elegant eighty-year-old French municipal buildings. I had made plans to see an official, but the reception clerk, in the morning, told me she could probably help me. She told me this in Vietnamese, and I'd had to ask her to repeat herself three times before I got the gist of it.

"May I speak with someone who speaks English?" I asked.

"No one here speaks English," she said.

"This is the foreign ministry, and there isn't anyone here who speaks English," I said, reverting to English. I mustered a smile, mindful of Thuy's admonishment two days earlier. "Not like Hang's office," she'd said about my visit to the foreign ministry.

"I made an appointment yesterday," I said. *"Ten o'clock."*

She directed me to a seat, where I was sitting twenty minutes later when a Vietnamese official with a fine, leather satchel and a pocket protector stuffed with pens walked by and said, *"Bonjour."* Something about the way I said *bonjour* unmasked me, for a moment later, after consultation with the clerk, he turned to me.

"Quelle nationalité?"

"Americain."

"Bien, bien." He waved me after him. *"Suivez moi."*

In a room no larger than a spacious closet, I sat on the other side of what looked like a U.S. Army–issue desk. Ubiquitous Uncle Ho smiled down on me from the wall. I passed a parade of documents before this man: passport, visa, documents from my marriage application, pictures from our engagement ceremony, a photograph of me, Relin, and John Kerry we'd taken in Saigon before our bike trip.

The Vietnamese liked Kerry. He'd fought against them on the Mekong Delta during the war, but he was an ally against intransigent congressmen who supported the ongoing trade embargo against Vietnam today. I lied about my relationship to Kerry.

"My friend," I told the official. *"I've invited him to my wedding."*

The official offered me a cigarette and lit one for himself. He turned a floor fan out the window and began to talk in French about the trade embargo. He didn't look at me; he looked at a corner of his desk, sometimes angling his head, and craned forward with it as he made his point. He drew on his cigarette only to keep it alive, then held it pinched between his forefinger and thumb, daintily, as if holding a cup of tea.

"Parce que vous etes americain," he said. Because you are American. *"And because America does not have relations with Vietnam, perhaps it's better if Americans do not have relations with Vietnamese."*

He tore into another spiel, escalating the rhetoric, and made his case like a seething Russian in the U.N. I sat through it, listening to nothing.

"This is bullshit," I said quietly in English.

He'd been carrying on for five minutes and might have carried on ad infinitum. My remark halted him. He repeated the last word cautiously and with no appreciation of its meaning except for the context of my tone.

"You're a fool," I said, kindling the bridge before torching it. I was coming down off the high ground. I told him his country was fucked up. The sound of that word he knew.

"Communism sucks," I said in English, descending into the trashiest gutters as I stood. "You suck."

He jumped up and opened the door to his office. *"Di,"* he said.

"Assholes like you are why we should keep the embargo," I said, slowly gathering my things on his desk.

"Di."

"Gardons l'embargo," I said, passing him. And then louder, loud enough to turn heads down the corridor. *"Gardons l'embargo."*

CHAPTER SIXTEEN

Bangkok, five hundred miles from Hue as the crow flies. As far away as Boston from Cleveland, and yet a barrier between the two now, as unyielding as the Berlin Wall, as unbridgeable as places separated by a time machine. I'd dropped my visa like a roulette ball at travel agencies all over the city and then kept vigil with the vague, wild hope of someone who knows the odds are heavily against him but who also believes that by dint of perseverance all things are possible. I had only to shoulder the door from the right angle and it would pop. But everywhere the story was the same; everywhere there was confirmation of the tweed-jacketed agent's assessment in Hanoi: my case was special. And I'd made it twice as special in the foreign ministry.

"I'll have better luck in Phnom Penh. In Lao maybe," I said to one agent, rising out of the hard bucket seat of yet another Khao San Road travel agency.

"Maybe not," she said.

Usually, they just said maybe. The mantra all over Thailand was *mai pen rai*, no problem, but this agent had identified one and for whatever reason kicked the little bit of optimism I had out from under me. The next morning I retrieved it and made my rickety stand again.

For ten days, I went back and forth between the agencies and the Freddy III guest house. My room had jalousie windows with rusted cranks and brittle newspaper stuffed through rents in the screening. On the wall was a portrait of the great nineteenth-century Thai monarch Chulalongkorn, looking prestigious in Western military regalia. Freddy was a small, old woman who always had a cigarette going and who scolded me shortly after I'd moved in. The problem had to do with the three floor fans in my room. I tried telling her they were there when I arrived, I wasn't hoarding, but she'd have none of it. "One room, one fan," she'd said.

The room was cheap, five dollars per night, but after ten futile days of working the travel agencies, when I finally admitted that this problem was not a thing I could wrestle to the ground, that wanted finesse and strategy, I realized I needed a fax machine, and so made plans to move. Leaving that room for another guest house, the Freddy II, which had a fax machine, felt a little like leaving Thuy all over again. When I'd arrived at Freddy III, it had been less than thirty-six hours since I'd last seen her. The proximity of that contact was like a thing itself that I had brought into the room. It existed there; it had galvanized the arrangement of the furniture and the tilt of Chulalongkorn's portrait on the wall. I'd prayed I'd be able to leave this room and go directly back to her; instead this room was to intervene between then and however long it was going to take.

At night, I'd been imagining how days can slip to weeks, weeks to months. Me in the States. Thuy waiting in Hue. Months to years. Why not? Who was I? Who was Thuy? The cops in Hue had flagged my passport number; now, every time it showed up, an edit in their system kicked it out.

Thuy had vowed to wait. "I am waiting for you forever," she'd said when I phoned Hue after my visit to the foreign ministry. She didn't say much more. She was crying, and I was crying. We sobbed into our mouthpieces for minutes, fathoming the depths of our predicament that way. Later in Bangkok, remembering those words, they tightened on me like a tourniquet. I wished I hadn't heard them. I didn't want to be a beneficiary of that kind of love.

I found God in my foxhole and made promises. I swore off wanting things that were not intrinsically errant but tried to consider them so in the tiny deals I was trying to broker in my head. I'd quit traveling, quit my journal. Some accommodation had to be made, some sacrifice. The day before I left the Freddy III, I'd picked up a short paperback history of L.L. Bean, such an improbable find in Bangkok. A pair of the company's trademark boots, flopped leather uppers and gum-boot bottoms, were pictured on the cover. I read it twice, finding comfort in the crimped orbit Bean had made of his life in New England. Finding his story was like a message from tea leaves or chicken's feet. No more travel. No more chances. No more risk. I'd be done with that. I'd retreat and live out my life in a quaint place where nothing would ever go on the line again. Just so long as I had her with me.

At the Freddy II, I faxed several typed letters to agencies in Hanoi, seeking improbable business visas and sat in the lounge to wait on a response. At lunch, the receptionist let me know my room was ready. She was young and tall with lips so pouty I wondered whether they'd been surgically enhanced. It was a special room, she said, in the penthouse.

"Like the magazine," she went on. "You want me show you?"

I looked at her hands. They were large, and the knuckles were prominent. As she noticed me noticing, I looked and saw the faint bulge of an Adam's apple on his throat, something no amount of makeup or surgery could disguise.

"A regular room is fine," I said, giving him some *baht* as a deposit. "I'll move my things up in a bit."

When he left, a Brit spun a copy of *The Economist* he'd been reading onto a coffee table. "You know about Suppapohn?" he asked.

"I got it."

He lit a cigarette and exhaled thoughtfully, watching the ceiling fan turn overhead. His eyes were rheumy, and his hair was long and wretchedly kept, like a guy just up from the dungeon. His trousers were held up by a drawstring, and his shirt was a loose-fitting shift. But for all of that, his English was precise and smacked of a public-school education. "Bangkok," he said thoughtfully, "where men are men and sometimes the women are men too. Have you been had?"

"No."

"You've spent some time here?"

"Some."

"A bloke comes in last week, fresh from the real world, a Kiwi, young guy. It's three in the morning, and he's throwing a bleeding racket. He wakes up half the guest house when he finds ol' Suppapohn isn't what he thought she was."

The First World gears of the fax machine whirred. I went to the machine, as I had several times that morning, and found another fax that wasn't mine. The Brit meanwhile was still watching the fan.

"Going with a katooey is like getting stuck with the placebo," he said, ruminating the subject out loud. "She's never going to do you any good, and you never find out until it's too late.

Simon was a fixture in the guest house, as were several other expats, men of European heritage who sprawled over the bamboo furniture in an adjoining bar/TV lounge. They'd let themselves go, like Simon, putting even more distance between themselves and home, but for all these efforts—the displacement, the devolution of appearance—they spent a lot of time tuning in to what they'd left behind via CNN and broadcasts of European soccer. Several young Thai women, who seemed to both work at the guest house and work the *guess how*, as they called it, draped themselves over one or another of these guys. It was an incongruous spectacle, these young, meticulously madeup Thai girls, ever ready for a stroll down the catwalk, and these dissolute, chain-smoking, football-mad Europeans. They never spoke to each other. The men traded offhand commentary during the matches or engaged in spirited discussion in between, while the girls just looked smoky and jaded.

"Do they never talk to each other?" I asked Simon one day.

"It's better if they don't. Muddies up the whole effect, rather?"

At night, I could hear them at work in the small hours, the rhythmic beat of a headboard against my paper-thin wall, the hopping legs of a bedstead overhead, their groans and expulsions. There were twenty rooms in the guest house, and four were active every night. I pounded the walls and the ceiling. I appealed for silence *please*. My protests did nothing. I began to wonder whether I was capable of smashing down doors, of bludgeoning a human being. At breakfast one morning, I stopped in the doorway of the breakfast lounge.

"Tonight," I said in a volume and tone meant for everybody, "maybe you could shut the fuck up so the rest of us can get some sleep." I glared at each of the Europeans in turn, trembling with adrenaline, half-hoping one of them would stand out of his chair.

Two of the men looked up from their curry, deliberately bored. I became immediately conscious of myself as I looked to them, an uncool, wound-up American who'd just violated the sanctity of the *mai pen rai* spirit. I was the guy people laughed at in movies, the guy who couldn't hold it together. I didn't care. Fuck them. "Thank you," I said.

After I turned and started back to the second lounge, someone mimicked the low hum of a fax machine.

When I arrived in Bangkok, Beatty was out of town on a telecommunications assignment in Indonesia. After he returned and heard my story, he suggested we pull away for a weekend in the seaside resort of Pattaya. "If you think the girls in the Limelight or in King's Castle cut the mustard, wait till you see the Marine Bar," he said. After Pattaya, he flew to Phnom Penh.

Simon had ideas. I could lose my passport and apply for a new one at the American embassy. New passport, new number, new visa. Another time, he reported encouraging news from a traveler who'd obtained a visa at the embassy in Vientiane, Laos, and who managed to double the length of his stay with extra cash slipped under the table.

"And then of course, there's forgery. A new identity," he said one day, "although it's the rather costly option."

I began faxing letters to my congressional delegation and to a Boston newspaper columnist. Beatty returned from Phnom Penh for a couple of days and was surprised get a phone call from me. "You're still here?"

"I can't leave."

"You don't need an exit visa here."

"No, I mean I can't go back to Vietnam. I'm having trouble."

I'd spelled out that trouble to him the first time we'd talked, but he'd not understood that I was really stuck. Or if he had, he'd forgotten, perhaps because I was bad at asking for help, because when I'd first talked to him I'd played stoic and shrugged off just how bad it was. My friendship with Beatty had always been casual, a light-spirited friendship borne of two-dollar keg parties in college, intramural leagues, quadrangles, and study corrals. Desperation never stalked us there, and it was hard for him to believe—as it might have been hard for me to believe had the roles been reversed—that I was prone to it.

"I need help," I said.

Beatty said he'd talk to the lawyer who handled immigration affairs for the firm.

One morning, he was at the guest house when I came down to breakfast. Several of the house harlots had taken seats at his table, attracted no doubt by his dark suit and tie; one had managed to engage him in a game of connect four while he worked his way through breakfast.

"Sully," he said. "You didn't tell me Jiap was staying here? I know Jiap from when she was at the Limelight."

It was tough to tell at first glance whether Beatty was here for me or Jiap or for one of the other harlots. The nonchalance in his greeting and his casual rapport with the girls led me to believe he'd been here before.

I nodded at Jiap, who hardly acknowledged me. She knew me as the morose, bad-humored guy who paid scant attention to any of them.

"Got a fax from Relin," he said abruptly. "He's been over in Burma. Plain of Jars, I think, buying his way through the country with scotch and cigarettes. I've been meaning to get over there myself." He drifted with that thought a moment and then, prodded by Jiap, dropped another checker. "Relin's on his way to Bangkok after Burma. He thinks you're here."

"Any word from your buddy, that immigration lawyer?"

"Bad news there, eh." He held my gaze a moment in numb shock. "They're tough, those guys in Vietnam. He's had some good luck there, Reginald has, but bad luck too. One guy he knows, whose brother is a high-ranking official in the U.S. government, hasn't been able to get in for a year. But let me have your documents. Let me look at those, let's see what's what and go from there?"

I retrieved a photocopied packet of papers from my room, wondering what the hell for, crushed by Beatty's allusion to this official and feeling on the verge of hyperventilation. When I came down Beatty was trumping Jiap in another game of connect four. Jiap looked at my papers with disgust.

"Tell me again, what's wrong with the visa?" he asked.

"My name must be on some list."

"Which list?"

"I don't know, the master list."

"Were you there on a journalist's visa?"

"God, no. It was garden variety."

"Tourist?"

"Yeah."

"Why not go in on a business visa?"

"I've got no business in Vietnam, no sponsor there, no sponsor abroad."

"Go in for us. Poke around a little. Explore some opportunities."

"Right." But I'd already tried that. One fax I'd sent to Vung Tau Invescon included language to that effect. Nothing, I was convinced, would turn the gears of the fax machine for me. My passport number lit switchboards all over Vietnam.

"In the meantime," Beatty went on, dropping another red checker for a new game with Jiap, "what do you think about some golf this weekend?"

Mornings now after rush hour, I walked long distances with no more purpose than the consumption of hours. As my homecoming steps neared the Freddy II, my pulse would crank up, plateau by plateau, in switchback fashion, as I considered the possibility of a fax from Vietnam, or the States, or word from Suppapohn on yet another visa application. But as I entered my fourth week in Bangkok, I'd begun to exhaust all my reserves of optimism. I'd been successful at finding and tapping new tanks after reading newspaper headlines that alluded to an imminent resumption of relations between the United States and Vietnam, in scuttlebutt at traveler's cafés, and once, desperately, in the marketing-speak of a new Bangkok travel agency that called itself Best! Travel. A respiratory infection settled in my chest—no doubt from breathing Bangkok's noxious air—and my year-old supply of antibiotics made it worse, blowing fog into my ability to think clearly and act rationally.

On one of my walks, I followed a young woman on her bicycle for several blocks. It was the same model and color bicycle that Thuy rode, the same balloon tubing and plush bench seat, the same white wire basket affixed to the handlebars, the same black hair fanned out against a cream-colored shirt. In all of Hue and Vietnam as far as I'd seen, Thuy's bicycle was unique, a gift from her sister Oanh, who'd bought the bike from a cache of Thai imports. "I like it because it's strange," she told me once, meaning "singular." But in Thailand, they were everywhere, these bikes, navigating the alleyways off Bangkok's boulevards, parked in the gated courtyards of neat Thai homes, like cruel jokes. I began to count how many of the bikes I saw each day, and when I began to analyze the string of numbers to see if there was anything to be read from the pattern, I knew I was reaching a place I'd never been before.

One afternoon, I phoned Beatty's office and found out he was unexpectedly called away. I asked for Reginald, and she asked who he was. It was a large firm; she couldn't have possibly known every-one, but her failure to know him, and to refer me to him, was unacceptable.

"I'm not stupid," I told her. "I know he's there."

"No Reginald here."

"May I speak to your boss?"

"He not here."

I doubted that. He was in, so was Reginald, and Beatty's assis-tant was in league with the entry-exit police in Hue, with the for-eign affairs official in Hanoi, with all of the travel agents who'd returned my passport and application, with the bacteria that wouldn't quit my chest and the virus in my liver. They'd all trans-mogrified into each other. There was collusion at large. I was the only guy in the world, paranoid now and full of rage. I slammed down the phone and ordered a beer in the lounge. Why worry about nursing my liver back to health when everything else was going to hell? The expats around me were watching *The Sheltering Sky*, the scene in which Port Moresby sleeps through the pricklings of a swarm of flies that have lit upon his face. The scene irked me. I guzzled the rest of my beer, looked at a couple of the expats, then took off out of Freddy II.

That afternoon, I went indulgently from café to café, persuading myself that my weeks-long failure to relieve pressure was more wrong than consideration of my recuperating liver. Rudderlessly, I walked through parts of Bangkok I'd never visited. Off the city's main arteries, the alleys turned at right angles, baffling the incessant white noise of the buses and tuk-tuks, the motorbikes that shot through traffic like heroin. I bought one cold Kloster out of a Sty-rofoam cooler and sat under a canopy of bougainvillea, pressing the bottle against my forehead, my mouth, my cheeks before taking it down in three long pours.

It rained late that afternoon, but the reprieve was temporary; the late afternoon sun cranked the temperature back into the nineties before retiring through wounded cloud cover. The sun was setting on a day that wouldn't come to me now, the way a day won't after a long nap on a summer afternoon. I thought the beer had got in the way of knowing, and I let the uncertainty hang a moment. I was giddy with dislocation. After a couple of minutes, figuring enough was enough, name it and be done with it, I bore down on it, remembering, but the day shirked my reach. I'd lost track.

Passing through a bar district, young Thai women swiveled on their stools, shilling "Where you go?" In Vietnam, they wanted to know where you are from, but in Thailand that didn't matter. If you were a *farang* and male, you had money, and your destination was relevant. In Vietnam, they were still making sure you weren't Russian.

I played connect four with two bar girls and bought them each a cola. When I bought them each a second cola, one of the women started to massage my shoulders. Her fingers were slow and expert; she dammed arterial flows of blood, then released them in warm floods that spread halfway down my arms.

"Tonight, where you go?" she asked, lifting her chin over my shoulder.

I didn't know. I'd exhausted faith in my ability to get anywhere. Or to accomplish anything. Until I'd muffled it with the Kloster, I hadn't been able to stop the revving in my head and couldn't kick the brakes out from beneath it.

"You go with me one hour, you know everything about Thailand," the girl went on.

A *farang* across the bar nodded the neck of his bottle at me. I closed my eyes. How easy to just give in. To quit the resistance and lay down here, certain of my ability to make at least one thing happen. But as I closed my eyes, I saw Thuy standing at the train station in Hue, moments before my departure, a purple shirt with the collar upturned, the warped brim of her hat. "That day at Phu Cam cemetery?" she'd said, raising her voice over its tremors. "When I told you about the day we would say good-bye to each other this train station? You go back to America, and I stay here? This is not that day. This is not saying good-bye like that."

Her letters had begun to reach me now in Bangkok, not with stingy frequency but every other day, sometimes daily long letters to match my own, effusively written and that I tended to inhabit with an intensity that was wrought with self-pity.

I've always known I was going to leave Hue some day, she wrote. *That's my confession. That's what I never told you and what I tell now because I know it's still true, even though it seems so black now. I knew that I would leave Hue because of some weakness in me, because I can never forget how different I felt from other kids. My family had money after the war, not a lot but enough so that we shouldn't have had to go to school wearing sandals cut from black rubber tires. But because of the war, and because my mother was worried about money so much, she saved. That shame started something in me. Later, when kids made fun of me, because the teacher often called on me to speak English and because my voice was soft, it pushed me more and more until I knew—not on the top of my mind where we ask ourselves questions and give back answers, but in a deeper place—that I would leave Hue. I still know that truly, but I also know that when I leave, I'll leave with you.*

The bar girl was addressing me, "Mr. Jim . . . Mr. Jim," using the honorific with the first name as they did all over Southeast Asia.

"One hour," the bar girl whispered, her chin nuzzling into my shoulder. "Everything. No price."

I stood up and paid my tab. "I'm sorry," I said.

On the other side of another maze of alleys, I heard the skirling music of a single horn, like someone trying to charm a snake out of a jar, seeping between the hum of night traffic. The source lay on the other side of a bazaar of makeshift food stalls, blazing with light and jammed with Thai men. Electrical wires crisscrossed overhead. Beside one stall, a street bitch with drooping tits marched through the vendors leading a pack of four pups toward the horn.

"Ah, you're very lucky?" a young Thai man said, cupping my elbow in his hand. "A special night for you to see fights."

"Special?"

"Very special."

"A government promotion?" I asked. "All tickets are sold out? But you have one? You can help me?"

He wore a Michael Jordan tank top, and the bangs of his hair fell in pincers over either brow. His English, however, was excellent, studied. "I know how you think. But I have one ticket. It's for me. I don't sell it because I am going to see the fights too. Special night."

Percussions joined the horn, and soon a tumultuous chanting drowned out the music. "Chee, chee, chee . . . ahooooy." As the chant subsided, the music billowed back out and resumed its steady pace until the crowd roared again, "Ahooooy, ahoooy."

Seni said he was an English student at the university, as were most of the touts outside the Grand Palace and Bangkok's renowned Wats. The day before, one tout had spoken knowledgeably to me about Clinton, quoting him, "I still believe in a place called Hope." This student studied English only because he had to; otherwise he told me he would be majoring in Thai history.

I bought a ticket and followed him inside the arena. Tiers of benches rose away from a boxing ring where two fighters were engaged in a stylized form of prayer. They wore woven headgear shaped like tennis rackets. Their prancing ritual was a request for a blessing.

As the fight got under way, the spectators egged on the contestants. They held Thai *baht* notes twined between their splayed fingers, waging bets with other men in the crowd. Through the first two rounds, the fighters spent more time clasping than fighting, but as the music's tempo increased in the third round, the jabs and kicks began landing hard. Every time a punch or kick hit home the spectators surged, shouting *"Ahoy."*

As kids, we'd always thought that only sissies kicked during a fight. Here, all over Asia, the kick was integral. But some kicking was better than others. And it turned out that Seni was right. It was a special night. After several bouts between *muay Thai* fighters, a Japanese black belt climbed into the ring against a Thai kickboxer.

The Thai fighter worked him close, leaving the Japanese no quarter to traffic the advantages of his martial art. Another Thai fighter dispatched a kung fu master in similar fashion. Then an Aussie heavyweight stepped into the ring against a lighter *muay Thai* boxer. While the slight Southeast Asian performed his prancing, one-legged genuflections, the Aussie huddled heads with his trainer, an older man who clasped his fighter by the back of the head and stared off into the infinity of middle distance while he mouthed his ministrations, more like a priest at absolution. This was serious. These fights were billed as an exhibition, but it seemed the outcome carried consequence.

A *farang* in my section waved down the twirling hand of a Thai in the tier below us, waging a wad of baht notes at him, as if the Aussie had a chance. Seni said they'd only bet the first round.

"All countries want to beat Thailand, but they cannot," Seni said.

"The Portuguese, the French, the English, and here too, Khmer, other countries in Southeast Asia, they want to conquer us. But Thailand always survive."

"Burma beat the pants off you guys," I said. "They sacked Ayuthaya. That's why we're in Bangkok now."

"Right, right. But we beat Burma. Cambodia beat us, then we beat Cambodia. Same Lao. But England, France, Portuguese, they don't beat Thailand. Mongkut, he is very wise."

"Mongkut?"

"Rama III."

"The King and I."

"That movie is terrible. That woman is a liar. Mongkut was very wise. He didn't kill the French priests. He let the English businessmen to do business. But he always kept Thailand for Thailand. His son, Chulalongkorn, the same. That's why today Thailand is smooth as silk. The land of smiles, Mr. Jim."

I'd been calling him Seni, and he'd been calling me Mr. Jim. If earlier that day I'd asked for Mr. Reginald, no Mr. Reggie, at Beatty's firm, I might have been transferred. I hadn't asked for Mr. Reggie because I'd stumbled into a cultural gap between the way we addressed each other. These gaps were as prevalent as minefields, and I was tripping them everywhere.

The Aussie didn't last the first round. They danced around each other, testing jabs. The Thai landed a few ineffectual kicks, and the Aussie closed the space between them, mindful perhaps of the Thai's strategy against the black belt. Let it be a weight contest. Allow his feet no quarter. But he'd made no allowances for the knees. After a frenetic exchange of combinations, the opponents collapsed into each other's arms, momentarily exhausted. But as the Thai pulled away, he clasped the Aussie's head and drove it down into the upcoming thrust of his knee. The Aussie flopped back like a cartoon character.

He hadn't anticipated the knee.

I slept through the night, through the high-jinks bedroom play, if any, and into the swamp of morning heat that filled my room within an hour of sunrise. Unabbreviated sleep inspired by the beer, no doubt, but by a sense too that I didn't have to get up for anything. Drool flowed out my mouth all night, soaking the pillow; that was how Relin found me.

"Very elegant," he said, standing over my bed. "Great flow."

I opened my eyes on a pair of knees and looked down, first at a pair of high-tech Gore-Tex cross-training, bushwhacking shoes, then up as he unshouldered a tidy knapsack of purple rip-stop material, shaped like a delta. Relin had a goatee, and I couldn't remember whether he'd had one last time I saw him.

"Your door was open," he said, gesturing. "Nice. Very inviting." He glanced at the mess I'd made of my gear. "I rifled through your things, and you don't have anything I'd want. No dough, neither."

I sat up, and the magnitude of the acute kernel of pain behind my right eye made itself known. I wasn't going to get off easy, not in the head and who could say about the liver, which had wanted more recuperation.

"How'd you know where I was?"

"The gorgeous reception clerk downstairs. He says you're a snob."

"No, here. This place."

"Beatty."

"Beatty? I thought he left again for Penang."

"Not as of yesterday afternoon. We stopped by last night, and then looked for you on Patpong. No show. He said your visa was a breeze, and that he and I ought to throw you a bachelor party. So we went to the Limelight, and Lek didn't know where you were. None of the girls at King's Castle I, or II, or III. We checked the Rose Bar, and some of the second-floor places."

"What did you say?"

"I said, you're not a great one for sitting on a bar stool next to a guy getting a hummer. I don't blame you. You see it once, that's enough."

"Before that."

He backed through the King's Castle bars and flipped me a Polaroid of himself, frowning bad-boy hip-hop next to a young go-go girl. "Oh, the visa. Four months, on a business visa. Beatty says you're no good to go as a tourist and no good as a journalist, which I already knew, or as a student, but as a businessman, it's okay for you."

Relin had other news, from my mother, who was ready to disown me and who, when I phoned later that day, told me first thing after hello that she hoped I would have children one day so one of them could do to me what I'd done to her over the past month. "One day, I'm talking to you and Thuy on the phone, right after your engagement; next thing I get a postcard out of the blue from Bangkok," she said.

She was tempted, she said, to shut down the loan she'd taken and send me nothing. She went on, chiding me through the collect call, getting it off her chest. It was only by osmosis that I figured out that in lieu of a loan from Uncle Tom, she'd secured her own access at the Hibernian.

When she dumped a heavy breath into the mouthpiece, I knew that her harangue was over. "So, would you mind telling me what you're doing in Bangkok?"

I didn't trust my ability to speak then, at least not coherently.

Balloons, never mind words, were liable to come out of my mouth. "Just a break, Ma," I said. "It's a long haul over there in Vietnam. No McDonald's, no—"

"You know what, James," she said, stopping me. "You still suck at lying."

CHAPTER SEVENTEEN

THE SHELVES WERE PACKED from floor to ceiling with premium dry goods, the best stuff to be had anywhere in the city: tins of biscuit cookies from Holland, bags of Milky Ways and M&Ms, Ovaltine, bottles of cabernets and Bordeaux. A small crowd of jostling shoppers pressed against the glass display counter—a new shipment having just arrived—ogling the bright foreign packages, barking selections to a team of clerks fielding requests. It wasn't an auction but felt like one. Every time a clerk retrieved something new, everyone paused to watch its descent from the shelves, as if perhaps they'd made a mistake in not picking it themselves.

I kept close watch on two bottles of Johnny Walker Black, reigning high on the shelves, the glass dustless and sparkling in fluorescent light. "Thuy," I said softly. She was at my elbow. "Count out the dollars U.S. in dong notes and give them to me."

If anybody made a move for the Johnny Walker Black, I had to be prepared to outbid. There were a half-dozen bottles of Johnny Walker Red on the shelves. They'd be okay for the lesser officials, but they wouldn't do for the captain at the entry-exit office. "No Red," Boi reminded me that morning. "He only like the Black."

It had been nearly two weeks since my interview with two bureaucratic officials, a meeting that I knew prefaced the imminence of an approved marriage license. Graeme had told me. He'd finally hurdled his own troubles with his single paper and had learned, from Australian expats who'd married Vietnamese in Saigon, that once you got to the interview stage, it was all downhill.

Like the entry-exit police, these officials had a good grip on my story. They knew I'd written for newspapers in the United States. They had a photocopy of the article about the trip from Saigon to Hanoi I'd published with Relin in *Bicycling*. Incredibly, they knew I was trying to write a novel about Boston in the 1970s.

"Can you tell us about that book?"

One of the officials was writing down everything I said. My remarks would be graded later. "It's about class and oppression. About wealthy people who, to make their consciences easy, force poor black and poor white people to do something they don't want to do."

"What is that?"

"Go to school together."

Huong, my translator, closed his eyes and shook his head. "We know about the racial problems in America."

"Yes, but this problem was not about race. Not at first. It was about class first. Integration is a good thing." I paused to see if I had to say the rest. "I wouldn't be here if I didn't think so."

The translator laughed, and then the officials did after the translation.

"But it's not good if rich people exclude themselves. Like they did in Vietnam. Their sons didn't come here to fight. Only the sons of the poor came to fight."

I had been prepared to lie through my teeth here, to tell them whatever they wanted to hear. I was finished with the retention of principle, and pride and honesty. But it was turning out the truth worked.

"In Vietnam, you had French imperialists. In Boston, the poor Americans were forced to do what the rich wanted."

After the translation, one of the cops asked whether I was Irish or American.

"My name is Irish, but I am American."

"Your parents carried you to America when you were a baby?" Huong asked, translating the question.

"No, a long time ago."

"What do you think of the problems in Ireland?"

"Not easy to answer," I said. "The violence is not good, but I think the island has to be one country, not two."

After an hour, one of the officials took four cans of Tiger beer from the cooler. They told me I was a good friend of Hue, no matter what some said. They knew about my problems. But everything was okay now.

I expected a note from somebody the next day, informing us that our marriage license had come in. But the days ticked by. We checked with the People's Committee and the Justice Department, and they couldn't say where the snag was. The papers had been returned from Hanoi; the interview had gone well. Be patient, they told us. Soon.

Thuy's mother figured it out. The last few feet of our boomeranging paperwork passed through the entry-exit police, she reminded us. Anytime anything went through there, it needed a nudge.

When our turn came at the foreign-goods merchant's, the Johnny Walker Black was still available. I bought both bottles, four more of the Red, and asked for six cartons of their best brand cigarettes.

"Chocolate too," Thuy said.

We crouched against the glass counter and looked at neat stacks of imported chocolate bars wrapped in metallic foil and lavender wrapping. All the entry-exit officials had wives, except for Dich, so I ordered five bars of Lindt chocolate.

"Better to buy six," Thuy said. "Better not to remind him."

It seemed absurd to me that I should be getting anything for Dich. I was sure he'd been responsible for the incident at the Noon Gate and for my expulsion from the country. I had no proof. But all roads led back to Dich, including, it turned out, the one we had to take this afternoon.

Supply goods in hand, we made a pit stop at Oanh's boutique, where Thuy's place behind the counter had been competed for and won by a first cousin who believed the job held the promise of incredible fortune: Just look at Thuy.

We started wrapping the scotch in *Cuoi Tre*, the country's leading paper, which often pushed the envelope on social issues. Thuy thought better of the gesture. She went from stall to stall in the market until she found a copy of a paper published by the army. "Don't give them anything to think about," she said.

Several buildings ahead of the police station, Thuy steered her bicycle into a café where she would wait for me. She didn't take a table. Instead, she stood over the top tube of her bicycle. She took a deep breath, then looked off without moving her head. Her gaze fixed on nothing, and she was still for a long moment.

"Mulberries again?" I asked.

"What do you know about mulberries?"

"I read the *Kieu*. I know about them."

"You know about them from the footnote."

"Everything's changing. It's about to change," I said.

"Right. This life, huh?" She had deliberately started to say *huh*, as I did, for fun at first. *Wow*, and now *huh*. She patted my knapsack. "Good luck." She gave me a thumbs-up.

The gesture touched me in a place she hadn't ever moved before. Maybe it was the weak close of her curled fingers or the arched angle of her thumb. It was the physical novelty of the gesture, yes, but something else too, this notion that she was making transitions, and here was a sign. I had come East; she would go West.

"I've been talking to travelers," I said. "They're saying the border's opened up at Lao Bao, which means we can get out overland. We could cross there. You can get a visa to Lao. We'll make a way to Savannakhet, ferry up the Mekong to Vientiane, and get to Bangkok."

In Bangkok we could short-circuit the Vietnamese emigration process, which was bound to be lengthy and full of red tape.

"A week after our wedding, we could go," I told her.

She looked away from me for a moment, at a child shimmying up the bent trunk of a coconut tree across the street. Two other little kids were trying to beat their friend to the fruit with rocks, and a small spectator of a girl was clapping on the competition.

A sheeny film glistened in her eyes, and I knew that my hatched scheme had not carried her to Lao Bao, Savannakhet, the Mekong, Bangkok, and America but away from Vietnam. Going to the States was an inevitable part of our program, hers and mine together, but something that had always seemed as uncertain as a mirage. We rarely talked about what we would do in America; there was so much to do to get there. But now I had hauled her up into the crow's nest with me and asked her to look. I wished I hadn't. I wanted her to be with me forever, but I could see now that I didn't ever want her to leave Vietnam.

I tried to put the genie back in the bottle. I laughed. "You know what, on second thought, that'll never happen."

"My father and mother, I heard them talking late last night. My father, he told my mother he was worried because in America, if I need him, he can never reach me. If my sister, Nga is in trouble, he can go to Dalat. Everybody else, they are in Hue. But with me, new story."

"It'll be easy for them to come to America to visit," I said.

I had no idea, but I was prepared to say anything as the glistening in her eyes spilled over into tears. She shook her head. She knew it would not be easy, that everything had changed now that the mulberries had swept in.

The shock of success was resonating in all of us, and I could only imagine what it was doing to Dich. He'd had to acquiesce yet again. If his talk was not a lot of blather, he had an appointment with an airport runway in his future. As I pedaled away from Thuy toward the entry-exit office, I thought of that monk from Hue who had immolated himself in a Saigon intersection in the early 1960s. Here was a people who could make good on a dire pledge. But Dich had known for some time that our papers were in ship shape. If he was prepared to lay down on a runway, he would have prefaced that desperate act with one more shot at me. That hadn't happened.

There were backpacker travelers in the office when I cycled past, so I turned in the street and went back to Thuy at the café. *Tay ba lo*, I reported, the pejorative term for the backpacker traveler.

"Scruffy," Thuy said, which is how we referred to him.

After ten minutes, I tried again, and Scruffy was gone.

I passed through the gated entrance, parked in the courtyard, and felt the weight of the scotch on my shoulders. I hadn't been here

since the day one of the officials inside had told me my visa was
no good. So strong was its polarity that I'd begun to wonder
whether a real repulsive force emanated from it. State propaganda
was broadcasting from the sidewalk speakers, louder than elsewhere, as if they'd dialed up the volume here or mounted a few
extra tweeters to ensure receptivity in the entry-exit office. The
building's fenestration glared down on me, and I felt a heavy sweat
moistening my shirt. I wiped my palms on my hips, cleared my
throat, and started up the stairs.

I was looking toward Dich's desk when I entered. To him I'd
make my first greeting. But again he was not there. His absence
unnerved me momentarily. For a split second, I handled an unwieldy image of Dich as Dudley Do Right, staked to the runway
and speaking in tongues. I turned and glanced behind me. It
seemed unreal to go on unless he was present, as if it wouldn't be
made real unless I got this one person to see that it would be done.

At neighboring desks, two officials caught my eye and funneled
me with nods of the head toward a ranking official who was beckoning me to his desk. He stood as I neared and spread his arms at
the two chairs before his desk. "Ah, Mr. Jim," he said.

"I'd like to . . ." I said, launching the spiel I'd worked up for this
moment.

He held up his hand and looked over my shoulder. Two backpackers stepped over the threshold, rubbernecking the vast space of
the room, the ceiling fans, and each other, as if to confirm they'd
reached where they were heading. One of the officials waited out
their curiosity and then gestured for them to approach his desk.

I turned back to the official. He was waiting for me with a
question.

"How's your hotel?" he asked.

"The same," I said.

"The same?" He laughed deeply and translated our repartee to his unengaged neighbor, who chuckled lightly. I roamed around inside my head, looking for the punch line, but didn't get it, not then while the clock pendulum swung high against the back wall.

The official began to talk then about hotels in Hue and guest houses, the number of rooms coming on-line, how pleasant they were, how pleasant the weather in Hue could be, all the while glancing at the desultory movements of the engaged official. The ceiling fan overhead stirred on its slowest setting, like a metronome setting the pace for work.

After the tour-guide spiel, my official dropped into the dead space of silence. The awkwardness of the sudden quiet got to me, and I asked how Mr. Dich was. "I haven't seen him for a long time," I said.

"He okay. He okay," he said, as if arguing to persuade me. "Maybe his motorbike today, it's not okay."

Here was my explanation. Dich was having car trouble, or the equivalent of it. Here were the mundane facts of life. But I couldn't help reading into them.

"He had an accident?" I asked. He was at the body shop, I thought, banging out new dents.

"No, no," he said again effusively, beating back skepticism. "I don't know that word in English." He made an indecipherable motion with his hands, intimating the source of the motorbike's ills.

The table was pounded behind us, and I glanced back as the official put his imprimatur on what was likely to be another visa extension. The two foreigners walked airily out of the room.

"Now, how can I help you?" my official said hurriedly.

"I am here to thank you for all the help you have given me," I told him. "I know that my marriage application has been approved and that it's almost ready to be issued. I want to express my gratitude to your department for everything you've done." I patted the side of my pack, and the official nodded at one of his subordinates.

The subordinate ushered me behind a screen and withdrew the contents of my pack. He stood the scotch on the table, in a line, and once straightened the line so that it hewed to some military standard of neatness. He laid a carton of cigarettes before each bottle, then placed a chocolate bar on each carton but not before he scrutinized the details on one of the packages.

"Swiss?" he asked me.

I pointed out where it said "Switzerland," and he nodded, hiking his eyebrows reflexively and then, I suspected, regretted having done so. He frowned down hard but touched my upper arm as he went around the screen and made a detailed report to the ranking official.

The official stood as I came around the screen. He was smiling and shook my hand. "We're glad we could help."

The two foreigners walked quickly down the front steps of the hotel and started for the courtyard entrance. They carried enormous backpacks and an assortment of smaller bags slung over their neck. The chief receptionist chased them. "You pay ten dollar."

"No," the man said. "No hot water."

I looked down at my coffee, now dripping from the small tin filter onto a bed of condensed milk and hoped I'd mistaken their accent. It sounded American to me, and I'd been wanting to believe that things had changed. It was raining, and the woman backpacker pulled on the hood of her poncho.

"The sheets were dirty," she told the receptionist, tightening her drawstring. "We're not paying."

She was from the Midwest. The few other guests looked up from breakfast. Mr. Cu, the café's proprietor, was sitting beside me, showing me photographs he'd begun taking recently. "They don't know about a switch for hot water. Sometimes this happens."

The receptionist shuffled in front of the backpackers, from one to the other like a man trying to block a pass, meanwhile calling over his shoulder for reinforcements.

"Call the police," the woman said, swerving around him. "Go ahead, call them."

"She doesn't want that," Mr. Cu said.

"You wouldn't," I said.

The man jumped squarely in her path, arms waving, and she shoved him. He pushed her back.

"No hot water," the man said again righteously. "No pay."

Several more hotel employees joined the fray from several directions, and the woman began to pat her hair, as if to demonstrate that she'd had to wash it under cold water that morning. The man kept making the same argument.

"If you want hot water so badly, mate," an Australian at a nearby table called out, "you should stay home."

That morning, the entry-exit police had officially stamped our documents. They would have done it sooner, they assured me, but they'd lost their stamp and had to call up to Hanoi for two weeks. Boi confirmed this. They really had lost their stamp, and its loss had virtually shut the office down. But we had it now, and we'd entered the sweet, expectant days leading up to the wedding. Thuy and I had written invitations for my guests—there was no need to do so for the Vietnamese—and I was making my rounds this morning, delivering them.

As I finished my coffee, Boi parked his cyclo and dropped into a chair at my table, gesturing to Mr. Cu's wife for a black iced coffee. His brow was furrowed, and he took a big, restorative gulp of the coffee when it came. "The air is very heavy over there this morning," he said.

"At Number Three?"

He nodded.

"I was just on my way over." I slid his invitation across the table and tapped the several others I had for Graeme and Kim Anh's family.

"Better you go another time. Yesterday," Boi said, "Kim Anh, she declared to her family she won't marry Graeme."

"I thought they wanted her to marry him."

"Yes, they want her to marry the foreigner, one daughter to marry the foreigner, but they think Graeme, he is going to *Bia Om.*"

Bia Om literally translated as "Beer Hug" and referred to the kind of seedy café where you could order a beer and a fondling girl to sit down with you. In Saigon, you could hail *Honda Om* from a taxi girl who'd let you embrace her as she zipped through the streets on a motorbike.

"Graeme doesn't go to *Bia Om,*" I said.

Kim Anh was the real thing for Graeme. There weren't many like him, and I felt bad they hadn't seen this in him.

"Several days ago, one of Kim Anh's sisters saw him talking to some girls on Le Loi Street. They're pretty. They were students."

"More like mosquitoes," I said. You couldn't pedal down Le Loi Street without moving through a drove of them, and their questions. I'd taken to barging through, but Graeme was more tolerant. He stopped. He helped students with homework. He let them practice their English. They hadn't exhausted him.

"I know, students. But they say something else. *Bia Om.* Talk to other girls."

I pictured the scene at Number Three, at Kim Anh's father

sitting in a tiny chair at the edge of the sidewalk, fuming over a cigarette, a man who'd driven a truck during the war, who'd called Relin Saddam Hussein because Relin's whiskers were so vigorously evident in the evening. He fought frequently with his wife about how much money they were giving to his family or to her family, harsh, loud arguments blaring among the tables, among foreigners who couldn't understand them. It was for that reason I'd started coming over to 2 Le Loi more often. The air was indeed heavy.

"They call him a country person," Boi went on, "because he grew up on a farm. They say he has a big mouth. Kim Anh hears all this. And what can she think? She is going to marry him?"

Boi never talked about this stuff. "I don't want" was how he usually expressed his distaste for all of the squabbling. He couldn't believe that he was an audience to any of it.

When Graeme stopped by the café yesterday, he'd learned Kim Anh had called off the wedding. The family rehashed their gripes all over again, and Graeme fled. "No one has seen him since," Boi said.

I pedaled to Graeme's room on Ngo Quyen. The receptionist hadn't seen him since the day before, but he hadn't checked out either. Outside his room, I knocked, then looked in his window. The bed was tautly made, and his possessions had a remarkable, militarily efficient neatness to them, each rugby shirt exactly folded and stacked, his novels and nonfiction supported by bookends. On his bed was a copy of Robert Stone's *A Flag for Sunrise*, and on the night stand was a gold-framed photo of Kim Anh. I wondered whether she had a similar one of him.

"Ahhhh, Mister Sullivan," Gary said from behind me, emphasizing each syllable. "I was planning to do you the honor of a little visit today." In shorts and the same mustard-colored shirt, he stood in his doorway down the corridor. "I'm preparing a speech to deliver at the city planning conference they're having here next week, and I'd like your two cents on it."

"Have you seen Graeme?"

"Woman trouble," he said. "They're all the same. I was all set to buy a ring for my old lady when she dropped a bomb on me last week. A real fuckin' big one too."

His old lady had ceased to be the pharmacist I'd known him to be with. When I returned from Bangkok, I learned that he'd taken up with an eighteen-year-old pharmacy sales-clerk. I'd understood my own failure to say something to this woman's family as diffidence.

"Her birthday is coming up, and so I thought, okay, a ring. But then a couple of weeks before the occasion itself, she reminds me of the birthday again and says, 'Gary, for my birthday, buy for me one Honda Chally.' Who does she think I am? I'm not going to put one eighth of one second more into anything that little bitch wants."

Gary stepped back into his room and a moment later was back outside, snapping the speech he'd prepared for the convocation.

"Are you an invited speaker?" I asked.

"Not yet."

I read the speech. He wrote about the need for garbage cans on the city's street corners and regular garbage collection. Then he weighed in heavily against the city's police force, the corruption and shakedowns. It was a harangue that went on and on, judge, jury, and verdict.

"I don't think is going to go over. I can't imagine they're going to take to your going after the cops like this."

"It's the truth."

"Whatever it is, they're going to go ballistic on you for this."

Gary frowned, like a wounded boy, and I wondered at his lack of judgment. But not for long. However noble his intentions to trade every month at war in Vietnam for one of peace and to fix the fortunes of one Vietnamese family, Gary was still marching through Hue, an emissary from an enlightened world who was try-ing to get the dink bastards to see the light. He'd forged those prejudices in another time, and though the people and the places were the same, the prejudices no longer had currency.

He placed one sandaled foot on the banister and stared at the high, brick compound wall, as if there were revelation there. And maybe there was, for him. For Gary, I feared it was just going to be one brick wall after another. "I'll rewrite it," he said. Then he took a lighter from his pocket and held the flame to a corner until the whole thing flared.

I found Graeme that afternoon in Tho Duc, about four miles upstream from Hue on the river's south bank. We'd pedaled out here before to a place he'd been dreaming about, a little piece of land on the river where he might one day build a house and ride out the rest of his life. I had a hunch he'd gone back out there, and here he was, wandering now through some of the local shops that sold bronze works, tiny bronze cannons and vessels made in the foundry nearby. My arrival didn't surprise him.

"They've been making this stuff out here for hundreds of years, mate," he told me. "Since the 1600s, when they shanghaied a Por-tuguese founder from Cambodia and started him making artillery. Gongs for the pagodas. Urns. Imagine that. Some guy from all the way out to Portugal, making a go of it here more than three hun-dred years ago and pulling it off."

He stepped out into the street carrying one of the shop's urns, and I wheeled my bike beside him. His clothes had the wrinkled look of having been slept in. If Graeme had bunked out the night

on that piece of land, it wouldn't have surprised me. We started
back toward town.

"Can I ask you something, mate?"

"Go ahead."

"It's of a personal nature."

"That's all right."

"Do you and Thuy ever have any . . . let me call them domestics?"

"Arguments?"

He nodded.

"We do," I said. I was glad I could say it and glad Thuy and I
were airing out grievances in argument. At Children's Tet, I'd scattered a handful of candies among a bunch of kids who'd flooded
the doorway of her house; she thought I'd condescended to Vietnamese, treating them "like chickens." There was a culture gap
between us, and some misunderstandings were inevitable. But we'd
begun to grapple with other problems too. Occasionally, she deplored my habit of drifting away from her in shops. While it
seemed perfectly reasonable to me that she should look at what she
liked while I looked at what I liked, she had this idea that we
should look at everything together, "as a couple." At the same time,
I thought her appreciation of "a couple" was naïve. People moved
in tandem, not unison. They cultivated their own peculiar interests.
These issues weren't catapulted out of the culture gap. This is what
we got when all the window dressing of culture was stripped bare.
These were the things that were going to take work. I said as much
to Graeme.

"But do you get the silences, when she battens down all the
hatches and won't talk about what's bothering her for days?"

"After I scattered that candy, after she swatted my hands and shouted for me not to do so, I couldn't get her to tell me what bothered her about it until the next evening. I had no idea there was a connection between tossing candy for kids and condescending to Vietnamese."

I wish we'd spoken like this before. We were both blazing new ground here, embarked upon futures that, perhaps, lay beyond conception until recently. Everything was novel. Hearing that someone else was going through the same thing was solace.

For a long time I'd blamed Thuy's silences, like Kim Anh's perhaps, on a cultural tradition. It was a clichéd appreciation of the Vietnamese, and of Asians in general, that their minds, the Oriental mind, were inscrutable. During the Vietnam War, Americans were frustrated by the Vietnamese failure to be up-front and explicitly honest: They evaded direct questions and hid behind bland smiles. It was possible to believe this was how the Vietnamese handled problems; unilaterally and through a maze of unfollowable turns of the mind. Graeme had no idea what was to come out the other side of Kim Anh's thinking on his alleged infidelity. I'd believed Thuy's buttoned-up response to issues that Westerners aired out more freely was a liability that would always plague us. But that was only because of the distance in time between my interest in airing out the problem and hers. In the wake of any bout of silence, she got it all off her chest. The reason, she told me once, why she didn't speak out immediately was because she needed time to let her feelings settle. "So I can be reasonable about it," she told me. I couldn't chalk that up to a fundamental difference between us— because she was Asian and I was Western; it was a matter of personal style, impressed upon her by a cultural tradition that prized tranquillity in the face of difficulty. Beneath it, I found the same raw material that she was finding in me.

Graeme stopped and stared into the bronze urn he'd cradled in his palms, the concentric ribs rising up the sides, the nonbuffed cast of the vessel's bowl. "Has her family ever asked for anything, mate?"

This they had not done. I'd been afraid of this since the start. If anything might have put the genie in the bottle, it was that. I thought about lying to Graeme about this, but I knew he trusted me to give him an honest answer.

"No," I said.

He nodded and started walking. We walked in silence for some time. "Go ahead and ask," he said.

"Okay."

"Every single one of them."

"How could you not? I mean, looking at this place. Most people are living on dirt. They ride bicycles. How can we expect people not to look at us and hope? A pittance to us could make a huge difference in someone's life."

Graeme laughed as he listened to me work my way off his revelation into the disparity between the First World and the Third World. He ran his fingers through his thinning hair, then scratched his scalp hard. "You know, Jim," he said. "I came here looking. I'm under no illusions, mate. It is what it is."

My last morning in the Morin, through the clangs of the bridge supervisor's morning alarm, I thought I heard my name, or an approximation of it; "Chim. . . . Chim. . . . Chim." I kept still for a moment, listening to the distant sound of this summons, a single voice made lonesome and forlorn by the smallness of other, nearby noise: the dry rasp of a man sweeping banyan leaves off the hotel driveway, the tinny racket of a woman setting up her coffee concession against the Morin's back wall. It sounded like the Sunday mornings I'd known, hushed as if from reverence.

I'd been awake since before the alarm, flipping through scattered snapshot memories of my boyhood. Those remote faces, our long-ish hair and bothersome bangs. Bobby Leonard. Neil Leonard. Skinny Vinny, whose hair was the texture of sandpaper and who, all through our boyhood, smelled like a baseball glove. My paper route. Sitting on the polished-granite curbstone in our cutoff cor-duroy shorts, the indolence of hot summer days overtaking us. The cold orange soda we'd drunk while perched on the wall that ex-tended from the barbershop beside the corner store. Suiting up in surplice and cassock for Mass in the sacristy of the Star of the Sea with the Kid. We had been waking up to girls in those days, girls for whom I had no courage but dreams galore. Holly Flynn and Cary Hannon—impossibly beautiful, even at nine and ten years old, and for me, a smaller freckled boy, unreachable.

We had a confidante in Father Rock, a burly young priest who played goalie in a men's ice-hockey league and who pretended to none of the airs that removed other priests. We liked him, Costa and I did, and we wanted to talk to him about the big things, all those questions that haunted us through grade school. It had oc-curred to me then that there was a girl somewhere in the world out there, playing, doing stuff, whom I would marry. Even then her life was moving inexorably toward mine. The revelation of this— an incontrovertible fact, I used to think, as absolute as gravity— made me giddy with speculation. It wasn't like time travel. That never fascinated me, for there wasn't even a hint of possibility—in my mind, at least—that any of us would ever sit down with Abra-ham Lincoln. The math would never work. If it could, why weren't people from the distant future upon us now? But the math could work to reveal the girl. All the constants and variables were in place: my life, her life, and our mutual influences. All we had to do was run the equation.

We'd introduced my idea to Father Rock one day, as if we'd come upon a cache of some precious, heretofore undiscovered metal that needed validation. But Father Rock had Socratic tendencies and asked us to consider whether we might have a vocation waiting, instead of a girl. I knew I didn't have that vocation waiting. She was out there somewhere. I was certain of that.

I pulled the mosquito net from beneath my foam mattress and swung my feet to the cool tile floor, cognizant I'd never do this again. A series of thresholds lay between me and that day's ceremony. The last shave. A last cup of coffee. I wouldn't ever be single again. I could be divorced, or widowered, but not single.

As the clangs subsided, rippling away that last time, I wandered into my tenth birthday party. I remembered some of it vividly. The knotty-pine beadboard of our dining room, and the twirled ends of my father's mustache, where my mother was sitting, leaning over the table, still so young at thirty. My father was sitting against the windowsill when he said, "Double digits, you're in double digits now, kid, just like us." My presents were coins, very fine zinc pennies from World War II, and one I'd been pining for, a 1909 Lincoln-VDB penny. I'd really wanted the S-VDB penny, but I was realistic. It was expensive, beyond us.

I'd delivered my *Patriot Ledger*s that afternoon, May 1, 1975. Saigon, the day before, had fallen, and Vietnam was all over the headlines: VIET REDS CRUSH LAST RESISTANCE. Another front-page story detailed an exodus by nearly 30,000 South Vietnamese: 22,000 had escaped by small boat and been picked up by U.S. Navy ships; some 6,000 had been airlifted out of Saigon two days earlier. Kissinger thought the refugee count might rise to 56,000, and the United States would be obliged to resettle as many as 70,000 Vietnamese from South Vietnam.

Here was one of the variables in my equation, and if I could have run it then, I would have found her in Danang, a refugee out of Hue, living at the Phan Thanh Gieng School. She and her family had fled Hue ahead of the communists, streaming south on Highway 1 with more than thirty people packed in a single van. A Dodge, her father had interjected days before, while Thuy's sisters and mother pieced together their story in whispers.

In Danang, they'd heard, there were American ships offshore, and so they planned to try for them. But the reports coming back were grim. As smaller boats from the evacuation flotilla sidled up against ships and children were passed upward, people and children were falling to their death between them. Nga had told her mother that she would lose four or five children if they tried this. Now, at least, she had them all.

When word came into the school that planes were coming into the American airfield at Danang, Mr. Bang and his oldest son made an attempt to catch the last flight out. This was Mrs. Bang's idea. If they could get out, later they could retrieve the family from America. Thousands had had the same idea, and Mr. Bang never made it off the tarmac.

So what if you'd showed me that picture then, of a four-year-old girl with straight, short hair, an unkempt homemade dress, and a doll she'd made herself? Wearing black sandals made from rubber tires. I wouldn't have believed it. Holly or Cary, yes, but not her, not this. She'd been out there then, this girl I would marry, but beyond my imagination. How lucky, I thought then, to end up in a place with someone who existed beyond the limits of daydreams.

I crossed the tile floor to my door, shot the bolt, and stepped out into a lattice of morning sunlight. Two chambermaids giggled in the corridor—I was in shorts only—and pushed each other into a vacant neighboring room. I unlatched the louvered, French shutters and pushed them. On the roof across the courtyard, evaporating rainwater steamed off the terra-cotta tiles. On the windows below, a dozen bare-chested bridge workers were squatting on the corridor sill, smoking cigarettes and grinning as if they'd been waiting.

"*Chim,*" the bridge supervisor called up. "*Dac biet.*" Special day.

My entourage gathered at Marian Cadogan's house later that morning, milling outside a late-model washed and waxed van, courtesy of the E.C. Thuy's brother-in-law, Dung, checked the arrival of my guests against his wristwatch and his list. Boi arrived in a pink button-down shirt. His hair was combed, and though his skin was burnished from labor, it was possible to see in the way he carried himself the kind of life he might have made if he still belonged to that privileged class. He drew Marian aside, consulted quietly with her, and then beckoned me from her doorstoop. He looked gravely serious. I went around him into the house, and he hung back, looking up and down the street a moment, before he followed me inside.

In Marian's dining room was a colonial-era upright piano. I'd heard the plink of its keys in the past, usually when Marian was out and her housekeeper couldn't resist. Boi said nothing. He pulled the bench from beneath and lifted the lid. His fingers touched down on the keys in several places. He shook his head quickly at each, like a pitcher waving off his catcher's calls. In my chest, I felt something descend from the base of my throat into my gut, a heavy settling of suspicion. Boi brought one hand down on the keys and craned his upper body away. His other hand came down tentatively, and then he bent into it. In a moment, Satie's "Gymnopedique" filled the room. I leaned back against the wall and crossed my arms against the music. It was expert, but I couldn't really listen. This was Satie, but here was Boi, a cyclo driver who sometimes didn't have enough to eat, playing as if he belonged to a conservatory. His erratic work ethic made a kind of sense to me now, as did his choice of job. There were keyboards in Hue, here and there, and he knew where they were.

He stayed with the last note as it resonated to silence. "Satie wants a very light hand," he said deliberately, as if he were reminding himself again.

"I didn't know."

"It's true. But—" One hand crashed the keys, then the other, until we were getting a piano version of "Welcome to the Jungle." "Axl Rose does not, my friend."

He closed the lid hurriedly, nudged the bench under the piano, then charged into me, pushing toward Marian's door and onto the threshold. This was how to avoid the questions I'd never been able to stop asking.

"Tonight, you sleep across the river," he said.

"I'm finally taking your advice. A small hotel across the river."

"Much better, my friend. The B-52s and the Hueys here, they will be safe from you now."

"The monk, right. I remember."

He clasped his hands, except for the forefingers, which he lined up like a gun barrel and swiveled into the air around him. "But not from me," he said.

Gary was gone from Hue. He'd quit the city after his attempts to gain admission to the city planning conference were rebuffed by two cops who'd double-teamed him. "Like I'm Wilt the Stilt fuckin' Chamberlain," he'd said. On the morning he left, there was a note under my door, announcing his departure and the line "I know where I'm not wanted."

Kim Anh had renewed her engagement to Graeme, as he'd

known she would. They were part of my entourage, as was Gioang
and his wife, Kim Anh's parents, and Relin. We were waiting for
Relin. I'd awakened him on my way to Marian's, and I could picture him now in the midst of a morning routine I'd learned by
heart in the months we'd traveled together, his irregular plumbing,
the neatening of his bed and things.

"It's very important we leave on time," Dung told me, pacing
from the van to the small road that ran back behind the Morin.

"In Vietnam, we are often late," I said, mimicking one of Thuy's
allowances.

"No, this is different. Our mother . . ." he started to say, then
let it trail off.

"I see," I said. "Our mother. The ghosts . . ."

Dung nodded hurriedly and stepped away. He was a doctor of
physics and taught at the University in Hanoi. He spoke Russian
and English and had walked the galleries of the Hermitage in St.
Petersburg. He was an expert in string theory, but a son-in-law too,
and sometimes the mandates of the fortune-tellers trumped all.

I felt none of Dung's urgency. Officially, Thuy and I were already married. Four days earlier, we'd gathered at a conference table
in the Justice Department building. Thuy's mother had laid several
Jet-brand cigarettes on small plates at each table setting. Relin took
photographs of Thuy and me beneath a portrait of Ho Chi Minh.
Hang, wearing a white *ao dai* with a long-stemmed rose embroidered over the breast, asked Thuy's uncle to make a short speech.
He offered a benediction, then unfolded a paper from his pocket.

"Now he's going to read a special poem," Thuy had said.

Mr. Gioang rose and went to stand beside the Viet Cong hero.
He looked down at the poem, then nodded at uncle and waited for
him to begin. They alternated languages, uncle launching the poem

theatrically, like a stage actor, throwing a shielding palm overhead, then cringing beneath it, as if blinded. Gioang played straight man, smiling sheepishly as he translated the first line of the poem: "Don't look at the sun."

Afterward, Thuy turned over the fees in Vietnamese dong. A cashier from downstairs, who'd also decked herself in an *ao dai* for the occasion, fingered through the cash with a nimble, practiced forefinger, mumbling the tally in a soft voice as we sat in silence. She parceled the total and punched the subtotals into a keyboard. Toward the end of her reckoning she stopped and mentioned a fifty-dollar fee. Thuy had converted that fee to dong, and the cashier asked what exchange rate she used. Another woman went out of the room to check that day's exchange rate, since that was the one to be used, and when we came up several thousand dong short, I peeled a few thousand off a wad in my pocket.

Relin beat me to it. "Let me be responsible."

The cashier slid the piles to Hang, who double-checked the totals through another awkward series of minutes. Then she smiled and pounded a red stamp on a thick sheaf of papers. For the record, that was it.

By the time Relin showed up, Dung had ushered us into the van, and the driver had started the engine. Relin smirked in apology. He wore a Bugs Bunny tie. As we turned on Le Loi, one of the Morin guards waved. He wore a cream-colored doorman's uniform with shoulder braids and embroidered cuffs. The spiffy uniform was premature. SaigonTourist had only just acquired the hotel, and the homeless still pitched mosquito nets against the Le Loi Street facade at night, but change was in the air. And had been ever since I'd come back from Bangkok.

The U.S. Senate had passed a nonbinding resolution to lift the trade embargo against Vietnam, paving the way for President Clinton to finally take America's hand off the face of Vietnam. The Vietnamese thought the end of the embargo would kick-start the economy. Thuy's sister had come up from Dalat and told us about the golf course they were building on a hill near the city center. Everyone was talking about the need for more mini hotels. Thuy's sister Vui and her husband had sat down with a builder and sketched plans to build a sixteen-room hotel on their property, which overlooked the lake where the Nguyen emperors used to go boating with their concubines. Water theme parks were coming. Fast-food franchises. Supermarkets stocking Western conveniences. American sitcoms. T-shirts whose decorative phrasing made sense.

On my shortwave, I'd tuned in to one news report about the Senate action and heard someone say that, ". . . these people, many of whom have been waiting for twenty to twenty-five years, deserve better than that." But they weren't talking about the Vietnamese; they were talking about Americans who'd gone missing in Vietnam. The BBC interviewed American families who called the Senate vote a "sellout" and a "victory for Hanoi."

It was remarkable that Vietnam's economy had been held hostage for so long in the interests of a very small but very vocal minority. Politicians were reluctant to take issue with the families, and the American public wasn't about to lobby for just policy in Vietnam, of all places. Who cared, first of all, and who wanted to wake up to the legacy? Nineteen years after the war had ended, Vietnam was a hangover that people were still trying to go back to sleep on.

Up Nguyen Trai Street, we drove past the house numbering system that defied mathematics and logic but made sense to the locals. Here was the bridge I'd been spanning for more than a year, bridging water that was meant to keep out invaders. And here was the square pond where I'd made that first rendezvous with Thuy. How tenuous.

Through my time in Hue, I'd figured that my reasons for being with Thuy, for wanting to be with her and stay with her, would make themselves known to me, would crawl out of my intuition and stand explicably forth, reasons as smart and crisp as tuxedos. That never happened. I'd begun to believe that the force of my own will was part of what had brought me to Vietnam, but something else too, an immeasurable impulse borne of tropism and an innate desire to reorient the direction of lineage. We didn't talk about such things in America. That part of why you chose one mate over another had something to do with a biological force and was not purely a function of like-mindedness and free will was base. But true. It was part of why Miller insisted on papers. Papers meant breeding, and breeding meant mating. People had been coming East for answers for centuries, and in some way, I believed that I'd come East to answer questions I hadn't ever asked, though I knew them to be questions. Whenever I tried to focus on the answers, as on a ship on the horizon, I couldn't quite convince myself that they were really there. But if I looked askance, there was enough resolution for certainty. They were there. Which is all we can ever go on. An invisible jury comes in, and they don't say why, but you have your verdict.

Short of the house, we emptied out of the van and lined up parade fashion. Thuy's two nephews, Tuan and Nang, held two bulbous paper lanterns at the ends of short poles and led the way to number 116, disguised as sixteen. My entourage carried traditional groom's gifts: areca nuts, betel leaves, rice wine, a dozen red roses for Thuy, and a wheel of furled firecrackers as a bulwark. Spectators poured out of houses along either side of the street.

At the main gate, Thuy's mother and uncle beckoned Dung from the parade. They all began to consult watches. The courtyard of Thuy's house bulged with people. The older women wore *ao dais*; the men wore suit jackets and ties.

Thuy's father stepped outside the gate and walked the line of gifts, appraising them with mock solemnity. He stopped at my side and lifted the knot on my tie to check if it was real. I lifted his and noticed that he, like most of the men who wore them, was wearing a clip-on.

"Mr. Popsicle," he said to me, chuckling over the translation again.

"Yes, Mr. Blackboard," I said.

I looked for Thuy in the crowd, but she was inside. The Chinese character for "togetherness" hung from the ceiling of the verandah and served as a backdrop for an altar spread with urns and flowers. A ready wheel of firecrackers hung from a tree limb.

Finally, Dung turned, looking distressed. "I'm sorry, we have to go back. We're too early. They say it's bad luck for the couple if the wedding does not take off at exactly the right time."

Dung led us back to the van, where we regrouped and watched Thang light a stick of jasmine joss and apply the tip to the wick of the firecracker string. He held it for several seconds, frowning harder as if to will ignition. When it failed to light, the old technique no good, he produced a lighter from his pocket and used that.

The string snapped to life, writhing as hundreds of firecrackers began exploding in succession. At intervals, the burning wick touched off a cherry bomb, which seemed to interject a note of seriousness and authority in an otherwise pesky display of boomlets. Cordite stung the nostrils. Smoke fogged over the wedding guests. All of a sudden, the scene looked like one from a farce, the courtyard overwhelmed by a great cloud and the guests going down within it, smiling, too charmed by the joyousness of the occasion to be bothered by the fact that they could barely breathe and hardly see.

The temptation of firecrackers was too much for Thuy; she came to the window in her wedding dress. I could see her through the horizontal iron bars, covering her ears with lacy, gloved hands, to beam at the fireworks. I remembered her at Tet that first year, the way she'd laid her hand on Minh's forearm to enjoy the vicarious thrill of shooting bursts of color from the Roman candle in her sister's hand. This was her glory. These were her people. This was all the love she'd ever known. And I would take her away from this.

We'd filled the house with flowers, potted marigolds, roses, and white lilies. In my courtyard, my mother and father were welcoming the groom again, the sixth time they'd done this here as each of their daughters married away. He'd been so strict, my father, with my oldest sister, Nga, who, at his insistence, had married the son of his best friend. He had had so much to say about the choices Nguyet had made, but then less with Dieu, and less with Oanh, who'd been very smart about leaving one man and marrying another. Our father had tried to dissuade Vui from marrying her husband, a handsome truck driver whose charm could never compensate for what else we knew about him. But by then, he was old, and he couldn't muster the will to keep down Vui's own terrific will.

About Jim, he'd told me that Americans were very good at leaving. And Jim had left. But he'd come back, and he stayed. And I knew my father liked Mr. Popsicle. They weren't fluent in each other's language, but that wasn't the only way to get to know someone. Still, when I look at him, at that long nose and his spray of freckles, I'm sometimes a little shocked that he is the person for me.

As the firecrackers made their last few pops, I caught his eye and mouthed a line that I knew he knew, that every foreigner in Vietnam had heard. "Hello," I said. "Where are you from?"

When the fireworks quit sputtering, a herd of neighborhood boys charged into the tattered, red-papered remains, ferreting out unexploded crackers. Even Thuy's well-dressed nephews joined the fray, scrabbling in like crabs. Dung marshaled us to parade again, and we made our way up Nguyen Trai.

Thuy had retreated inside the house as I passed through the gateposts into a throng of relatives. An uncle laid a hand on my shoulder and guided me to the family's ancestor altar.

"Are you ready for your nuptials, Jim?" Minh asked.

She was finishing her sophomore year now, an English major and a French minor. I couldn't help wondering if she didn't resent me in some small way, for the distance I would eventually put between her and her sister. Or did she blame herself? If she hadn't selected English as a major, would Thuy have invited me and David to tea that first night? Thuy said she would not have. It was an incredibly rickety thought. If Minh had followed her desire to become a mathematician and not followed her brother-in-law Dung's advice, and applied herself to English, there was a very good chance I wouldn't have been standing there.

"I'm ready. Are you?" I said to Minh.

"For my own nuptials?"

"No, for Thuy's."

She narrowed her eyes at me. And maybe she saw the culpability in my face. "Thinking too deeply," she said. "Didn't you learn anything in Vietnam?"

"For example?"

"*Ong Troi* decides."

"I don't believe it."

"You believe, it's better."

Minh skipped away from me at Thuy's call, and for a moment, my focus fell on various guests. Thuy's relatives from the village. Her grandfather's surviving brother. Her uncle, who will forget he's already made a separate peace, and make another one.

Beyond the altar, Thuy's mother called my attention to two framed photographs she'd propped on a table. My mother and father, each in their own frame: my mother on the porch of the home her father had grown up in Boston's Dorchester and my father beside a granite headstone he'd purchased and raised over his plot already, fearing the precedent of his own father, grandfather, and great grandfather, whose own children, through some malignancy of the blood, had each failed to buy a stone for their father.

I could look at my own parents and see precedent too. That occurred to me as I pictured them here on the day that would initiate my own attempt at the big bold dream of lasting marriage. There was that history of severing, turning, and running for the next best thing, for something better, with an eye on the West, but I'd come all the way West. It was impossible to go any further than I'd come already. I was twenty-eight years old, and I could hardly suspect the challenges that lay ahead, through silences and shouting, but I told myself I knew this. It wouldn't get any better. I made my own vow, and I thought, *Okay, let's go.*

When Thuy finally came out of the house, she looked unimaginably different. A white wedding dress of shimmering sequins and a tiara, her face powdered, her hair piled high. Two twirled locks spiraled by her ears. Her eyes were made up with brown crimson, a color drawn from the juice of one of the trees in her front yard. She looked a bit like a Chinese opera singer and very much like each of her sisters in the photos I'd seen of their weddings.

"How can I be sure it's you?" I whispered, taking my place beside her.

She whispered back. "I'm the only one here who knows that marriage is the comfortable way to spend the winter."

I smiled.

"No smiling," she said. "Serious."

Her uncle offered obeisances to her ancestors, then ushered us inside, where we kowtowed again before the family altar.

As a proxy for my mother, Marian Cadogan stepped forward to hang Thuy's earrings, a gesture she undertook with great solemnity and some awkwardness. I glanced around the room then; it more than any other place resonated with our romance. It had taken wing here, from these walls of pastel blue, from that clutch of suitors, to soar through a courtship that neither of us could have dreamed, not me as a ten-year-old delivering the *Patriot Ledger*, or Thuy as a four-year-old refugee. As Marian fumbled the earring, I noticed Thuy's sister Oanh, wincing slightly and touching thumb to fingertip in a tiny moment of body language: "Like this, Marian." It occurred to me then that before not too long, Thuy would move beyond the pale of Oanh's help, and the vernacular of this room and the charisma of this family, to my colder country. My life, I suspected, would go on there with great familiarity and predictability, with my family and my friends, but hers was about to be changed forever. All along I'd thought it was me, but really it was Thuy who was about to go over the moat.

After the jewelry was hung, Thuy took my hand, and we turned to behold our guests together. If there was a moment in which the marriage was fixed, this was it. Relin started to applaud, a gesture so singular and foreign that the Vietnamese turned to look at him. In the back room, a new litter of piglets started squealing frantically. It went on and on, convulsing the children in laughter.

"Nhac heo," I said, pig music, the way Thuy had said it, the way she'd parried my First World glance at the grit of Third World living.

"Not right," she said. "I can tell you now, Jim. My family, we keep pigs."